Visitor's Guic
HUNGARY

About the Authors

Andrew Beattie read Geography at Mansfield College, Oxford, and now teaches the subject at Eltham College, London. He has travelled extensively in Central and Southern Europe and in the Middle East, and is the author of *The Visitor's Guide to Czechoslovakia* in Moorland Publishing's Country Traveller series.

Timothy Pepper was born in Chester and read History at Wadham College, Oxford. After leaving University he travelled widely in Eastern Europe, South Africa and Central America before joining forces with Andrew Beattie to write The Visitor's Guide to Hungary and also a book on the Czech and Slovak Republics in Moorland Publishing's Off The Beaten Track series.

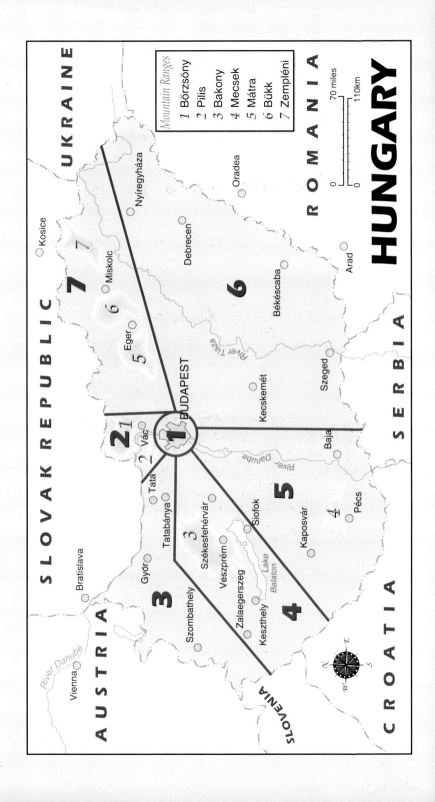

HUNGARY

Mountain Ranges

1 Börzsöny
2 Pilis
3 Bakony
4 Mecsek
5 Mátra
6 Bükk
7 Zempléni

70 miles
110km

VISITOR'S GUIDE
HUNGARY

Andrew Beattie & Timothy Pepper

MPC

Published by:
Moorland Publishing Co Ltd,
Moor Farm Road West, Ashbourne,
Derbyshire DE6 1HD
England

ISBN 086190 380 3

British Library Cataloguing in Publication Data:
A catalogue record for this book is available from the British Library.

Colour origination by: Forest Graphics (Nottm.) Ltd

Printed in Hong Kong by: Wing King Tong Co Ltd

Cover photograph: Hungarian Gypsy Musicians, Budapest
(International Photobank)
Rear Cover: Elizabeth Bridge, Budapest *(S. M. Wragg)*
Page 3: Parliament Building, Budapest *(S. M. Wragg)*

The illustrations have been supplied by: A. D. Beattie pp15, 19, 39, 42, 51,
58, 59, 62, 79, 98, 103, 119, 123, 126, 151, 154, 163, 166, 195, 198, 202, 207, 219,
223; T. J. Pepper pp51, 75, 78, 134, 139, 146, 170; C. M. Dixon
(Photoresources, Canterbury, England) pp10, 14, 23, 27, 110, 127, 163, 178,
179, 195; Hungarian Tourist Authority, Budapest pp 86, 110, 126, 171, 175;
S. M. Wragg pp38, 43, 46, 58, 59, 62, 63, 66

Authors' Proofreader: Helen Nield

MPC Production Team:
Editor: Tonya Monk
Editorial Assistant: Christine Haines
Designer: Ashley Emery
Cartographer: Alastair Morrison

CONTENTS

Key to Symbols Used in Text Margin and on Maps

▲	Church	*i*	Tourist Information
▥	Castle	✳	Other Place of Interest
⊞	Building of Interest	🦆	Birdlife
▣	Museum/Art Gallery	✿	Garden
🐐	Nature Reserve	⛰	Beautiful View/Natural Phenomenon
🚂	Railway	♣	Park
ᴨ	Archaeological Site	🦇	Cave
🚶	Walking	⛵	Water Sports
⛷	Winter Sports		

Key to Maps

▬▬▬	Motorway	⬠	City/Town
▬▬▬	Main Road	●	Town/Village
▬▬▬	Secondary Road	∿	River/Lake
┄┄┄	Minor Road	╌╌╌	National Boundary

How To Use This Guide

This MPC Visitor's Guide has been designed to be as easy to use as possible. Each chapter covers a region and gives all the background information to help you enjoy your visit. MPC's distinctive margin symbols, the important places printed in bold and a comprehensive index enable the reader to find the most interesting places to visit with ease.

At the end of each chapter an Additional Information section gives specific details such as addresses and opening times, making this guide a complete sightseeing companion.

At the back of the guide the Fact File, arranged in alphabetical order, gives practical information and useful tips to help you plan your holiday before you go and while you are there.

The maps of each region show the main towns, villages, roads and places of interest, but are not designed as route maps and motorists should always use a good recommended road atlas.

INTRODUCTION

H ungary lies in the very centre of Europe, yet, because of more than 40 years of isolation behind the Communist 'Iron Curtain', the country has only recently become a tourist destination popular with Western visitors. Hungary has always been thought of as being in Eastern Europe, which may have been right once politically but which is decidedly wrong geographically. Europe extends all the way over to the Urals in Central Russia, placing the country very firmly in Central Europe. This position has resulted in a variety of foreign powers gaining control of this small region of Europe through the centuries — each group of people leaving distinct reminders of their stay in the landscape, making modern Hungary a complex mosaic in which can be seen evidence of a number of different peoples and eras, from the Romans to the Turks, the Imperialist Habsburgs to the equally imperialist Soviets and, of course, the indigenous and unique culture of the Hungarians, the Magyars, who first arrived on the scene in the ninth century.

Hungary has always had more cultural and historical links with countries to the west, especially Austria, than with those to the east. Although Hungarian-speaking peoples originated from Central Asia and migrated into the Carpathian Basin from the east, by the eighteenth century Budapest (and Vienna) had risen to become the capitals of a vast empire which stretched, at its apogee, from the Alps and the Adriatic into modern-day Poland and Russia. Like Vienna, Budapest still maintains the vestiges of an Imperial capital; glorious palaces and broad boulevards and squares were laid out with all the confidence and arrogance of a city that once ruled a fair-sized chunk of Europe. In the eighteenth and nineteenth centuries the city became (with Vienna and Prague) one of the centres of Mitteleuropa (Middle Europe), an area hard to define but which was typified by the prominence of writers, intellectuals and artists, who became part of an elegant and sophisticated café society which characterised Budapest until the early part of this century. After 1945, the Iron Curtain came down over Mitteleuropa (Middle Europe), dividing it between two opposing spheres — capitalist Western Europe, and Marxist Eastern

Europe. Now, with the curtain lifted, the country is once again eager to throw off its eastern ties and affirm its position as a Western country; but, while Budapest is becoming more and more a Western capital, one does not have to travel very far to find scenes which would be unthinkable in most of Western Europe: the concrete housing blocks and huge industrial complexes that are the reminders of Stalinist days, or the pockets of rural poverty where the only vehicles on badly-made roads may be a horse and cart, carrying a farmer — and the produce from his tiny smallholding — to the local market.

As Hungary emerges from a 40 year period of economic and political domination by another country, and further back, from a more glorious history as an Imperial power itself, the future course of its development will remain a continuous balance between national desires and external pressures: between those anxious to develop and maintain the Hungarian state founded nearly a thousand years ago, which is now free from foreign domination, and those anxious to encourage more trading, economic, cultural and political links with the West, including eventual membership of the European Community. The developments which will take place in Hungary during the 1990s, and in the first part of the twenty-first century, remain unpredictable, but any change will take place rapidly as the country enters a new and decisive phase in its long history. It is for these reasons — in addition to the presence of Turkish mosques, Roman remains, Habsburg palaces and ancient peasant dwellings on the Plain, all of which are reminders of a long and complex history — that Hungary is fast becoming one of the most exciting and surprising travel destinations in Europe.

History

From Earliest Times To The Romans

The recorded history of Hungary starts with the Romans, but there is plenty of archaeological evidence to suggest that Stone Age man lived in the Carpathian basin 3 million years ago, hunting reindeer and living off what could be picked from trees and bushes. Half a million years ago, a small group established a settlement near what is now the village of Vértesszőlős, in northern Hungary, where some unique archaeological remains were discovered in the 1920s, including what is thought to be the earliest impression of a human footprint uncovered anywhere in the world. After the Ice Age these early peoples began to organise themselves into tribes and farming communities. Various different groups wandered into the country from different directions: the Kőrös culture from the Balkans, the Scythians from Asia and the Celts from Western parts of Europe. However, none of these peoples dominated the country, or left such an obvious mark, as the Romans. Their occupation of the land they called *Pannonia* lasted from AD10 to the beginning of the fifth century. The area was heavily militarised and consequently became very prosperous. There are reminders of the Roman occupation of Hungary all over the country, but the best preserved ruins are at Gorsium (near Székesfehérvár), *Aquincum* (in Budapest) and at Szombathely.

The First Hungarians

Roman withdrawal resulted in the occupation of the area by various warring tribes and invaders including the Huns and the Avars. The last of these tribes, the Magyars, under Árpád, arrived in AD896 and have occupied the Carpathian Basin ever since. The origin of the Magyar peoples is uncertain. Most of them migrated from an area around the River Volga in north-western Russia, but some tribes came from further south, and were formerly tent-dwelling nomadic herdsmen, living along the shores of the Caspian Sea. During the tenth century the Magyars established the first beginnings of a Hungarian state, and used the area as a base for daring raids into areas as far away as France and Constantinople — until a series of defeats led to them taking a more passive role as defenders of the territory which they had already conquered.

It is Árpád's great great-grandson, Stephen I (1000-1038) who has been credited with the foundation of the modern Hungarian state. Crowned with Papal blessing at Esztergom on Christmas Day, AD1000, Stephen forcibly dismantled the old tribal structure and replaced it with a feudal one, creating a new nobility to administer crown lands now organised into fifty rural counties. Desires to gain acceptance into the broader European political framework and to promote obedience and respect at grassroots level prompted Stephen to attempt to convert the Hungarians to Christianity and for this, in 1083, he was canonized. His mummified hand, held in a vault in St Stephen's Basilica in Budapest, is revered as a national and religious relic. By the beginning of the thirteenth century the Hungarian empire extended over Transylvania and parts of Croatia.

Medieval And Renaissance Hungary

In 1241 Mongol forces attacked from the east and caused widespread devastation and famine before their retreat. Under Béla IV the country embarked on the long and arduous task of reconstruction. The Árpád family line continued until the death of Andrew III in 1301. Three foreign rivals immediately claimed the throne: Charles Robert of the French Anjou dynasty eventually triumphed. A period of relative peace and expansion followed and by the time of Louis I (1342-82) the Hungarian empire stretched from the Adriatic to the Black Sea.

The reign of 'Renaissance King' Matthias Corvinus (1458-1490) has come to be viewed as Hungary's 'Golden Age'. The nobility were taxed without precedent to fund a 30,000 strong 'Black' army regularly used to raid Bohemia and Austria, and the artistic and cultural life of Hungary prospered; Matthias held court at the Palace of Visegrád (on the Danube) which for a time was one of the most glorious palaces of Central Europe. Two marriages proved childless and his second wife, Beatrice of Naples,

is thought to have poisoned him as he attempted to pave the way for the succession of a bastard son born of a Viennese commoner.

When Matthias died the nobles elected themselves a king (Ulászló II) who would allow them much more power. No one suffered more as a result of the shift in power than the rural underclass; taxes were raised and common land was filched. In response to this, in 1514, a peasant army initially raised to fight in a crusade decided instead to engage in a revolt against their noble lords. In the event, the crusade may have been the better option as the savage repression of the uprising saw an estimated 70,000 peasants killed and their leader, György Dózsa, roasted alive and eaten. After this episode the nobles treated the peasants even harder, binding them to virtual slavery under the Werbőczy Code of 1517.

Turkish And Habsburg Rule

The continual embezzlement of royal funds, and the neglect of the army and the country's fortifications led to the comprehensive rout of the Magyar forces at Mohács in 1526 by the Ottoman Turks under Seleyman the Magnificent. After Mohács the Turks easily took Buda and other important Hungarian cities in preparation for a final advance in to Austria and an unsuccessful attempt to capture Vienna. A three-way division of Hungary was formally recognised in 1568: Western Transdanubia and the north was controlled by the Habsburgs as a buttress to defend Vienna, Transylvania was controlled by the local nobility with the tacit agreement of the Turks, who controlled everywhere else. There are many reminders in Hungary of the long period of Turkish rule, especially in the mosques and minarets of Pécs and Eger, and in the many churches in some parts of the country which still bear signs of their use as mosques during the seventeenth century.

In 1699 the Turks were driven out by a multi-national army. The Peace of Karlowitz marked the end of Turkish rule. The Habsburg Empire immediately extended itself over the vacated territories which in 1703 prompted an 8-year-long War of Independence. It failed, and the subsequent resettlement of Swabians, Serbs and Romanians in the sparsely populated formerly Turkish-held regions resulted in the Magyars becoming a minority race within their own country. With Habsburg domination came rebuilding and renewal — especially of the palaces and churches in Budapest and elsewhere — and Baroque architecture, art and music flourished. But there was also an increasing 'Germanisation' of the country, and fears grew for the survival of the Hungarian language and culture. Many Nationalists, such as the Parliamentarian Lajos Kossuth, soon began to campaign for greater Hungarian independence, and many artists and architects began to develop a uniquely Hungarian, as opposed to Austrian, style. In 1848 there was a revolution in Hungary led by the poet Sándor Petőfi which was partly a revolt against Habsburg rule, and

One of the most pervasive images of Hungary: a horseman on a cattle ranch on the Great Plain

partly a peasant revolt against their still semi-feudal status. The revolt was only put down with the aid of a Russian army sent by Tsar Nicholas, anxious to see such subversive ideas quashed. However, the events of 1848 were not entirely in vain as they paved the way for the diplomatic 'Compromise' of 1867 which transformed the Habsburg Empire into an Austro-Hungarian one, with separate governments and parliaments in Budapest and Vienna. Over the next 50 years there were great developments in Hungarian cultural and economic conditions, as the country at last began to find its own voice. The Austro-Hungarian Empire, which lasted from 1867 until 1918, was vast, incorporating all of present day Austria and Hungary, the Czech and Slovak Republics and also parts of Italy, Romania, Poland, the Ukraine and Croatia. However, the Empire had defence, foreign and finance ministries which were common to both parts, and as a result Hungary was dragged into World War I on the side of Austria and Germany.

Between The Two World Wars

After defeat in 1918, Hungary declared itself a republic; then in 1919 the Communists swept to power with initially large support, though the large-scale nationalisation policies and anti-clericalism alienated many and alarmed the West. A French-backed Romanian army entered Budapest in August 1919 and forced the resignation of the Revolutionary Governing Council. The new Head of State was Admiral Miklós Horthy, who led the right-wing backlash that has come to be known as the 'White Terror'; Communists and Jews became the targets for fearful violence. Meanwhile, the Treaty of Trianon (1920) dismantled the Austro-Hungarian Empire and deprived Hungary of two-thirds of its historical territory and 3 million Hungarian speakers (including 1.7 million Hungarians who found themselves in Romania, a bitter loss still today).

During the 1920s and 1930s the political repression and economic hardships of the Horthy regime forced many Hungarians to emigrate. Government propaganda meanwhile blamed the country's problems on the Jews, and the Trianon powers of France, Great Britain and Romania, hence the increasing support for Nazi Germany within the country. This turned into an alliance when Hitler promised to (and indeed did) return lands lost by Hungary in 1920 to Czechoslovakia, Romania and Yugoslavia. Thus in 1941 Hungary entered World War II on the side of Germany, though the permitted transit of Nazi forces across Hungary to Yugoslavia (with whom Hungary had recently signed an 'eternal' Treaty of Friendship), proved too much for Prime Minister Pál Teleki and he promptly committed suicide. Winston Churchill declared that an empty chair would be left for Teleki at the table of any future peace conference, though none was. Early in 1944 Horthy saw that the Nazis would be defeated and tried to negotiate Hungary out of the war. The Germans responded to this by sending troops in and installing the Arrow Cross fascists in power. The Arrow Cross set about exterminating what was left of the country's Jewish Community — over half a million Hungarian Jews were shipped to

German concentration camps — while the German army concentrated its efforts on blowing up the capital's bridges to forestall the advancing Soviet army. Budapest was finally liberated in February 1945.

Communism And Its Eventual Collapse

In 1948, at the suggestion of the occupying Soviet army, the Communist Party and the National Social Democrats united to form the Worker's Party and formed a government, despite their failure to win a majority in the national elections. Matthias Rákosi ruled the country as a dictator, taking his orders from Stalin. Nationalisation was re-introduced and industrialisation given firm priority. As a result, many peasants flocked to the towns, and those left behind were forced into collective farms. Opposition was strong; in the late 1940s and early 1950s an estimated half a million people were imprisoned, tortured or shot, many in local concentration camps. Discontent finally erupted in 1956. For the immediate causes of the uprising one must go back to 1953 when, in the aftermath of Stalin's death, Kremlin power-struggles resulted in the replacement of hardliner Matthias Rakósi with the more liberal Imre Nagy, who became President. Two years later, Rakósi (who had remained Party Leader) replaced Nagy and announced a return to full-blooded Stalinism. This provoked general resentment which manifested itself in public debates and condemnatory literature. In response to this, Moscow sent in another hardliner Ernő Gerő. Mass demonstrations in Budapest and Szeged followed and on 23 October 1956 50,000 Budapest students besieged the radio building. The ÁVH secret police responded with live rounds, prompting a city-wide, then country-wide uprising. On 1 November, the reinstated Imre Nagy announced the Hungarian withdrawal from the Warsaw Pact and asked the United Nations to support Hungarian neutrality. Three days later, on 4 November, with Suez occupying world attention, the Soviets invaded and resistance was crushed. Thousands were imprisoned, and 200,000 fled to the West. Cardinal Joseph Mindszenty, the head of the Catholic Church who had been imprisoned by the Communists in 1949, was freed during Nagy's brief 4-day premiership, and when the Soviets invaded he sought sanctuary in the United States Embassy. He remained in the building for 15 years, until 1971, when he was allowed to leave the country. In 1958 Nagy was secretly tried and hanged in a prison on the outskirts of Budapest. He was buried in an unmarked grave with carcasses from the local zoo.

Yet changes occurred in the 1960s, with a softening of the former hardline attitudes. From 1961 prisoners were released and Prime Minister János Kádár proclaimed that 'He who is not against us, is with us' — a reversal of the famous slogan used by Stalin. Hungary's economic system became based on compromise and in the 1970s a private sector emerged under the title 'Market Socialism', or 'Goulash Communism' as it was sometimes called by some cynical Western commentators. Hungary became known as the most liberal of the Eastern Bloc countries; virtually all its citizens were allowed to travel to the West, and consumer goods

*Part of Hungary's
Roman heritage: a bust
of the marble head of
Julia, wife of Tiberias
Caesar, in the
Museum of Fine Arts
in Budapest*

appeared in the shops which were unheard of in the USSR or other Communist countries. Some Hungarians set up private businesses and were allowed to become relatively wealthy. The 1980s, however, saw increasing economic problems, including inflation, unemployment and a large foreign debt. An awareness of the need for more substantial economic changes coincided with the arrival in the USSR of Gorbachev and Perestroika. The declared illegality of the trial and execution of Imre Nagy and the intense publicity surrounding his formal reburial in June 1989 provided the spark for the changes. Hungary was the first Eastern Bloc state to announce multi-party free elections and to propose the withdrawal of Soviet troops. The decision in September 1989 to open the Hungarian-Austrian border to East German refugees, over 20,000 of whom crossed into Austria (and then to Germany) in the space of a few weeks, rendered the Berlin Wall moribund (and paved the way for the unification of the two Germanies in October 1990). In October 1989 the Hungarian Communist Party dissolved itself and passed legislation to legalise other political parties. The words 'Socialist Republic' were removed from the country's official title. Within 3 months the Communist regimes in East Germany, Czechoslovakia and Romania had also fallen. The first free elections in over 40 years were held in Hungary in March

1990, and the winning coalition became the country's first non-Communist government for over 40 years.

And The Future ?

As an unwilling victim to the avaricious desires of Turkish, Habsburg, German and Soviet empires, Hungary has very little history that is particularly its own, and very little democratic heritage. When Hungarians were last in control of their political destiny the country veered from one end of the political spectrum to the other. At the time of writing Hungary is probably the most politically stable of the former Eastern Bloc states, but the country faces severe economic problems and is receiving only partial help from the West to counter them. The transition to a full Market Economy will be painfully slow, but hopefully the Hungarian people will see the 1990s through with patience and perseverance in anticipation of better things to come in the early part of the twenty-first century.

Geography

Hungary lies in Central Europe. At the end of the 1980s and the beginning of the 1990s the political boundaries of this part of the continent were being redrawn (and in the case of Yugoslavia, fought over), but Hungary itself has remained immune to any changes of this sort. It is bordered by seven states: Austria lies to the west, Slovakia (formerly part of Czecho-

The River Danube at Budapest, Hungary's most important river

slovakia) to the north, the Ukraine (formerly part of the USSR) to the north-east, Romania to the south-east and the former Yugoslav Republics of Serbia, Croatia and Slovenia to the south. The area of the country is 93,033sq km (35,762sq miles), making it about a third the size of the United Kingdom, or just over two thirds the size of New York State. Hungary has a population of 10.6 million, a fifth of whom live in Budapest; other large cities are Debrecen, Miskolc, Pécs, Szeged, Győr and Székesfehérvár.

Hungary is situated in the Carpathian Basin. The country is surrounded by high mountain ranges — the Alps to the west, the Carpathians to the north and east, and the mountains of the Balkan peninsula to the south — but has no high mountains itself. The highest ranges of hills (or low mountains) are along its northern border where Mount Kékés reaches a height of 1,015m (3,329ft) above sea level. The longest river is the Tisza which is a tributary of the Danube, the country's most important river which flows through Budapest and into which all the other rivers in the country drain. Much of Hungary's external and internal trade is shipped along this river.

Most of the land in Hungary is flat or gently undulating. A belt of low mountains across the north-western part of the country divides the Plain into the Kisalföld (Little Plain) in the north-west, and the Puszta (Great Plain) to the south-east. The Kisalföld is the area that anyone travelling between Budapest and Vienna will pass through. It is an intensely culti- vated region, and the site of the major historical settlements of Sopron, Győr and Szombathely as well as a string of picturesque small towns. The southern part of the Kisalföld breaks out into the pimple-like volcanic hills which are part of the Bakony range which stretches along the northern shores of Lake Balaton. The Bakony is an ideal place for rambling and provides the setting for a dozen castles (the most impressive are at Sümeg and Nagyvázsony). Balaton is one of the largest lakes in Europe and is the country's most popular holiday destination away from the capital.

The Danube cuts through a low range of mountains just north of Budapest, at a place known as the Danube Bend. This area is popular with hikers and there are spectacular views from many high points above the river. In north-eastern Hungary there are a number of low mountain ranges which lie along the country's border with Slovakia, including the Mátra, the Bükk and the Zempléni. These hills are popular winter and summer destinations — fine for walkers, and, though virtually no West- erners will come to Hungary to ski, there are a few small winter resorts in this region. South of these hills is the Great Plain, which covers two-thirds of Hungary and is the chief agricultural region. The Danube and Tisza, which run across it, divide it into three natural regions. There are also many large towns in the Plain, of which the most important are Szeged (in the south) and Debrecen (in the east).

Flora and Fauna

The characteristic covering of the Transdanubian lands and mountains is deciduous woodland. Oak, beech, lime and chestnut trees cover many areas, whereas the Great Plain is intensively cultivated crop land, interspersed with areas of rough grassland and marsh. The Great Plain was once wooded, but it was cleared by early invaders from Asia, a process which continued during the long wars against the Turks. Thick forests cover the mountain and hill ranges — the silent, eerie pine forests of the Northern Uplands and the hills around the Danube Bend are home to boars, deer, foxes, and hares. Hungary is an important station for bird migration between Europe and Africa. The most common birds are storks, cranes and swallows. Part of Lake Balaton is kept as a reserve for birdlife; hundreds of species are seen here, of which the heron is probably the most beautiful. Carp is the most prominent freshwater fish; two-thirds of the commercial catch from the Danube belong to the carp family. There are numerous nature reserves where Hungary's diverse wildlife can be seen in its natural habitat. The best known are the reserves on the Great Plain, the Kiskunság National Park near Kecskemét, and the Hortobágy National Park near Debrecen, where the typical natural and human life of the Great Plain can be seen to greatest effect.

Food and Drink

Eating Out

Hungarian cooking is typically wholesome and nourishing, and is often not particularly good for you. This is no place for those on a diet, and the expanding girths of many middle-aged Hungarians point to a national cuisine which comprises such calorific staples as red meat, potatoes and rich desserts. The cooking, like that of Germany, Austria, and other Central European countries, is heavily meat based (pork is easily the most common meat, followed by beef and poultry) but with some more distinctive Hungarian elements such as the addition of spices to many dishes. Paprika is the most common spice, introduced to the country by the Turks. Sour cream and yoghurt, important ingredients in many dishes, are popular in other Balkan countries, while all the rich meat dishes and cream-drenched desserts show the German influence in Hungarian cooking. Visitors will find that eating out is good, and by West European standards, often outstandingly cheap, with restaurants providing generous portions and offering their clients a wide choice of food and good-quality wines, and often laying on some form of entertainment as well. The dour nature of restaurants and food still found in some of the old Eastern Bloc countries is not common here: in Hungary people take their food seriously, making eating out a pleasure rather than the grimly-borne necessity that it is elsewhere. Only a brief indication of the type of food available can be given here. Visitors will need a good phrase book to navigate around the menu, which is seldom available in English (though German speakers will often find that restaurants provide menus in that language).

Hungary's most famous speciality is undoubtedly goulash *(gulyás)*. In Hungary, this is not a stew (though it may be served as such in the most touristy areas) but it is actually a thick beef soup *(gulyásleves)* cooked with onions and potatoes and seasoned with paprika, peppers or caraway, often with whole pieces of meat, carrots, other vegetables or bits of pasta floating around in it. It was originally the basic dish of shepherds; now it is an integral part of Hungarian cuisine, served everywhere — and, since there are no real 'rules' as to how it is made, it is different everywhere you try it. Other soups *(levesek)* to look out for are fish soups, often made from a variety of types of freshwater fish, a meat soup called *Újházi tyúkhúleves* which is chicken based but which is normally flavoured with spices, vegetables and other meats, or *hideg gyümölcsleves*, a cold fruit soup.

One ingredient rarely missing from goulash, and many other main dishes, is paprika, a red or yellow spice originally introduced to Hungary by the Turks, which is usually used to add flavour and colour to dishes. It is from paprika that Hungary gets its reputation for having a 'spicy' cuisine, though it actually comes in six different strengths, from *különleges* (very mild) or *csemege* (mild) through *édes nemes* and *félédes* to *rózsa* (rose) and *erős* or *csipős* (very hot). Most dishes are prepared using the mildest form, but stronger forms are usually placed on restaurant tables next to the salt and pepper. In markets, paprikas are usually bought whole. In restaurants and in supermarkets it usually appears as a finely-ground powder, the strength of which is determined by the ratio of seeds to flesh of the plant that is used.

The majority of Hungarian dishes are meat-based; pork, beef and poultry predominate, often in the form of *pörkölt* where the meat is stewed in lard with onions and paprika and then served with either rice or boiled potatoes, or even chips. The chicken version of this is called *paprikáscsirke* and is served with sour cream. Another popular main course is *töltött káposzta*, cabbage stuffed with meatballs, smoked ham and sausage and served with sour cream. Other meats available are veal, bacon, lamb, steak, turkey, hare, wild boar, venison, pheasant, or duck. They are often served up with *galuska* — balls of flour, egg and dough — or *zsemlegombóc* (dumplings), though thankfully these do not come in the bewildering varieties that the Czechs are used to. The salad served with these dishes will often be a token gesture only. Lake Balaton is a major source for freshwater fish. Carp, pike and trout are widely available, though sea fish are understandably hard to find. Many fish dishes are, like meat dishes, served up with paprika, vegetables, sour cream or onions. *Halászlé* is a soup made from a mixture of several kinds of fish, tomatoes, green peppers and paprika. It is very filling and can appear as a main course or starter. Many fish and meat portions are coated in breadcrumbs. Many main dishes are specialities of a certain region or town in Hungary. For example, anything called *Szegedi* will be a speciality of the city of Szeged.

Desserts *(édességek)* are typically rich and bear some resemblance to what you might find in Germany or Austria. The favourite ingredients in desserts are chocolate and chestnuts, walnuts or hazelnuts, and everything seems to come with rich amounts of cream or chocolate or nut sauces. Desserts include various assortments of pancakes *(palacsinta)* with a choice of fillings, and strudels *(rétesek)*, thin pastries filled (again) with a choice of anything from apple or cherries to almonds, nut-based pastes or soft cheeses. The most famous strudel is called *Gundel palacsinta*, named after a Budapest restauranteur whose deluxe restaurant can still be found on the edge of the city park in the capital, which consists of pancakes filled with a walnut, raisin and chocolate paste, topped with more chocolate (often grated) or cream. Hungarians are also fond of ice cream *(fagylalt,* available everywhere in summer) and sweet cakes (available in bakeries or cafés, to eat there or take away).

Facilities for vegetarians are poor, but getting better. For a long time the concept of vegetarianism was simply unknown. However, there are now

Eating out in open-air restaurants throughout Hungary is a good way to enjoy local cuisine

vegetarian restaurants springing up in Budapest and meatless dishes are available in some restaurants. *Gombapörkölt* is a mushroom stew, *rántott sajt* is deep-fried cheese coated in breadcrumbs. Egg-based dishes are also available in a variety of different forms, look for the word *tojás* (egg). Yet one must be careful as to what one orders as even vegetable soups may contain meat stocks.

Wines, Beers And Spirits

The finest Hungarian wines *(bor)* are produced on the Volcanic soils of the Badacsony, on the northern shores of Lake Balaton (from where Roman Emperors once had the wine shipped to Rome), and also around Eger, Tokaj, and Sopron, in north-eastern Hungary. In the south of the country, Pécs, Villány and Szekszárd are surrounded by vineyards. Most wines are named after the region in which they are produced. Look for the name of the place with a letter 'i' on the end of it (eg wines called *Soproni* come from around Sopron in north-western Hungary). The most famous Hungarian wines are *Egri Bikavér* (Bull's Blood from Eger) which is a very full-bodied and dark-coloured red wine, the opposite to which is *Egri Leányka* (Maiden of Eger), a delicate, sweet white wine and *Tokaji Aszú* which is a very sweet (almost port-like) dessert white wine which has many famous admirers. Louis XIV of France called it 'the King of wines and the Wine of Kings', Schubert wrote a song about it and Peter the Great was so impressed with it that he bought a Tokaj-producing vineyard. Tokaj wines are marketed abroad as Tokay and in Hungary many varieties can be bought in supermarkets. For Tokaj and other wines, *száraz* on a label means dry, *félszáraz* means medium-dry, while *édes* means sweet. Wines may also sometimes be known by the recognisable names of the variety of grape used — eg *Rizling* (Riesling) or *burgundi*. Pinot and Cabernet grapes have also been introduced to Hungary and, conversely, Hungarian vines have been introduced to California. The words *Minőségi bor* on labels are the Hungarian equivalent of *appellation contrôlée*. Red wine is *vörös*, white is *fehér*. It is a common practice to add mineral or soda water to table wines at restaurants.

Another popular drink is *pálinka*, a clear and very potent brandy made from apricots, apples, cherries, peaches, pears or plums. Different areas produce their own specialities — amongst the most well-known is *barack pálinka*, apricot brandy made from fruit grown around the city of Kecskemét on the Great Plain. *Mecseki* and *hubertus* are two delicious Hungarian liqueurs. The beers *(sör)* available in Hungary are of the lager variety, available in 0.33cl or 0.5cl bottles. German and Austrian beers are widely available, though Czech, Slovak or Hungarian varieties are good quality and also cheaper. Russian vodka is available cheaply in supermarkets.

Where To Eat And Drink

Restaurants come in four different classes (I to IV, with I being the highest rating) and introduce themselves under a bewildering number of names.

Conveniently, many restaurants are increasingly calling themselves 'restaurants', though until recently the term has not been used much in Hungary. *Étterem* or *vendéglő* are what Hungarians call restaurants. The first term is often used by slightly classier establishments. A *csárda* originally meant an inn, but is now used to designate 'traditional' (expensive) establishments where gypsy musicians are virtually guaranteed and which are specially geared towards serving foreign visitors. Lower down the scale are the *bisztró*, which will offer a few hot dishes besides cold snacks, and further down still the *büfé*, which is often little more than a café or pub which may sell hot food and normally found in stations or by the road, open long hours. Right at the bottom is the *Önkiszolgáló*, a very cheap self-service restaurant popular with factory workers, in which Western visitors may cause a raised eyebrow or two.

Lunch *(ebéd)* is the main meal of the day (often there is more variety of food on offer at lunchtime rather than in the evenings). It is served between 12noon and 2pm. Some restaurants offer a set lunch of soup, main course and side salad, and sometimes dessert. Dinner is *Vacsora* and in areas that are used to tourists it will often be accompanied by live music or 'native' gypsy musicians, who will expect to be tipped. Breakfast *(reggeli)* is not really served outside hotels, where it is usually of the continental variety — often without a paprika in sight. Menus are often available in German and, less frequently, English. Everywhere provides two or more set menus *(napi)* which, by law, must be cheaper than buying the same food à la carte. Bread is usually supplied with the meal. Service charges are not usually included in the bill; 10 per cent is an appropriate figure, simply tell the waiter how much change you would like when paying. Service in Hungarian restaurants can be variable. It is generally believed that foreigners are treated better because they are more likely to leave a bigger tip. Bills must normally be requested from, and paid to, the head waiter, who will not necessarily be the one who served your food. Tips in hard currency will be gratefully appreciated.

For drinking purposes one can visit a *söröző* (beer hall), *borozó* (wine bar) or *borpince* (wine cellars, found in wine-producing areas where the products of the local vineyards can be tasted). Alternatively, Hungary has numerous cafés *(kávéház)* the cafés of Budapest in particular have a great reputation as the focal point for intellectual activity, though nowadays they are beyond the price that most Hungarians can afford, and many now exist for visitors. The coffee in most establishments is of the small, black espresso variety, and is usually extremely strong. Coffee with milk is *tejeskávé*. Coffee with cream is *tejszínhabbal*. It is drunk throughout the day and so usually comes in extremely small cups. Fast-food establishments will normally serve something a little more substantial. Another place to look for coffee is in a *cukrászda*, which are very common. These establishments are basically patisseries, offering cakes, ice creams and other sweet desserts, though they can vary from classy places with nice décor to run-down establishments along side streets.

Many street stalls sell drink and hot or cold snacks. These may sell anything from corn-on-the-cob to fried fish from the local lake, but there are also many places selling the all-pervasive hot dogs, fries or hamburgers, and many American fast-food establishments are mushrooming in Budapest and in provincial cities. Other popular street eats are *lángos*, huge ring-shaped doughnuts which are served hot, with either sweet or sour flavourings, and waffles which may come with melted cheese or sliced meat on top.

Cultural Life

Literature

Hungarian literature has, for the most part, been the literature of a politically repressed people. Consequently, the writing of political poetry has been almost a moral obligation for Hungarian writers. This, together with the general inaccessibility of the language (its nearest relations are Finnish and Estonian) may be why so few Hungarian writers are known outside its borders. Hungary's national poet is Sándor Petőfi (1823-49), an inspiratory figure in the 1848 revolution. He wrote the Hungarian *National Song* and is thought to have actually died in the fighting although no grave has ever been found. Lyric poet and revolutionary Endre Ady (1877-1919) also died young (of a blood disorder) as did Attila József (1905-37) whose short life ended under the wheels of a freight train at Balatonszárszó. József was a tragic figure, an outcast from society with schizophrenic tendencies, who has nevertheless become one of Hungary's most revered sons. Hungary's most famous post-war poet is János Pilinsky (1921-1981). His grandly impotent verse has been widely championed in the West and is available in an English translation by Ted Hughes.

Hungary's most important novelist is the nineteenth-century story teller Mór Jókai (1825-1904). In the revolutionary era that he wrote his novels they were dismissed as light entertainment but widely read. Jewish-Hungarian schoolteacher Milán Füst (1888-1967) was being considered for the Nobel Prize for Literature in the year of his death. A fearful eccentric, awe-inspiring and shockingly rude, Füst led a largely uneventful life and produced his masterwork *The Story Of My Wife* while in self-imposed exile in his Budapest villa during the Fascist era. In 1862 Imre Madách (1823-64) wrote what has come to be Hungary's most enduring play, *The Tragedy of Man*. Madách was a reclusive country gentleman, unknown in the literary world at the time of the play's publication, who died before he could give any precise clues as to the philosophical meaning of the work. After the 1956 revolution, many writers whose works were seen as anti-Communist were imprisoned or were forced to flee the country, but in the 1960s some of these rules were relaxed to allow writers to have more freedom of expression.

*Scenes of rural
Hungary*

Cinema

In 1928 Mihály Kertész (1888-1962) emigrated to America, changed his name to Michael Curtiz and became probably the most colourful and versatile director of Hollywood's 'Golden Age'. An acknowledged sadist, Curtiz directed his films wearing breeches and riding boots, chomping cigars and brandishing a fly-whisk. He directed such classics as *Twenty Thousand Years in Sing Sing*, and *Casablanca*. Another emigré, impressario Alexander Korda (1893-1956), was responsible for most of the major British films of the 1930s and 1940s including *The Thief of Baghdad* and *The Private Life of Henry VIII*. István Szabó and Miklós Jancsó stand out amongst modern-day directors. In 1982 Szabó won an oscar for his film *Mephisto*.

In Communist days Hungarian films were subsidised by the government and the country's cinema was allowed to be more critical of the country's society and political framework than that of other Eastern Bloc states. With money from the government, Hungarian directors tended to make films which catered for the high-brow rather than populist tastes — a situation which is now changing, as films become more geared towards the needs of the market place. Budapest's annual film festival, in February, is the showcase for new Hungarian films, shown dubbed or subtitled for the benefit of foreign critics and distributors. But few Hungarian films see the light of day outside the country in which they were made, and most Hungarian cinemas show Western films which have been dubbed for the benefit of Magyar audiences. Nevertheless, a few of the smaller cinemas in Budapest sometimes exhibit oddities — even if it is just a subtitled Western art-house film that you may have missed when it was on back home. More information about actually seeing films in Hungary can be found in Chapter 8 'What to do in Hungary'.

Art

Hungarian painting reached its zenith with the nineteenth-century school of Romantics. Mihály Munkácsy (1844-1900) became the most famous internationally, painting mainly historical and religious paintings in a realistic style. In 1872, he left Hungary for Paris, ending his days in a lunatic asylum on the outskirts of Bonn. The best examples of his work are in the Hungarian National Gallery and in the Déri Museum in Debrecen. More modern trends are represented in the work of Impressionist Pál Szinyei Merse (1845-1914) and the 'Group of Eight' (Nyolcak) who combined expressionism and cubism with a didactic socialist fervour. The best examples of the work of the Group of Eight are to be found in the Szombathely Gallery. During the Horthy period before World War II and the Stalinist period after it, artistic creation was rigidly controlled and many progressive artists were forced, either through personal taste or by active persecution, to emigrate. Pressure, however, eased quite substantially after 1956.

Another strand of Hungarian art is folk art, the existence of which is now relegated largely to tourist areas and to isolated villages deep in the

Northern Uplands or on the Great Plain. Folk art in its many forms (costumes, handicrafts, and paintings, in addition to music and dancing) can be seen mainly at festivals. For more information, see Chapter 8. The most popular places to see folk art are Hollókő (Chapter 7), where villagers still wear traditional, brightly-coloured costumes on certain festival days and Kalocsa (Chapter 5) where, in addition to costume wearing, there is folk art in the form of embroidery, decorated pottery and ornaments, and floral decorations on the town's traditional buildings. The folk artefacts that tourists buy and see in Hungary are traditional forms of ceramics, embroidery and wood-carving whose form often dates back to medieval times.

Music

Franz (properly Ferenc) Liszt (1811-1886) spent the majority of his life abroad but he did return to his homeland to become the first President of the Hungarian Academy of Music. The Academy is now the most prestigious music school in Hungary, producing many outstanding young composers and performers who benefit from five free and intensive years of musical education from established and internationally famous musicians. Liszt's Hungarian Rhapsodies reflect his interest in gypsy music and the nationalism of the era; he also wrote some prodigiously difficult piano music and was widely known as a virtuoso pianist. Liszt grew up on the Eszterházy Estate and studied music in Vienna from the age of 11. Another Hungarian composer who found fame in Vienna was Franz Lehár, who wrote many famous operettas including *The Merry Widow*. In the eighteenth and nineteenth centuries many composers spent some time in Hungary. Beethoven is supposed to have composed the *Moonlight Sonata* in a villa at Martonvásár, near Budapest, while between 1760 and 1791 Joseph Haydn worked as a court composer to the Eszterházy family at their mansion at Fertőd (formerly Esterháza) in north-western Hungary, where many of his works were premiered.

The history of twentieth-century Hungarian music is dominated by the names of Béla Bartók (1881-1945) and Zoltán Kodály (1882-1967). They were the first people to seriously compile and analyse Hungarian folk music and both used it as the basis for some of their own compositions. Soon after the outbreak of World War II Bartók left Hungary for America where he found illness and obscurity; he died in New York. Like many composers, his genius was only recognised after his death, and the huge increase in the popularity of his music since World War II encouraged the Hungarian government to bring his body back to Hungary in 1988 for reburial in his homeland. Many Hungarian emigré musicians, such as the conductor Sir Georg Solti, specialise in interpreting the music of Bartók and have succeeded in making his music known to a wider audience. Bartók's works feature in the repertoires of major orchestras all over the world, and some of his operas such as *Duke Bluebeard's Castle* are often staged outside Hungary. Kodály, however, stayed in Hungary, made important innovations in music education (see under Kecskemét, in Chapter 6) and wrote subtly subversive music during the Communist era.

Unless they go to concerts (for more information see Chapter 8 'What to do in Hungary'), the music which most visitors to the country will come into contact with will be folk music. Bartók and Kodály both identified Hungarian folk music with gypsy music, and many modern folk groups play music which was catalogued and collected by these two composers earlier this century. Traditional folk instruments include the Shepherd's Pipe or flute, and the Hungarian bagpipes. The zither and cymbalom are both stringed instruments, the latter played using specially shaped carved wooden sticks with which to strike the strings. The *Táncház* (dance house) has revived interest in Hungarian folk songs, but it is difficult to differentiate between gypsy and genuine Hungarian folk music; folk music from Transylvania and Serbia is played in areas which traditionally have links with these countries. Popular Hungarian dances, such as the wild and foot-stamping *czardas*, originated at the end of the eighteenth century and form another distinctive strand of Hungarian music. Many restaurants have a group playing traditional Hungarian or gypsy music to guests.

People, Politics And Economy

There are presently 10.6 million people living in Hungary, of which 96 per cent are ethnic Hungarians, descendants of the Magyar tribes that moved into this area from Central Asia in the ninth century. The next largest groups are Gypsies and ethnic Germans, and there are also small numbers of Slovaks, Romanians, Serbs and Croats. Hungary is probably the least ethnically troubled country of Eastern Europe, in part due to the Treaty of Trianon in 1920 under which the Hungarian Empire lost two-thirds of its territory, creating an ethnically cohesive Hungarian state but leaving large minorities of Hungarians living in neighbouring countries. Over 2 million ethnic Hungarians live in Romania, 750,000 in the Czech and Slovak Republics, 450,000 in the former Yugoslavian Republics and smaller numbers in the Ukraine and Austria. Due largely to the mass emigration which took place in the 1920s and 1930s, there are Hungarians spread right across the globe. About 250,000 live in Western Europe (including 25,000 in Great Britain), and a further 600,000 live in the United States, with smaller numbers in Brazil, Argentina, South Africa and Australia, all of which have small but significant Hungarian communities. There are also a quarter of a million Hungarian-speaking Jews living in Israel.

The 2 million Hungarian speakers who live in Romania constitute the largest minority people living in any country of Europe. Their treatment by the government of Romania under Ceauşescu resulted in bitter disagreements between the two countries, and in widespread public outrage in Hungary. They live in north-western parts of Romania, on the Plains around Arad and Oradea, and in the valleys of Transylvania. In some of these regions, Hungarians form the vast majority of the population and Romanian speakers are unwelcome visitors. Control of this area has long been disputed: the Romanians say that their own descendants, the Dacian peoples, originally came from this part of Romania, and that when the Hungarians colonised the area in the tenth century, they expropriated land which was rightfully Romanian. The Hungarian version of the story is that Transylvania was unpopulated when colonisation began, so the Romanians have few historical rights to the area. During the Ceauşescu era the culture of these native Hungarian speakers was regarded by the Romanian government as subversive, and much was done to suppress the language and traditions of these people, a fairly easy task in Ceauşescu Romania where the feared *Securitate* (Secret Police) infiltrated every factory and school, and where people were openly encouraged to turn informer against members of their own family. In 1988 Ceauşescu imple-

Children wearing traditional Hungarian costume

mented his policy of *sistematizare*, which involved the destruction of thousands of Romanian villages and the setting up of large rural communities on greenfield sites, which the government thought would be a more efficient way of organising agriculture, but which would also (usefully) break up rural communities, giving ethnic minorities in Romania (especially the Hungarians) even less of a chance to organise themselves and to voice their disagreements with the Romanian government. With the ending of the Ceauşescu regime in Romania at the end of 1989, this policy stopped, and things are now looking brighter for the Hungarians who live in the country. But, nevertheless, many of them are moving into Hungary to take advantage of that country's higher living standards and, of course, its more sympathetic government and people.

Two-thirds of Hungarians can be broadly defined as Roman Catholic. About a quarter are Protestant, living particularly in the north-east of Hungary where many people are adherents to Lutheranism and Calvinism. There are small communities of Jews and Greek Orthodox. Communist pressure on all these religions eased during the 1960s, although Hungarians were not granted complete freedom of religion until 1989. The average life expectancy in Hungary is low in comparison to the West. Hungary also has very high levels of suicides, violent deaths and chronic diseases. Sociologists blame these on the stress of the political and economic changes which also manifests itself in an increasing addiction to tobacco and alcohol, also the fact that it is not unusual for Hungarians to have to take more than one job to make ends meet — consequently leisure time is considered something of a privilege.

Hungary has a one-house parliament called the National Assembly. Parliaments are elected for 4 year terms. The Head of State is the President whose duties include serving as Commander-in-Chief of the Armed Forces, authorising elections and carrying out the duties of the National Assembly between sessions. The National Assembly appoints a Council of Ministers, members of which head the various government departments. The chairman of the Council is the Prime Minister. After the elections of March 1990 the Hungarian Democratic Forum emerged as the largest single party and they formed an alliance with the Christian Democratic People's Party and the Independent Smallholder's Party (who actually won the last free election in 1945). Árpád Göncz became President and József Antall became Prime Minister. At Local Government level, Hungary is divided into 19 counties and 6 cities (including Budapest) that rank as counties. These are governed by local councils elected every 4 years.

In 1990 the new government introduced reforms to further limit government control over businesses. This continued a trend which stretches back to the New Economic Mechanism of 1968, which introduced elements of a Market Economy into Hungary's planned, Marxist Economy. Already in the 1980s, the government had stopped funding loss-making companies, encouraged the formation of private businesses and allowed successful ones to pay their workers higher wages. Yet the transformation to a full Market Economy has brought with it many problems as much of Hungarian industry is uncompetitive and inexperienced in the ways of the market. The government lacks the money for the necessary major restructuring and so has tended to wash its hands of the problem either by simply withdrawing subsidies and leaving companies to fend for themselves (usually unsuccessfully; unemployment is becoming a major problem, especially in the north-east where much of the country's heavy industry is situated), or by simply selling companies off, usually to foreign investors. Many foreign companies have had their fingers burned, having bought inefficient industrial plants in the expectation of a protected, and indeed larger, domestic market. Rising prices in the country have not helped the situation. The companies that are left have a major problem concerning markets. In the Communist era, half of all the trade was conducted with the former Eastern Bloc countries who now lack the hard currency to maintain trading links. In such an economic climate, every penny earned in hard currency from tourism is very important. Having said this, the Hungarian economy is in a much better shape than that of many other formerly Communist countries, and in April 1994 the country formally applied to become a member of the European Union.

Hungary's Attractions: What There Is To See And Do

The city of Budapest is the most important destination for most visitors to Hungary. A considerable proportion of any amount of time in the country is likely to be spent seeing this beautiful and, until recently, comparatively undiscovered city. Budapest's fascination rests in its blend of architectural styles — from Turkish to Baroque, and nineteenth-century palaces to Roman remains — and also in its fusion of the old East and West: brash commercialism and the hedonism found in its all-night wine bars and clubs contrast with an antiquated but reliable public transport system, and prices that are still absurdly cheap by the standards of other European capitals, all of which can be savoured in a city whose cultural attractions are enormous and whose Imperial splendour is still readily apparent. Budapest is now awash with tourists at all times of the year. However, the rest of the country is less well known, and although this book has a lengthy chapter devoted to the capital, the chapters that follow it allow the visitor to escape the city crowds and head for the scenery, castles and historic towns in the other parts of the country.

Many provincial cities, while lacking the pulling power of Budapest in what there is there to see and do, have a fair amount to offer visitors, in terms of their historic sites and a varied set of cultural attractions. The three nicest provincial cities in Hungary are probably Eger (Chapter 7), a wine-making centre in the foothills of the Bükk Mountains; Sopron (Chapter 3), a town in north-western Hungary very close to the Austrian border which boasts many fine medieval buildings and streets; and Pécs (Chapter 5), in the sunny south of the country, where the Turks and Romans made striking contributions to the city's architecture and history. These three towns also have much to offer in terms of places to see in the areas surrounding them, and are good centres to head for if visitors want to experience a small piece of what Hungary has to offer outside Budapest. Other towns worth visiting are Kecskemét and Szeged in the western part of the Great Plain, which, like Debrecen in the eastern part, are important farming centres that have some varied architecture and cultural attractions (all Chapter 6); Győr and Szombathely, the largest towns in north-western Hungary, which have a certain charm about them, despite being large modern industrial centres (Chapter 3); and two very different former religious centres — Esztergom (Chapter 2), with its huge nineteenth-century basilica overlooking the Danube, is the place where King Stephen was born and was crowned, whereas Székesfehérvár (Chapter 4), half-way between Budapest and Lake Balaton, is the place where he died, and the city's long history as a religious centre has resulted in its offering a number of attractions to visitors. All these centres have the usual clutch of museums (which vary in quality and interest, and rarely have anything available in English for visitors), and a number will also have concert halls and theatres which will offer a programme of events that is likely to include something to appeal to non-Hungarian speakers (see Chapter 8 'What to do in Hungary' for further information).

In a land lacking any high mountains (the highest peaks are really only foothills compared to those of neighbouring countries), the biggest scenic attraction must be the River Danube which, in Hungary, flows through some of the most outstanding gorges and scenery anywhere along its whole length. Between Esztergom and Budapest the Danube turns in a huge U-shape, before turning again, abruptly, and heading south. This is the area of Hungary known as the Danube Bend, a popular destination for weekend excursions from the capital. The Pilis and Bőrszőny Hills, through which the river cuts so breathtakingly, are good hill walking country, and a number of settlements along the river here, notably Szentendre, Visegrád and Esztergom itself, offer historical sites that are well worth visiting. All these attractions can be reached easily by boat (or bus, train or car) from Budapest. Another area noted for its natural beauty is Lake Balaton, the largest lake in Central and Western Europe, which is shallow enough for the temperature of the water in summer to be warmer than that of the Mediterranean, a natural destination for many thousands of Hungarians to take their summer holidays. Despite the crowded resorts and beaches, it is possible to escape the throngs of people. The hills of the Tihany Peninsula, on the lake's northern shore, and the rounded, volcanic landscape of the Bakony Highlands, offer welcome retreat and peaceful scenery. The highest hills in Hungary are along its north-eastern border with Slovakia. Here the Mátra, Bükk and Zempléni ranges offer eerily gloomy scenery, with silent pine forests, villages where livestock roam at will and women still wear dark shawls and traditional long, multi-layered skirts, and where travellers will find a succession of castles, fine views and vineyard-covered slopes. Hungary's most famous wines, Tokay (from Tokaj) and Egri Bikavér (from Eger) come from this region. In addition, the area boasts one of Europe's deepest and longest limestone cave systems, at Aggtelek, a remote spot on the Slovak border north of Eger which receives many thousands of visitors each year. All these upland areas have a network of mostly well-kept and well-marked paths, which makes exploring easy. Some walks have been described in this book, but it is easy for visitors to buy a map of any area and plan out walks themselves (for more information, see the Fact File section at the end of this book). Scenery of a very different sort can be seen in the Great Plain, where mile upon mile of flat farming and pasture land exerts a curious pull on visitors, if only because parts of it *are* awesomely flat and expansive. In some areas the Great Plain gives way to marshes and lakes, which are havens for wildlife, the most notable examples being in the Forest of Gemenc (Chapter 5) and in the Bugac and Hortobágy National Parks (Chapter 6).

Hungary is as much a 'doing' country as a 'seeing' one, which is why a separate chapter has been included at the end of this book, detailing the many ways visitors can get the most out of a visit to Hungary besides the usual round of sightseeing and museum-going. Hungary has a famous cuisine and a good selection of wines, which make eating out an integral part of enjoying any trip (there are more details earlier on in this section). Concerts and festivals can be enjoyed in many towns. The fare on offer in Budapest is world-class and things like opera and ballet are far more affordable, and often of a comparable standard, to that offered in Western capitals. Budapest has a varied nightlife, and boasts oddities such as a laser theatre and many sporting events (such as the annual motor-racing Grand Prix) to keep visitors busy. It is also a great place for shopping and bargain or souvenir hunting. In the countryside it is possible to go horse-riding (the horseman has been a symbol of Hungary ever since the first Magyars arrived in the country on horseback), and skiing (though opportunities are limited — no Westerners come to the country with the sole intention of skiing). There are watersports around Lake Balaton, and also opportunities for birdwatching (around the country's many nature reserves), wine-tasting (many private vintners now let visitors taste the product of their vineyards and will sell you a bottle or two if you like it), and of course walking. There is a tremendous variety of things to see and do in Hungary, enough for visitors to seek out their own tastes and interests, possibly discover some new ones, and all the while enjoying the famous hospitality, and friendliness, of the Hungarian people themselves. The country is easy-going, and fast-changing enough for some parts to appear modern, yet for others still to maintain an air of traditionalism which has been subsumed by the pace of development in most West European countries. No wonder that the country is fast becoming one of the newest and most exciting tourist destinations in Europe.

1
BUDAPEST

Budapest is one of the great cities of Europe. Newly liberated from enforced semi-isolation behind the Iron Curtain, its attractions and charm are being enjoyed by millions of Western visitors every year. For many visitors, the capital is their only experience of Hungary and although this gives a very narrow impression of the country, there is no denying that not only is Budapest by far the most important tourist destination in the country, it is also very important to Hungarians themselves. All major roads and railway lines in the country lead there. It is home to one in five Hungarians, with no other city coming close to matching its population size of about 2 million; it is where the money is made. It is the centre of cultural and intellectual life, of politics and business, commerce and industry. Budapest always had a reputation as the most liberal and Western-looking city behind the old Iron Curtain. The death of Communism has given Budapest a new surge of energy and vitality which makes it an exciting place to visit. Like all cities, it has its negative aspects but these merely highlight the other side of the city, one of elegance and a slightly faded sophistication, of wide, tree-lined boulevards and the sweeping panorama of Castle Hill and the Royal Palace gained from the East Bank of the Danube. It is where most people will begin their tour of Hungary, which is ideal, for afterwards, leaving the capital for many of the provincial towns will be like entering another world entirely.

Initial Orientation: A View From The Citadel

When visiting a great capital city like Budapest for the first time, it is always difficult to know where to start. Arguably, the place to begin one's visit, from where it is possible to get to grips with Budapest's geography and visual splendour, is the Gellért Hill, a huge, craggy limestone cliff which rises above the central part of the city on the Western Bank of the

 River Danube. It is crowned by the Citadel and the stark Liberation

Monument. Its name derives from the fact that St Gellért, who converted the Magyars to Christianity at the behest of King Stephen, was thrown off the cliff in the year 1046, by pagans who took objection to him trying to convert them to the new religion. Its significance for visitors, however, is the panoramic views that it affords over the whole of Budapest, and beyond the city into the countryside and hills that surround it. To stand at the Citadel at the top of Gellért Hill, with a map of the city, and from there to get one's bearings, is as good an introduction to the capital as any.

From the Citadel, a number of Budapest's most distinctive monuments and features stand out. First and foremost is the River Danube, which flows beside the vertical cliffs of Gellért Hill and divides the capital into two areas: Buda, on the West Bank, and Pest, on the East. Much of the city's magnificence and charm comes from its position astride this great European river; elegant bridges cross it, vibrant promenades run along both sides of it, and the capital's most famous landmark, the Royal Palace, rises above its Western Bank. A steady stream of traffic constantly plies the river — small motor launches, passenger cruise ships of various sizes and degrees of luxury, industrial barges loaded with coal or minerals and towed by one or two smaller tugs, probably heading for the large dockyards on Sziglet Island, in the south of Budapest. The river has always been the life-blood of the capital, its spiritual and geographic heart. No city along the length of the Danube turns itself so obviously towards the river. Of the eight bridges that cross the Danube at Budapest, two or three stand out. These include the elegant Erzsébet híd, just below the Gellért Hill and, immediately upstream, the distinctive nineteenth-century suspension bridge known as the Chain Bridge (Széchenyi lánchíd), which crosses from the centre of Pest to the Royal Palace.

Buda is the historical heart of the capital. It has only been formally linked to Pest since 1873. Its most distinctive feature, again, visible from Gellért Hill, is the complex of buildings that make up the Royal Palace, a wealth of museums and galleries to which many visitors head first. These buildings are situated on Castle Hill, a superbly fortified area where steep slopes on all sides formerly deterred would-be attackers. The northern part of Castle Hill, where there are well-preserved old streets, buildings and churches, is also very popular with visitors. Behind Castle Hill (ie to the west) is Moszkva tér, an important transport interchange and also the Déli railway station, one of the capital's three mainline termini, from where there are trains to Vienna, and destinations throughout western and southern Hungary. From the Citadel it is possible to look beyond Castle Hill to the Buda Hills, a popular recreational area where there are a number of things to see and do, including walks, visits to ancient caves and an opportunity to ride the Pioneer railway, run entirely by young people for the benefit of children, which takes one beyond the suburbs of the city and into the forested hills.

Pest, on the other side of the river, is entirely different. While the main attractions of Buda are its historical landmarks, Pest is the centre of the

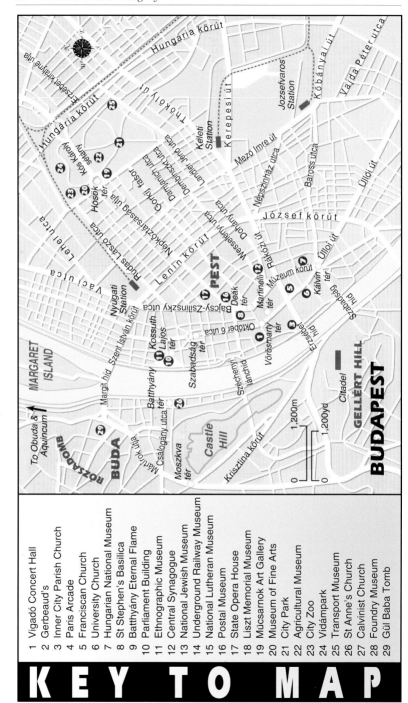

KEY TO MAP

1 Vigadó Concert Hall
2 Gerbeaud's
3 Inner City Parish Church
4 Paris Arcade
5 Franciscan Church
6 University Church
7 Hungarian National Museum
8 St Stephen's Basilica
9 Batthyány Eternal Flame
10 Parliament Building
11 Ethnographic Museum
12 Central Synagogue
13 National Jewish Museum
14 Underground Railway Museum
15 National Lutheran Museum
16 Postal Museum
17 State Opera House
18 Liszt Memorial Museum
19 Műcsarnok Art Gallery
20 Museum of Fine Arts
21 City Park
22 Agricultural Museum
23 City Zoo
24 Vidámpark
25 Transport Museum
26 St Anne's Church
27 Calvinist Church
28 Foundry Museum
29 Gül Baba Tomb

modern city. Its few historic monuments are lost amidst the bustle and hubub of a large and growing European capital. In contrast to the stately, somewhat refined atmosphere of Buda, Pest is unashamedly bold, brash and noisy. It is where Budapest's claim to be a Western, commercial capital, with all the attendant noise and detritus and excitement of a big city, is staked. Viewed from the Citadel, one's main impression of Pest is of the string of smart (and rather ugly) international hotels which line the Danube's East Bank, the riverside promenades outside their glass and steel walls alive with crowds and street entertainers. Behind these are Vörösmarty tér, a pedestrianised square which is arguably the heart of modern Budapest, and slightly beyond that are Deák and Erzsébet squares, where the three metro lines meet and where Budapest's main bus station can be found. Pest is not, however, merely a collection of smart shops, sophisticated nightclubs and overpriced restaurants. There are historical sites here that are worth exploring, including the old Jewish Quarter, and there are many fine museums and galleries. The other more functional aspects of Pest include the presence here of most foreign embassies, and also that of many government buildings, the police head-quarters, many banks, businesses and airline offices, and also Nyugati and Keleti railway stations, the capital's other main line termini.

A Brief History Of The Capital

The site on which Budapest is built has been occupied for many thousands of years. From the first to the fifth century AD the Romans governed their province of *Pannonia Inferior* from the garrison town of *Aquincum*, now part of the northern suburbs of Buda, where a number of Roman remains can still be seen. When the Magyars arrived on the scene in the ninth century, and began to colonise the area of modern day Hungary, Budapest remained undeveloped, and Esztergom, then Székesfehérvár, became the capitals of the newly created state.

Buda and Pest were developed more during the early Middle Ages, first as a trading port on the Danube inhabited by German and French settlers, and then as a defensive site, when a series of castles and palaces were built on Castle Hill. The remains of these medieval fortresses can still be seen beneath the buildings that currently stand there. King Matthias, who developed the splendid palace at Visegrád, further upstream along the Danube (see Chapter 2), is also credited with building an important castle at Buda.

Habsburg rule during the eighteenth and nineteenth centuries resulted in the building of many of the capital's most important monuments. Count István Széchnyi, a patron of Hungarian engineers and designers and also a commited anglophile, built the first railway lines into the city and also linked Buda and Pest for the first time, with the steel-built Chain Bridge. In 1867 the Austro-Hungarian Empire was created and Budapest became an Imperial Capital, with the lands of the Hungarian Crown stretching from the Adriatic into what is now the Ukraine, Slovakia and Romania. Pest was replanned, its new, wide streets and elegant boulevards a reflection of the confidence of the Hungarian rulers, and the esteem in which they held their capital. Hősök tere and the Heroes' Monument were built for the 1896 millenial celebrations, when the thousandth anniversary of the foundation of the Hungarian state was celebrated. Also at this time, Andrássy utca, which leads from the centre of Pest to Hősök tere, was built as a wide, stately avenue, and continental Europe's first metro line was constructed underneath it. Budapest became a bustling centre of *Mitteleuropa*, its cultural and intellectual life flourishing in the cafés and bars, its name becoming associated with a sophisticated brand of hedonism that was also found in the other great cities of the Empire, Prague and Vienna. Yet this golden period in the city's history was short lived, ended abruptly by two World Wars, invasion and foreign domination.

After World War I, when the Hungarian Empire was broken up, the country was briefly occupied by the Romanian army, and was then ruled by Admiral Horthy, who was deposed by the Nazis when Hungary became regarded as an untrustworthy ally of the Germans during World War II. The Nazis established the Arrow Cross Fascists in government, and killed or deported the capital's once thriving Jewish population. Fierce fighting during World War II led to the destruction of much of the city, including the Royal Palace on Castle Hill. The Nazis blew up all the Danube bridges in an attempt to prevent the advance of the Red Army.

Under Communism, Budapest witnessed pronounced sea-changes in the attitudes of the political masters of Hungary. In 1956 50,000 of its citizens marched on the parliament building to press for political reforms, and were met by live gun fire from the Secret Police which triggered a city-wide uprising and the Soviet invasion. After the uprising, Hungary's leaders adopted a hard-line Communist stance, which softened during the 1960s and 1970s as Hungary grew comparatively wealthy and its citizens could afford luxuries only dreamed of in other Eastern Bloc states. Váci utca, the capital's main shopping street, became a symbol of Hungary's new 'Goulash Communism' which allowed individuals to amass private wealth and allowed private enterprise and free market economics to play a greater part in the country's economy. After the collapse of Communism the city authorities set about removing all traces of the old style of government from the city. Streets and squares formerly named after Marx, Lenin, Engels and noted Hungarian Communists were soon renamed, and the city fast began to take on the look of a Western capital, with neon advertising appearing on every corner, the appearance of beggars and street hawkers in central Pest, and a noticeable amount of money-spinning consumerism. The future of Hungary may still be uncertain, but Budapest is confident of its new-found role as the capital of a fast-changing European state that desperately wants to be modern.

Getting The Most Out Of A Visit To Budapest

Budapest has a lot to offer visitors, and it is important that visitors plan their time in the city carefully in order to get the most out of their stay in the city. Firstly, all practical information relating to Budapest, including notes on accommodation, where to get information, using the transport systems, and lists of important addresses and telephone numbers, can be found in the back of this book under the relevant headings in the 'Fact File' section. Secondly, information about entertainments in Budapest, and what there is to do in the city beyond conventional sightseeing, is contained in Chapter 8, 'What to do in Hungary'. Here, there is information on everything there is to see and do in Budapest, including where to find information on eating out, theatres, cinemas and other entertainment, and on Budapest oddities such as the planetarium and laser theatre, where to take a boat trip on the Danube, the city's many thermal baths, and even where to go to use the public observatory. A visit to Budapest is certainly not complete unless visitors make use of the tremendous opportunities in the city that there are for entertainment and other activities away from the more conventional round of museums, churches and other historical sites.

This chapter covers the sites and sights of Budapest in a logical order. The first section deals with Pest, including the central shopping area around Vörösmarty tér and Váci utca, and then looks at the Jewish Quarter and the rich variety of museums that can be found on this side of the river. The second section deals with Buda, including the old Royal Palace and other attractions on Castle Hill, and also Gellért Hill which lies on the same side of the Danube. The islands in the Danube are also considered here. The third section goes further afield, to the Buda Hills on the outskirts of Buda, where the attractions are mainly based around walking in these wooded hills which stretch to the north-west of the city.

Finally, it is worth noting the many excursions which can be taken from the capital. Details about places to visit on day trips from Budapest can be found in the chapters that follow this one, and it is impossible to suggest a comprehensive list of possible destinations since many of these depend on how far one wishes to travel. Virtually all the places mentioned in Chapter 2 can be visited on day excursions from Budapest. Certainly many visitors to the capital visit the picturesque town of Szentendre, on the River Danube, getting there by road, bus, suburban railway or boat. Many places on the shores of Lake Balaton (Chapter 4) can be visited in a day's excursion from Budapest, as can those places (Martonvásár, Székesfehérvár and Lake Velence) which are described at the start of that chapter. Kecskemét, on the Great Plain (Chapter 6) can be seen on a day trip from the capital, perhaps combined with a visit to Szeged — which is much further afield, in the very south of Hungary. Even Pécs (Chapter 5) can be visited in a day's excursion from the capital, by those who do not mind too much travelling in one day.

PEST

Buda is the historic part of the Hungarian capital, with its carefully preserved buildings, Royal Palace and ancient (if heavily rebuilt) churches. But Pest is the true heart of the city, beating with a pulse and vitality that comes from a new-found freedom after years of repression under Communism. On a functional level, this is the business and political centre of Hungary, with most of the city's embassies, government offices and major offices of national and international firms being located here. To the north of the city centre, by the banks of the Danube, is the country's parliament building. Pest is the place to begin one's stay in the city, if only to visit the principal tourist and information offices here, to change money and to check transport or other details. But visitors to the city will also spend a lot of their sightseeing and leisure time in Pest: most of Budapest's major museums are here; the capital's most elegant and varied shops can also be found here, as can most of its theatres and cinemas, its restaurants and night clubs and big hotels. After dusk, Buda might as well not exist. In comparison, Pest seems to come alive at night, as people head for the lights and variety of the big city. Here, too, are the contrasts one experiences in any large city. The presence of large cars and expensive shops give an added poignancy to the ever-increasing signs of poverty on the streets — beggars, drunks, and, more recently, homeless refugees from what used to be Yugoslavia, who have entered Hungary in their thousands. Much of Pest has a turn-of-the-century feel to it in terms

Overlooking Pest from Buda

Sightseeing by cruise ship on the River Danube

of its stately architecture and wide streets. If it was to be compared to
another city in Europe, then that city would be Paris, without the pomp-
ous grandeur and chic elegance, perhaps, but also without the high costs
and huge crowds.

The Romans established a tiny garrison town here, as an offshoot of
their many fortifications in *Aquincum* on the other side of the river. In the
Middle Ages the town grew, becoming a prosperous trading post, but
Buda was always the more important of the two settlements. Only in the
twentieth century, with the growth of shops and theatres and transport
terminals on the East Bank of the river, has Pest grown to compete with,
and finally overwhelm, its western neighbour. The ancient core of Pest —
the old walled medieval city known as the Belváros (Inner City) — now
corresponds with the city's District V. It is bordered to the west by the
Danube, and to the north, east and south by wide boulevards that encircle
it — Vámház körút, Múzeum körút, József Attila utca. The centre of
modern Pest, and of the city of Budapest, is Vörösmarty tér, a few blocks
inland from the Danube. Váci utca, the city's main shopping street, runs
south from the square. Strung out along the Danube waterfront are a
number of large international hotels. By Vigadó tér, which opens out onto
the water, are the landing stages for boats (the international boat terminal
is just south of Erzsébet híd). A number of wide roads radiate out from the
Belváros, the most famous of which is Andrássy utca, Budapest's widest
and most stately boulevard which links the centre of the city to the
Városliget, the City Park, a peaceful area of lakes and woodland on the
north-eastern outskirts of the city centre. The very central area of the city

is encircled by another half-ring of wide, fast streets — Szt István körút, Erzsébet körút, Ferenc körút and József körút — and it is around this continuous boulevard that two of the capital's major railway stations are found. Keleti station, east of the city centre, is the main terminal and departure point for long-distance trains to Western Europe, while Nyugati station, to the north-east of the centre, is another important internal and international gateway. The city's two main bus stations, one in the very centre of the city at Erzsébet tér, the other much further out at Népstadion, are both in Pest, and the city's airport at Ferihegy is in the south-eastern suburbs of the city. All these facilities are linked by the extensive metro, bus and tram systems that all centre on Pest. It is the obvious place to begin one's stay in the city.

Central Pest

A Walk From Vörösmarty Tér To Kálvin Tér

In the centre of Pest — and arguably at the heart of the city of Budapest — is **Vörösmarty tér**, a bustling, leafy, pedestrianised square named after the nineteenth-century poet and dramatist Mihály Vörösmarty. There is a monument to him in the centre of the square. A line from his *Szózat* (Appeal) to Hungarian Nationalism is inscribed on the monument. It reads 'Be faithful to your land forever, Hungarians'. The monument also shows people reciting the *Szózat*, which is widely regarded as the country's second National Anthem. Also in the square are a fountain, featuring sculptured lions, and a small area of grassland which seems to be a popular gathering and meeting place come early evening. The square is always alive with street musicians, entertainers and artists who will encourage you to pose while they draw your portrait in any one of a number of different styles. Around the square there are various airline offices, tourist offices and banks. Along the western side of the square, however, is the back wall of the **Vigadó Concert Hall**, the entrance of which is round the other side of the building on Vigadó tér. The original concert hall was opened in 1832, and Liszt, Wagner, Brahms, Bartók and Prekoviev have all performed here. The name, in Hungarian, translates as 'merry-making'. The present auditorium was much restored in the 1980s, although it is concealed behind a front entrance of ornate nineteenth-century Hungarian-oriental stonework, and an effusively decorated entrance hall of lavish carpets and huge chandeliers. This is one of the most popular venues for concerts in the capital. Back on Vörösmarty tér, a pastry and coffee house attracts many of the capital's visitors, who congregate on its outside tables, drinking strong coffee and guzzling the rich cakes and pastries on offer. This is **Gerbeaud's**, Budapest's most famous patisserie, named after the Swiss family of confectioners that bought it in 1884 and refurbished it in elegant style. The prices charged now mean that few Hungarians can afford to eat here, but plenty of tourists come to experience something of the old central European traditions of refined hedonism, and they each seem to spend a couple of hours talking, reading or people watching.

Váci utca leads off from the south side of the square. This is Hungary's ❄ most famous shopping street. In Communist days, tourists from the Soviet Union and other Eastern Bloc countries would come here and gaze astounded at the quality and variety of goods that were on offer, a reflection of Hungary's unique degree of wealth and market freedom that could not be found anywhere else in the Communist world. The shops in Váci utca and the streets immediately around it still offer many opportunities for a good browse, and the street arguably still offers a greater choice and quality of goods for sale than anywhere else in Eastern Europe. This is the place to search for books (Hungarian and foreign language), jewellery, fashion goods, clothes and handicrafts. The street is narrow, pedestrianised and invariably crowded. Some of the buildings along the street have interesting art nouveau adornments or sculptures above shop level. Offices and hotels mingle with the shops and restaurants. In the Pesti Szinház (Pest Theatre), along the street on the right (number 9), Liszt made his Pest performing debut when he was a boy of just 11, and further along are interesting modern buildings which house the International Trade Centre and the Central European International Bank. Beyond this an unmissable sign points the way to the MacDonald's restaurant in Régiposta utca, just off the street. When it opened, in 1988, it was the first American fast-food restaurant to open behind the Iron Curtain, and for a time it was the busiest MacDonald's outlet in the world.

Along Régiposta utca (the other way) is **Martinelli tér**, a triangular ❄ shaped and rather haphazard square which was once the site of an eighteenth-century outdoor market. The building at number 5 boasts some extraordinary art nouveau decorations on its upper floors, made from ceramic tiles and considered revolutionary when they were added to the building in 1912. On the same side of the square, another building is adorned with ornate sculptures, embellishments and mosaics. The Servite church on the square dates from the eighteenth century, and has very fine interior decoration. Just off the far side of the square, in Városház utca, a huge Baroque building, formerly a hospital for soldiers disabled in the war against the Turks, now serves as Budapest's City Hall. The Pest County Hall is just beyond it in the same street.

Back in Váci utca, and a little further on along the street, Pesti Barnabás utca runs off to the right. A small Baroque mansion along here at number 2 now serves as one of the city's most fashionable restaurants. A marker by the doorway records the height of the Danube Flood in 1838. The short street opens out into a spacious square, **Március 15 tér**, one side of which ❄ is open to the Danube. The name of the square commemorates the date in 1848 when the revolution for Hungarian independence from the Habsburgs broke out in Pest. In the centre of the square is a much restored pile of stones, set in a sunken park, which are all that remain of the Roman

Budapest is a city of music

Street entertainment, Budapest style

fortification of *Contra-Aquincum*, built in the third century AD to support the much larger Roman settlements on the other side of the river. The modern fountain in the square shows Roman soldiers. The most striking building on the square, however, is the **Inner City Parish Church** 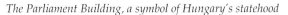 (Belváros Templom), the oldest building of any kind in Pest. The church was founded in the twelfth century and some of the original Romanesque parts remain, but the towers and the rather grimy façade are eighteenth century. The interior of the church is bright and airy. The *mihrab* (prayer niche), carved in the chancel wall betrays the building's function as a mosque in the days of the Turkish occupation. Despite its history, the church was nearly knocked down in the 1960s to make way for the road access way to the new Elizabeth Bridge, which crosses the Danube here. Behind the church is part of one of Budapest's largest universities, famed in the past for its rebellious students and for being a seedbed of radical ideas. The building is a former monastery that was once attached to the church. The promenade along the Danube that starts from the square is always alive with buskers, street entertainers and strollers, who mingle on the leafy terrace between the string of international hotels and the Danube.

At the southern end of Váci utca is the **Paris Arcade** (Páriszi udvar), a ☀ covered shopping arcade which was built in the early part of the twentieth century, and which still has its original ancient outsize telephone boxes to prove it. The arcade is squeezed in between Kigyó utca and Ferenciek tér (formerly Felszabadulás tér), a busy square crammed with traffic lanes

The Parliament Building, a symbol of Hungary's statehood

and tram lines, and served by Ferenciek metro station. Across the square is the Baroque **Franciscan Church**, which is unfortunately usually locked. The High Altar inside is magnificent, and there are also beautiful side chapels, wall frescoes and carvings. On the outside wall of the church (the Kossuth utca side) there is a relief showing a local baron saving people from the 1838 Danube flood. Along Károlyi Mihály utca, very close to the church, is a shop which sells all things ecclesiastical — from icons and statues of the Virgin Mary, to vestments for priests, other dignitaries (and even for boy choristers) who serve in the city's churches; an interesting shop in which to poke around. Károlyi Mihály utca itself contains many University buildings. The Petőfi Literary Museum is also along here. On Egyetem tér is the **University Church** (Egyetemi templom), built originally by the Monks of St Paul, the only monastic body created in Hungary. The monks themselves were responsible for the elegant wood carvings inside. This is one of the most beautiful Baroque churches in Budapest. The frescoes on the ceiling, the copy of the Tschenstochau (Czestochowa, Poland) Black Madonna, and the two massive towers all date from the eighteenth century. The church is often used for organ recitals.

A little way beyond Egyetem tér is **Kálvin tér**, another busy interchange (served by Kálvin tér metro station) on the busy semi-circle of boulevards that follow the line of the old city walls. The Kecskemét Gate was once located here and remains of it were discovered during building work. A few eighteenth- and nineteenth-century buildings surround the square. The Reformed Church on the square dates from the early years of the nineteenth century, and is rather severe in character, although in the church treasury there are valuable pieces of religious art dating from the seventeenth and eighteenth centuries. Heading south-west along Vámház körút brings one to the huge indoor market building by the Danube, and then Szabadság Bridge. Across the bridge is the famous Gellért Hotel with its thermal baths. Heading the other way from Kálvin tér, along Múzeum körút, is the Hungarian National Museum. The Jewish Quarter of Budapest is also very close by.

A Second Walk In Pest

The second suggested walk in Central Pest also begins in Vörösmarty tér, but heads north, past the basilica to the city's Parliament Building. This covers a more relaxed part of Pest than the first walk, passing through small parks and along quiet avenues where embassies and government departments have their offices. As before, any museums encountered en route are mentioned here, and full details of them can be found in the special section dealing with museums in Pest.

Start by heading north from Vörösmarty tér along Harmincad utca, past the whitewashed stone mansion that now houses the British Embassy, and then turn left along Bécsi utca. Erzsébet tér here is a spacious square which contains the city's main international bus terminal. Things get quieter as one crosses József Attila utca and heads along Október 6 utca, until — when you look up Zrínyi street, to the right — the imposing dome and façade of **St Stephen's Basilica** (Szt István Bazilika) seems to domi- nate everything.

The basilica, the largest church in the capital, was built between 1851 and 1905, under the supervision of three architects, and holds 8,000 people. It is a huge, airy place, dimly lit but crammed with neo-Classical decorations and columns and topped by a 96m (315ft) high dome (the height alludes to the date AD896, when the first Magyars arrived in Hungary), a replacement of the original one which collapsed in 1868 (during the inaugural ceremony, Emperor Franz Joseph was seen to glance nervously up at the new dome, hoping that the same thing was not about to happen again!). Inside there are many statues and paintings, including a statue of St Stephen on the High Altar, carved from Carrara marble. In a small chapel behind the altar it is possible to see St Stephen's mummified right hand, a sacred relic nationally revered which is brought out into the main part of the church on 20 August, St Stephen's Day. At the front end of the church is the Treasury, containing various religious vestments, chalices and monstrances.

From Szt István tér, outside the basilica, head north along Alpári Gyula utca to **Szabadság tér** (Freedom Square) a wide, spacious and quiet square, lined with elegant buildings which include the American Embassy, and the head offices of Hungarian State Television and the Hungarian National Bank. At the northern end is a sombre memorial to fallen Soviet soldiers, more discreet than other memorials which are on a similar theme. From the memorial, head north-east up Aulich utca to another quiet square in the centre of which is the **Batthyány Eternal Flame**. This spot used to be an army base, where, in October 1849 Count Lajos Batthyány was executed for his part in the Hungarian uprising against the Habsburgs. Not liking Habsburg rule from Vienna, a group of Hungarians tried to claim independence for their country, but were crushed mercilessly by their Habsburg masters. Batthyány was the revolutionary government's Prime Minister, and is now regarded as a hero of Hungarian Nationalism. The Eternal Flame here, lit in 1926, keeps alive his memory, and the memory of all those who died in the uprising.

From the square, walk west along Báthory utca to Kossuth Lajos tér, the large square outside the **Parliament Building** (Országház). The building is neo-Gothic in style and is supposed to have been modelled on the Houses of Parliament in Westminster, London. It was built at the end of the nineteenth century when the Austro-Hungarian Empire was created and Hungary gained partial independence from Vienna, with considerable autonomy in its own home affairs. The dome is exactly the same height as that of the basilica, a piece of architectural diplomacy designed to show that Church and State were equal in status. Statues of eighty-eight Hungarian rulers adorn the façade. Arguably, the building is best viewed from the river (or from Batthyány tér, on the West Bank of the Danube). Either way, tourists are only admitted to the building on group tours.

Most travel agencies in Budapest organise tours of the building, normally coupled with a look round one or two other sites in the capital. It is not possible to turn up at the front door of the building and wait for a tour group to turn up — a visit must be arranged beforehand (see Additional Information section at the end of this chapter). Those who do see inside will be shown works of art, the grandiose staircases and hallways, and the Assembly Chamber itself, formerly a rubber-stamp organisation which passed laws that the Communist government told it to, but now a forum for democratic argument and law-making. Tours of the building are not

The imposing metal and glass façade of Nyugati Station

conducted when parliament is in session. Opposite the Parliament Building is the **Ethnographic Museum** (Néprajzi Múzeum), while in the square
itself is a large statue of Lajos Kossuth, after whom the square is named.
Kossuth was the leader of the 1848 revolution. On 23 October 1956, many
thousands of people came to the square to demonstrate against their
parliament, evoking the memory of Kossuth and their actions became the
prelude to the 1956 Uprising.

Continuing north, one could either walk on along the embankment by
the Danube and then across the bridge to Margaret Island. One could nead
north-east to Marx tér, a cosmopolitan traffic interchange where, on one
side, there is the huge Skála Metró department store (worth a look round,
even if nothing is actually purchased) and, on the other side of the road,
the imposing metal and glass façade of Nyugati Station. This is one of the
three main line terminals in the capital, and it was built by the Eiffel
company of Paris who later built the Eiffel Tower.

The Jewish Quarter

District VII between Andrássy utca and Rákóczi utca is known as the
Erzsébetváros (Elizabeth Town) and is traditionally the site of the Jewish
Quarter of the city. At 2-8 Dohány utca stands the **Central Synagogue**
(Zsinagóga), the largest in Europe, which was built between 1854 and
1859 in romanticised Moorish-Byzantine style and which can hold up to
3,000 people. The building is undergoing extensive renovation. The synagogue is part of a large complex of buildings which include the birthplace
of Theodor Herzl, who in the early years of the twentieth century became
the leader of the World Zionist movement, campaigning vociferously for
the creation of a Jewish state of Israel. The first floor of the annexe to the
left of the synagogue is the **National Jewish Museum** amongst whose
displays is an exhibition of photographs from the war years. The garden
behind contains a weeping willow memorial to the dead of the ghetto.
Each leaf bears the names of families lost. Special city Jewish tours depart
from outside the synagogue every Sunday, Monday and Thursday.

Centred on Klausal tér and stretching out to Király utca, the Budapest
ghetto is the only major European Jewish ghetto to have survived World
War II largely intact. Wondrous and eerie by turns, this is one of the most
fascinating and evocative districts of Budapest and rewards for an in-
quisitive eye are numerous. Worn and bullet-scarred façades and courtyards betray a prosperous and characterful past, many of the dwellings
having been beautified with various Hebrew motifs and inscriptions. This
is history at its most immediate and nostalgia at its least sentimental.
Anyone searching for actual sights may inspect the newly-restored late
nineteenth-century synagogue on Rumbach utca, or alternatively the
unrestored one on Kazincsy utca. Along Dob utca is a monument to Swiss
emigre Carl Lutz who saved numerous Jews in World War II by issuing
them with false identity papers.

The Jews In Hungary

Documentary evidence suggests that Jewish presence in present day Hungary dates back at least as far as the Roman occupation. The first documented period of persecution came courtesy of Stephen I's attempts to Christianise the country back in the eleventh century. Mixed marriages were forbidden, Jews were not allowed to hold titles and it was made mandatory for them to wear a yellow patch on their clothing. There is, however, evidence to suggest that these regulations were imperfectly carried out and the Pope even excommunicated the country because of its failure to observe the anti-Jewish decrees.

Whatever imperfections there were, however, disappeared in the fourteenth century when zealous Christian King Louis the Great expelled the Jewish population from his lands. Within a few years the ban was lifted but those who returned tended to be poor refugees who were shunned and ghettoised by the established communities. In the aftermath of the peasant uprising of 1514, the 1517 Werbőczy Code stripped Jews of any rights they held claim to. In 1541 the Buda ghetto was completely destroyed by the Turkish army and the Jewish Quarter was once again looted and burned down when Austrian troops liberated the city in 1686. Under subsequent Habsburg rule Jews were banned from settling in all of the larger towns and refused entry to most professions. A special annual Jewish tax was also levied.

Jewish rights became bound up with the revolutionary fervour of 1848 and the rebel National Assembly voted to support the emancipation of the Jewish people. What failed in 1849 eventually bore fruit in 1867 when the law of emancipation was finally accepted. Respite, however, proved brief. The initial violence under the auspices of Horthy's post-war Nationalist regime was followed in 1920 by Europe's first anti-semitic law of the century (excluding Jewish youths from Hungarian high schools and universities). In 1938 Jews were banned from all white-collar professions and at the outbreak of World War II all able-bodied Jewish men were called up for forced labour — malnourished and frozen, some 40,000 died this way, another 20,000 were deported to Polish camps before the German army finally entered Hungary in March 1944.

In April of that year the first Hungarian ghettos were established, from where was begun the 3 day journey in cattletrucks to the Auschwitz-Birkenau concentration camp. The only surviving photographs taken inside the Birkenau camp are actually of Hungarian Jews. Deportations lasted until July when the route north became unsafe. Meanwhile in Budapest the Arrow Cross Fascists tortured and killed at random until 18 January 1945 when Soviet troops finally liberated the city. In Debrecen the temporary government immediately revoked all the anti-Jewish legislation and Ferenc Szálasi, the leader of the Arrow Cross, was publically tried and hanged along with the rest of his government. An estimated 600,000 Hungarian Jews had died in the conflict. Under Communism anti-semitism was constitutionally forbidden, and today an estimated 90,000 Jews live within Hungary's borders. It is to be hoped that the revived Nationalism and economic frustrations borne of the post-Communist era will not once again find as their scapegoat the country's Jewish population.

Towards The City Park

This walking route runs from Deák tér in Central Pest to the Városliget (the City Park) beyond which the city's grim suburbs begin. As with the last section, the presence of museums is noted in the text but details about them can be found in the separate section dealing with museums and galleries in Pest. Further details on the Opera House, theatres and medicinal baths which can be found in this part of Budapest are included in Chapter 8 'What To Do In Hungary'.

Deák tér, just east of Vörösmarty tér, is one of the busiest squares in the capital. Underneath it is the only metro station where interchange between the three metro lines is possible, while above ground traffic screeches to and fro and buses rumble into and out of the large international bus station in Erzsébet tér next door. The fountain in Deák tér is called Danubius. The bearded man symbolizes the Danube, while the female figures represent the river's tributaries — the Tisza, the Drava and the Szava. In the metro subway is the entrance to the **Underground** **Railway Museum** (Földalatti Vasúti Múzeum), while the **National Lutheran Museum** (Evangélikus Országos Múzeum) is in a building on the south side of the square. The huge domed pile on the eastern side of the square is the so-called Anker Palace, one of the few buildings in the capital to have escaped the war unscathed.

Take Bajcsy-Zsilinszky utca north, then **Andrássy utca** which runs ❋ north-east. This 1 mile (1½km) long boulevard is the grandest street in Budapest, built in the 1870s and modelled after the Champs Elysées in Paris — a tree-lined avenue full of smart shops, elegant buildings and expensive restaurants whose tables spill out onto the street in summer. Formerly named, in true Communist fashion, the Avenue of the People's Republic (the Hungarian translation is predictably unpronounceable), it also carried Stalin's name for a time. Now it is back with its original name, that of one of Hungary's most noted aristocratic families. Continental Europe's first metro line (now metro line 1) runs just underneath the surface of the road and there are frequent stops.

The **Postal Museum** (Postamúzeum) is at the very south-western end of the avenue. Further on, on the left, is the **State Opera House** (Operaház). Above the entrance there are statues of sixteen composers including Beethoven, Mozart and Wagner, but next to the portico are more prominent statues of Liszt and of Ferenc Erkel, who composed the Hungarian National Anthem and who was director of the Opera House when it opened in 1884. Technically, the Opera House was very advanced for its time, and the original stage machinery lasted for over a 100 years. During World War II many people sheltered in its cavernous cellars. Those who manage to see an opera here will be overawed by the sumptuousness of the interior which includes much decoration in 23 karat gold leaf. Opposite the Opera House is the State Ballet Institute, housed in an ornate nineteenth-century palace.

Further up still is the Oktogon, a wide, traffic-clogged square which is arguably at the centre of Budapest's theatre land. As the avenue continues beyond the Oktogon, getting perceptibly wider, a street to the right, Vörösmarty utca, contains the **Liszt Memorial Museum**. The last part of the street is lined with foreign embassies and government buildings. Andrássy utca finally ends in a windswept open square, Hősök tere — **Heroes' Square**. The most dominant landmark here is the huge Millennium Monument, an ostentatious and rather brutal affair, the construction of which was begun in 1896 to celebrate the thousandth anniversary of the foundation of the Hungarian state. Most of the figures are allegorical. At the top of the 36m (118ft) high central column is the Archangel Gabriel, who according to legend, offered King Stephen the throne of Hungary in a dream. The seven tribesmen on horseback represent the seven Magyar tribes that entered Hungary in AD896. The statues in the colonnades represent Hungarian monarchs. In front of the monument is the Memorial to an Unknown Soldier. Two large neo-Classical buildings face each other across the wide open space in front of the monument. To the south is the **Műcsarnok Art Gallery**, while to the north is the **Museum of Fine Arts** (Szépművészeti Múzeum), one of the most important art collections in the capital. Both buildings, and the form of the square itself, were designed by the architect Albert Schickedanz.

Behind the Millennium Monument is the **City Park** (Városliget), a pleasant place to wander and relax. To the right of the main entrance gate there is an artificial skating rink (operates only in winter). In the centre of the park is an artificial lake with a make-believe castle (the Vajdahunyad Castle) situated on an island in the middle of it, its toothy turrets and ballustrades reflected in the water. Built for the celebrations for the 1896 Millenary Exhibition, and supposedly incorporating every architectural style that can be seen in Hungary, part of it now houses the Agricultural Museum. Opposite the palace is a chapel, incorporating a copy of the great doorway of the Church at Ják in western Hungary (see Chapter 3). Outside the palace are statues of Anonymous — an unknown thirteenth-century scribe, who wrote the first *Chronicles of the Kingdom of Hungary* and peers out from behind a monkish hood — and a statue of George Washington, erected in 1906 by Hungarians living in the United States. On the northern side of the park is the **City Zoo** (Fővárosi Állatkert), with everything one would expect to find in a zoo. The hippos wallow in water from the thermal springs which are also used in the Széchenyi Baths, nearby. Next to the zoo is the **Vidámpark**, Hungary's biggest amusement park, though very tame by Western standards. Budapest's municipal circus is situated between the zoo and the Vidámpark, reputedly, an entertaining spectacle. Between the castle and the Vidámpark is the Széchenyi Baths, a huge complex with a metro station named after it nearby. It is one of the largest bathing complexes in Europe (see Chapter 8 'What To Do In Hungary'). In the south-eastern part of the park is the Petőfi Csarnok, a popular venue for rock concerts and other events. It also houses some of the exhibition rooms of the **Transport Museum** (Közlekedési Múzeum), the main part of which is in the south-eastern corner of the park.

The Archangel Gabriel rises above Heroes' Square

The make-believe Vajdahunyad Castle in the centre of the City Park

Museums And Galleries In Pest

Agricultural Museum (Magyar Mezőgazdasági Múzeum)
A museum of limited appeal that does no justice whatsoever to the wonderfully exotic Vajdahunyad Castle in which it is housed in the City Park.

Hungarian National Museum (Magyar Nemzeti Múzeum)
Founded in 1802 by Count Ferenc Széchenyi, the collection is housed at 14-16 Múzeum körút in an impressive neo-Classical building erected specially for the task in 1847 and which itself is the scene of one of the most celebrated events in Hungarian history. It was from these steps that poet Sandor Petőfi first recited the *Hungarian National Song* to a huge crowd during the 1848 Revolution. Consequently every year on 15 March the museum is the scene of impressive nationalistic celebrations. The prime exhibits are Hungary's Crown Jewels. The crown is said to be the original one that Pope Sylvester II sent to King Stephen for his coronation in AD1000 (the leaning gold cross on top always appears in reproductions). Also included are a Byzantium coronation robe, a sixteenth-century Venetian sword and a fourteenth-century sceptre and orb. At the end of World War II the Crown Jewels were smuggled into Germany by Hungarian Nazis before being taken to the United States from where they were only returned in 1978. The ground floor of the museum covers the history of Hungary from the Paleolithic Age to the Magyar conquest while the first floor takes the events up to 1849. Captions are in English and highlights include a superb third-century Roman mosaic floor from Balácapuszta (near Vesprém) and a Renaissance pew from the Calvinist Church in Nyríbátor. The second floor contains a natural history collection while the grounds feature various memorials to worthy Hungarians and a 3m (10ft) high marble column from the Forum in Rome.

Literary Museums
Budapest's main literary museum is the **Petőfi Literary Museum** (Petőfi Iródalmi Múzeum) at 16 Károly Mihály utca (entrance through the courtyard). A major part of the museum is dedicated to Sandor Petőfi (1823-49), the National Poet, but there are also other rooms dedicated to lesser writers such as Mor Jokai and Attila József as well as temporary art and photographic exhibitions and a room devoted to Mihály Károlyi, Hungarian President from 1918 to 1919 who formerly owned the building. Information sheets in English are available. Anyone so disposed may also like to pay a visit to one of the small memorial rooms in the city; 3 Gát utca is the birthplace of Attila József, 4 Veres Pálné is the former residence of Endre Ady while over in Buda, at 48 Városmajor utca, there is an exhibition concerning the influential *Nyugat* literary journal that was published between 1908 and 1941. By their nature these will be of limited appeal but entrance fees appear discretionary and it is an excuse to go wandering around some of the more obscure districts of the capital. At the very least a visit will have some anecdotal value, these are very much out of the way places and the excitement of a visitor will be tangible.

Museum Of Fine Arts (Szépművészeti Múzeum)
The finest art gallery in Hungary and easily comparable to anything in Western Europe. The Old Master's Gallery boasts works by Titian, Raphael, Brueghal, Rubens and Durer while the Modern Foreign Gallery has a good collection of French Impressionists (including Manet, Monet and Renoir). Picasso and Chagall are represented in the Twentieth Century collection and there are

a substantial number of drawings on show where works by Rembrandt and Leonardo stand pride of place. In addition to this there are also interesting Egyptian, Greek and Roman collections. Directly opposite the museum is the **Műcsarnok** which plays host to various temporary art exhibitions.

National Lutheran Museum (Evangélikus Országos Múzeum)
Displays various relics of the Lutheran faith including a facsimilie of Martin Luther's last will. Situated on Deák tér.

Postal Museum (Postamúzeum)
An exhibition of items connected with the post and telegram systems and the early days of radio and television. Situated at 3 Andrássy útca inside a former private residential apartment.

Transport Museum (Közlekedési Múzeum)
Situated at the back of the City Park, includes various antique cars, steam trains and the like. The aviation section is on the first floor of the Petőfi Csarnok (also in the park).

Underground Railway Museum (Földalatti Vasúti Múzeum)
A former section of metro tunnel is the setting for the underground railway museum. Various trains and other railway memorabilia dating from the 1890s are on show here. Access is from the pedestrian subway adjacent to Deák tér metro station.

Cemeteries In Pest

Situated 400m (1,312ft) to the south of Keleti station along Fiumei utca **Kerepesi Cemetery** contains the final resting places of some of Hungary's most famous sons. A map detailing the exact location of each of the fallen famous is available at the entrance. Of particular note are the impressive mausoleums of Lajos Kossuth, leader of the 1848 revolution, Ferenc Deák, engineer of the 1867 'Compromise', and popular novelist Mor Jokai. Also worth a look is the 'Pantheon of the Working Class Movement', erected in 1958, which contains the remains of top-brass party officials, including János Kádár, party leader from 1956 to 1988.

To the south-east of Kerepesi Cemetery along Salgótarjáni utca is the **Old Jewish Cemetery**. Today the gates are permanently padlocked and patrolled by a very fierce guard dog, nevertheless many of the once-proud mausoleums are visible from the street and further along at the end of Salgótárjani utca it is possible to peep over the wall and view the haunting spectacle of broken stone choked by undergrowth and daubed with Nazi insignia. Untended since its closure in 1950, the cemetery is an ever-increasingly expressive memorial to an age lost and a culture exterminated.

On the outskirts of the city, **Új Köztemető Cemetery** is the infamous site of the secret burial in 1958 in unmarked graves of Imre Nagy and the other leaders of the 1956 uprising. Their ceremonial reburial in 1989 was one of the sparks that eventually led to the downfall of the Communist regime (the whole event was relayed live on national television). The entrance to the cemetery is along Kozma utca and may be reached by a 20 minute bus journey from outside Keleti station. Plot 301, where they are buried, is in the far left hand corner and is a good 20 minute walk.

※ # BUDA

Castle Hill

Budapest's most striking and elegant panorama is that of the complex of
buildings that stretch along Castle Hill (Várhegy), as seen from the East
Bank of the Danube. Castle Hill attracts more tourists than any other part
of the capital. They come here to wander around the museums and
galleries, see the old medieval streets and churches and to admire the
views back over the Danube towards Pest. By day the area is alive with
street entertainers, open-air cafés, souvenir hawkers and people, but
everything seems to be done in a more relaxed and refined pace than
down in Pest. By late afternoon, however, places begin to close up, and
most of the throng moves down to Pest to enjoy themselves in the city's
restaurants and bars, leaving the long summer evenings on Castle Hill to
small numbers of concert goers and lingering couples. Castle Hill can be
divided into three main areas: the Royal Palace, occupying the southern
third of the hill; the area around the Matthias Church and the Fishermen's
Bastion, the busiest part of the hill; and the quieter district of medieval
streets, lined with churches,
dimly-lit restaurants and ornate houses, which extends to
the west and the north of the
Matthias Church.

Across To The Castle

There are several ways up to
the summit of Castle Hill, including some little-used roads
and paths that approach the
hill from the west, or from
Moszkva tér, to the north
(where the nearest metro station to the castle can be found).
But by far the most obvious
approach to the castle from
※ Pest is via the **Chain Bridge**
(Széchenyi lánchíd). This elegant structure, very much a
symbol of Budapest, was the
first bridge built across the

KEY TO MAP

1 Royal Palace
2 Budapest Museum of History
3 Hungarian National Gallery
4 Széchényi Library
5 Matthias Church
6 Arany Sas Pharmacy Museum
7 Fishermen's Bastion
8 Museum of the History of Music
9 Hungarian Museum of
   Commerce and Catering
10 Military History Museum
11 Labyrinth of Caves
12 Semmelweis Museum of the
   History of Medicine

Danube in the city. It was constructed as recently as 1849, before which
time boats and temporary pontoon bridges were the only way of crossing
from Pest to Buda. The piers at either end of the suspension bridge, as well
as the cables which hold up the roadway, are illuminated at night. The
structure was blown up by the Germans towards the end of World War

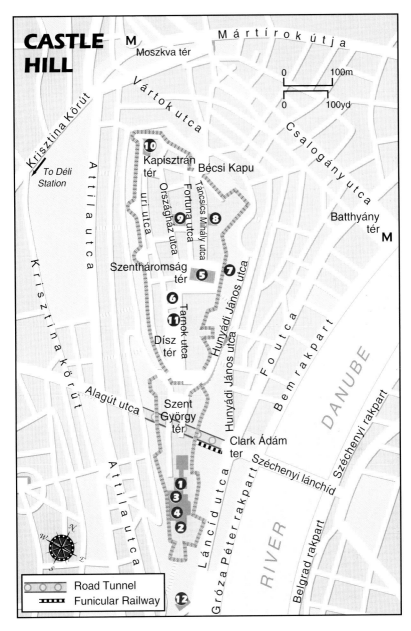

II to prevent the advance of the Soviet Army, but it was rebuilt quite soon afterwards, reopening on 1 November 1949, exactly a hundred years after the original opening. The designer of the bridge was an Englishman, William Tierney Clark, who also designed Hammersmith Bridge which crosses the Thames in West London, and which resembles the Chain

Bridge. It was engineered by a Scotsman, Adam Clark (no relation), after whom the square (more of a roundabout, really) at the Buda end of the bridge is named. He was also responsible for the construction of the tunnel under Castle Hill, which runs from the square. A Budapest joke is that the tunnel was built for the bridge to be stored in when it rained. In 1849 Adam Clark personally stopped the Austrian army blowing up the bridge, by flooding the chain-lockers with water.

A path runs up from Clark Ádam tér to the main entrance to the castle, but the best way up is by the funicular railway (*sikló*) which runs up from the square. The railway was originally opened in 1870, powered by a steam winch and, at the time, was the second oldest funicular railway in the world. After being hit by a shell in World War II it remained unoperational until 1986 since when it has been powered by electricity. However, the original principle, of the descending and ascending cars balancing one another and passing in the middle, remains unchanged. In front of the lower station is an odd egg-shaped sculpture, the 'zero kilometre' stone from which all distances in Hungary from Budapest are measured.

🏛 The Royal Palace

The top station of the funicular brings one to Szent György tér, a spacious square from which entrance is gained to the Royal Palace, formerly an Imperial residence, and now a collection of galleries, museums and sumptuous courtyards. This building, like most on Castle Hill, suffered extensive damage during the World War II (when it was used as a Command Post by the German army of Occupation), but it has since been restored to its original Imperial splendour.

The original fortress on this obvious defensive site was constructed by Béla III in the thirteenth century. Successive monarchs who ruled in more stable times built ever more grandiose palaces here, the most famous of which was that built by Matthias Corvinus (1458-90), whose lavish court attracted artists and scholars from all over Europe. However the palace was virtually destroyed when the Turks besieged Buda in 1686, and the form of the current buildings date from the eighteenth and nineteenth centuries when the neo-Baroque Habsburg Palace was constructed.

There are now three museums and galleries contained in the complex of buildings that make up the palace. The **Budapest Museum of History** (Budapesti Történeti Múzeum) is a survey of 2,000 years of the history of the city, from prehistoric times to the present day. Parts of the medieval castle that stood here have been excavated, and they form part of the museum. The most interesting rooms are the Gothic Knight's Hall, and the tiny Royal Chapel in which a beautiful fourteenth-century triptych has been installed. The **Hungarian National Gallery** (Magyar Nemzeti Galéria) occupies the central part of the palace, and contains a fine and large collection of Hungarian art from the Middle Ages to the present day, everything from Gothic stone carvings to examples of Hungarian Modern

Art. One ticket gives access to the whole collection, though each section has its own entrance. Finally, the **Ludwig Collection** contains various pieces of modern art and temporary exhibitions, while the foyer of the **Széchenyi Library**, which, by law, receives a copy of every book pub- ❊ lished in Hungarian, sometimes has temporary exhibitions.

At the front (Danube side) of the palace is a large equestrian statue of Prince Eugene. Behind the National Gallery building, in St George's Square, is the **Matthias Fountain**, which recalls the legend of Szép Ilonka. She was a peasant girl who fell in love with King Matthias while he was out hunting, not initially realising whom he was. After she discovered his identity, however, she died of a broken heart, realising that her love could never be returned. The statue also shows King Matthias' Italian Chronicler, who wrote down the story for posterity. In the southern part of the castle complex is the South Tower, a medieval bastion dating from the sixteenth century and in the small park below, several gravestones dating from Turkish times.

The Matthias Church And Bastions
The **Matthias Church** (Mátyás Templom), in the centre of the Castle ⛪ District, is another very distinctive landmark in the area. The church, like the castle, was founded in the thirteenth century, and is also known as the Church of Our Lady and as the Coronation Church (although most of Hungary's medieval kings were crowned in Székesfehérvár). In the fifteenth century, King Matthias married Beatrice of Aragon here, while in 1867, when the Austro-Hungarian Empire was split in two, Franz Joseph was crowned king of Hungary here, and Liszt composed his *Coronation Mass* especially for the occasion. Although medieval in origin, the church has been rebuilt several times. In the seventeenth century the Turks adapted it as the main mosque of the city, and the church was rebuilt almost from scratch in the nineteenth century, and then again, in the twentieth, after it had been partially destroyed in World War II. The style of the church is now one of riotous neo-Baroque decoration and ornamentation, whose richness cannot fail to impress, even if most of it is not as old as it looks.

In the Loreto Chapel, under the South (Matthias) Tower, there is a medieval red marble statue of the Virgin Mary, which according to legend is supposed to have been bricked up by the Turks but which emerged from the walls during the siege of Buda in 1686, a portentous event which showed the Turks that they would lose the siege and the Hungarians would regain control of Buda. Other items in the interior of the church that are worthy of note include the magnificent High Altar and the stained glass in the windows, both of which date from the nineteenth century. In the Holy Trinity Chapel, on the north side of the church, are the sarcophagi of the medieval King Bela III and his wife, originally buried at Székesfehérvár but interred here in 1848. In the Church Museum, which is housed in the rooms to the side and underneath the church, there are

Visiting the Royal Palace is made easier by using the funicular railway from Clark Ádam tér

The Chain Bridge, very much a symbol of Budapest, was the first to be built across the Danube in the city

Matthias Church, one of the most beautiful in Budapest

Old meets new; the spires of Matthias Church, reflected in the glass façade of Budapest Hilton Hotel

displays of religious ornaments, vestments and relics. The Hungarian Crown Jewels shown here are copies of the originals, which are kept in the Hungarian National Museum in Pest. One can also see coronation robes and thrones, and St Stephen's Chapel, the walls of which are decorated with scenes from the king's life. A Catholic Mass, with full choir and symphony orchestra, is held in the church every Sunday morning, and in spring and summer the church is a venue for organ and chamber concerts.

In Szentháromság tér, outside the western doorway of the church, a statue comprising various saints and angels dates from 1713 when it was put up by the survivors of an outbreak of Bubonic Plague. Horse and carriages leave from the square, ferrying tourists around the sights of Castle Hill. On the far side of the square is the old Town Hall of Buda, redundant since the formal merger of the two parts of the city in 1873. Below the balcony, a statue of Pallas Athena carries a shield, decorated with coat of arms of Buda. A little way along Tárnok utca, at number 18 is an old chemists shop, named Arany Sas (The Golden Eagle). The medieval building is now a museum, with exhibits relating to various crude and gruesome medical tactics that were practiced in days gone by. By the south-western wall of the church there is a modern statue of King Stephen astride a horse. He is Hungary's first king, and also its patron saint which is why the statue shows him with both a crown and a halo.

In the eighteenth century, a fish market was held in this part of the castle and fishermen were responsible for defending part of the fortifications, which is why the ornate collection of turrets, stairways and terraces here is known as the **Fishermen's Bastion** (Halászbástya). The whitewashed stonework and ornate frills do nothing to conceal the fact that the bastions here are a folly, built in the early years of the twentieth century as part of reconstruction work on this part of Castle Hill. Now, the archways provide outstandingly framed views over the Danube (particularly of the Parliament Building) and outdoor cafés have been set up on the terraces. Further along the bastions are reflected surreally in the glass façade of the Budapest Hilton Hotel, a controversial modern structure seemingly all at sea, surrounded by ancient and historic buildings and whose interior incorporates part of a Dominican monastery which once stood here. In the lobby of the hotel is an ancient piece of stonework, unearthed during its construction, which once marked the northern boundary of the Roman Empire.

The Northern Part Of Castle Hill

The area around the Matthias Church is always buzzing with tourists, but the streets to the west and north of the church are usually much quieter. Each one of these medieval streets is lined with elegant houses, and seemingly every other building has its own history to tell. Witness the plaques on the outside walls which declare the building to be a *műmelék* (monument). Along these streets are shady courtyards, ramshackle churches, tiny museums, small restaurants and gift shops. The area is well worth wandering in, but it is pointless trying to fix an itinerary — just head out into the area. A number of important buildings in the area are described here.

In Táncsics Mihály utca, at number 5, is an art gallery belonging to the Creative Circle of Etchers, where prints, drawings, and water-colours can be bought and viewed. Beethoven once lived in the house next door at number 7 and Bartók had his workshop here, so, fittingly, the building now houses the **Museum of the History of Music**. Most of the exhibits are of ancient musical instruments, but there are also rooms devoted to the life and career of Béla Bartók, recommended for fans of his music only. Number 9, next door, was once a prison which held the politician after whom the street is named. Further along the street, number 26 serves as a tiny **Jewish Museum**. The building was once a medieval synagogue and there are Jewish gravestones inside the door. The street ends in Bécsi kapu, the Vienna Gate, a reconstruction (1936) of one of the medieval entrances to Castle Hill. Around the small square (Bécsi tér) are ornate eighteenth-century houses. The huge neo-Romanesque building houses the National Archives (closed to the public). Thomas Mann, the author of many novels including *Death in Venice*, lived at number 7 during the 1930s. Between the first floor windows of the house are portraits of Roman poets and writers.

Fortuna utca is another attractive street, running north from the square by the Matthias Church. The **Hungarian Museum of Commerce and** **Catering** (Magyar Kereskedelmi és Vendéglátóipan), in an old hotel at number 4, includes mock-ups of old restaurant and hotel rooms, an interesting assortment of all things culinary, including old posters and shop signs. The next street to the west is Országház utca (Houses of Parliament Street). Parliamentary sessions were originally held in the house at number 28. This street and Úri utca, to the west, lined with rebuilt medieval houses of subtly different pastel shades, end up in Kapisztrán tér, in the northern part of the castle district, where a bleak medieval tower is all that remains of the Church of Mary Magdalene. The rest of the Gothic church was destroyed by the German army in the last days of World War II. The westerly-most street in the castle district is Tóth árpád sétány, a leafy promenade from where there are views over the western districts of Buda (the ultra-modern Déli Railway Station is below the Castle Hill) and over towards the Buda Hills. At the northern end of this road is the **Military History Museum** (Hadtörténeti Múzeum), where huge bleak rooms document Hungary's military history, from prehistoric swords to the defences of the former Warsaw Pact, including a courtyard full of armoured vehicles.

The final attraction in this part of Budapest are the **caves** dug into the hill, the entrance to which is down a narrow passageway at Úri utca 9. These tunnels date from the Middle Ages, when they were used during sieges. Many houses in this part of Castle Hill had direct access to the caves from their cellars, and they were used as a refuge and a hospital as recently

Eating out on the terraces of the Fishermen's Bastion

Sightseeing in style around the Castle District of Buda

as World War II. Now they are a waxworks, where bloody events in Magyar history are depicted using life-size models.

Beyond The Castle

The castle area is the part of Buda to which most people head, but the attractions of this area of the capital do not end there. Beyond Castle Hill, particularly to the south and north, along the western embankment of the Danube, there are a varied clutch of attractions, comprising Roman remains, a number of museums, and more vantage points over the city, particularly that which can be gained from the summit of Gellért Hill. The two very different islands in the Danube itself provide a contrast to the rest of the city and show visitors yet another side of the capital. It is well worth escaping the crowds and tourist traps of Castle Hill to find out what else lies on the west bank of the Danube.

Gellért Hill

Immediately to the south of Castle Hill is **Gellért Hill** (Gellért hegy), a distinctive limestone mound whose precipitous eastern slopes fall down right to the edge of the Danube. The hill is a stubborn block of dolomite which reaches a height of 235m (771ft). It is named after St (Bishop) Gerard (Gellért in Hungarian), a Benedictine monk and abbot of the Monastery

The Liberation Monument, Gellért Hill

of St Giorgio in Venice, whom Stephen I brought to Hungary in order that he could tutor his son. He converted many Hungarians to Christianity, but some citizens of Buda who did not like his message decided to throw him off the hillside in 1046. He is much venerated in Hungary.

Paths snake up the hill from the Danube, crossing through a pleasant area of woodland peppered with small sculptures and manicured flowerbeds. The most obvious way to walk up is via the path which starts opposite the western end of the Elizabeth Bridge (Erzsébet híd), although there are other paths. A road, with a bus route, runs up to the summit of the hill from the west. The main reasons for going up the hill is for the superb views over the city from its slopes and from the summit. However, there are some other, definite points of interest on the hill. On the north-eastern slopes is a large memorial to St Gellért (1902), in the form of a statue surrounded by a pillared portico, with a man-made waterfall beneath it. At the summit is the rather brutal Liberation Monument, built in 1947 to commemorate the liberation of Budapest from the Nazis by the Soviet Red Army (the figure, a woman holding a palm branch, is 14m/46ft high and can be seen from many parts of the city). Also at the summit is the Citadel, built by the Austrians in 1851 to intimidate the city with its cannons, but now housing a restaurant, hotel and viewing galleries and terraces.

Between Castle and Gellért Hill, on Apród utca 1-3, a restored Louis XVI mansion was the birthplace of an obstetrician named Ignac Semmelweis (1818-1865), who discovered the cause of the childhood disease septicaemia. He also discovered the dangers of infections during operations and made his medical students at the University of Pest disinfect their hands and surgical instruments before entering maternity wards, thereby considerably reducing death rates amongst pregnant mothers. His house is now the **Semmelweis Museum of the History of Medicine** (Semmelweis Orvostörténeti Múzeum).

The Danube: Islands And Bridges

The most interesting bridge which crosses the Danube at Budapest is the Chain Bridge (Széchenyi Iánchid). But a few of the other bridges are worthy of note. Immediately south of the Chain Bridge is the **Elizabeth Bridge** (Erzsébet híd), a modern construction whose predecessor — built at the turn of the twentieth century, and for a time the largest arched bridge in the world — was destroyed during World War II. The present suspension bridge, built in the 1960s, is a stately modern structure which crosses from the Belváros Parish Church to Gellért Hill. The longest of the capital's six bridges is Árpád híd, in the northern suburbs, which is 1km (½ mile) long and crosses the northern tip of Margaret Island.

There are two very different islands formed in the Danube, to the north and south of Central Budapest. Part of **Csepel Island**, to the south, forms District XXI of the capital, an industrial area with the city's docks and a huge metal foundry whose traditionally leftward-leaning and militant workers have given the island the nickname 'Red Csepel'. The island extends a long way south, almost to the city of Dunaújváros (Chapter 5), and much of it is open countryside with many small towns and villages. Understandably, few tourists go there. However, some of the derelict industrial sites may yet come in to good use as they may stage some of the events of the 1996 Budapest/Vienna world exposition.

In contrast, **Margaret Island** (Margit-sziget) to the north is a pleasant area of parks and woodland, ideal for strolling. Access to the island is either from Margaret Bridge, on the southern tip, or Árpád Bridge, on the northern tip. A bus route runs along the length of the island, but generally it is traffic-free. The island is 2½km (1½ miles) long and only 500m (1,640ft) wide at the widest point. The main attraction here is simply to wander. However, there are a number of more definite sights. In the very south of the island is the Union Monument, a huge metal flower which celebrates the union of Pest, Buda and Óbuda. The pictures on the inside of the leaves depict the modern history of Budapest. Nearby is a pleasant fountain. On the western side of the island is the Alfréd-Hajós sports bath, with its large swimming and diving pools. It is named after an athlete who competed for Hungary in the 1896 Olympics, and who also designed part of the complex. Further on, still on the west side, is the Palatinus Baths, one of the capital's largest thermal bathing complexes, which includes medical facilities and thermal swimming pools complete with water shute and wave machines, and nude sun-bathing terraces and pools for children. In the centre of the island are two scant historical remains. Fragments still exist of a fourteenth-century Franciscan church, and, beyond it, towards the eastern side of the island, are the ruins of a Dominican nunnery. The most famous nun was Princess Margaret, daughter of King Béla IV, who gave her name to the island. She spent virtually all her life as a nun, died here in 1271 and is buried in the remains of the nunnery. Between these two ruins is a very pleasant ornamental rose garden.

In the centre of the northern part of the island there is a permanently installed open-air theatre, which stages concerts, operas and plays on summer evenings. It seats 3,500. Next to it is an old Water Tower, the top of which gives excellent views over the island and beyond. On the northern tip of the island is the exclusive and rather swish Thermal Hotel, where there are more thermal baths which can be used by non-guests. Outside the hotel is an artificial rock garden, where thermal streams and pools are filled with tropical fish and are surrounded by many rare tropical plants.

The Watertown District

The Watertown District (Vízíváros) is an area of Baroque houses and churches on a narrow ledge between Castle Hill and the Danube, stretching north from Clark Adam tér. Traditionally the area was inhabited by fishermen and merchants. When the Turks occupied Budapest they turned the churches into mosques and fortified the area. Now, there are

Elizabeth Bridge spans the Danube south of Chain Bridge

Trams are a popular and convenient way of travelling around Budapest

a few points of interest in an area where modern and ancient buildings exist in a rather cheek-by-jowl fashion.

The biggest church in the area is **St Anne's Church** (Szent Anna templom) in Batthyány tér, completed in 1758 and restored in the nineteenth century and after World War II. Both the interior, and the main façade, are fine pieces of Baroque architecture. The magnificent High Altar shows St Anne with her daughter Mary in the Temple of Jerusalem. Batthyány tér itself is surrounded by a variety of fine eighteenth- and nineteenth-century buildings. On the west side is the old White Cross Inn, once the setting for the Watertown's lavish carnivals and festivities, and now a night club, named after Casanova who reputedly stayed here. The square is served by a metro station and is the terminus of the HÉV suburban railway line to *Aquincum* and Szentendre (see Chapter 2). The east side of the square is the best place from which to view Budapest's Parliament Building.

South of the square, on the Danube Embankment, is Szilágyi Dezső tér, where there is a **Calvinist Church**. In January 1945, as the Russian Red Army was encircling Budapest, officers of the Arrow Cross Fascists, installed in government by the Nazis, rounded up many Jews in Budapest and brought them to this spot, where they shot them and threw their bodies in the Danube. A small plaque commemorates the events.

Just north-west of Batthyány tér are the Király Baths (see Chapter 8 'What to do in Hungary' for more information) and beyond them, at Bem József utca 20, an old foundry that was in operation from 1845 to 1964 is now the **Foundry Museum** (Öntödei Múzeum) which traces the history of foundry technology and products from the Iron Age to the present day. The foundry here produced everything from tram wheels to ship propellers and bells, and was established by the Swiss engineer Ábrahám Ganz. Beyond this again, streets and steps curve up the hill from the approach road to Margaret Bridge and the **Gül Baba Tomb** (Gül Baba Türbeje), the entrance to which is at Mecset utca 14. Gül Baba died during a festival in the Matthias Church which was, at that time, a mosque. The tomb, set on a quiet, secluded hillside surrounded by back gardens, is of a Turkish dervish who died in the sixteenth century; the tiny chapel has been restored with the aid of a gift from the Turkish government, and the whole place forms a small shrine to his memory — there is a small museum here. The tomb is the most northerly place of Moslem pilgrimage in the world. The area of Budapest to the west of the tomb, the suburb of Rózsadomb, is one of the wealthiest parts of the capital, home to rich entrepreneurs or film directors who live in villas secluded by high walls, with swish Western cars parked in the driveways.

Óbuda And Aquincum

The principal remains of Budapest's Roman heritage lie on the West Bank of the Danube, north of the centre of Buda, in the city's District III. Óbuda is the oldest part of Budapest. In the early years of the first century a military camp was established here by the Romans. By the end of the century there had developed a civilian town at neighbouring *Aquincum* which became the principal town of the province of *Pannonia Inferior*. The settlement declined after the defeat at *Hadrianopolis* in AD378, compounded by subsequent Barbarian attacks. In the fifth century the Huns settled here and supposedly named Buda after the brother of Attila. A royal residence was established here, but from the fourteenth century the site became eclipsed by the castle when Béla IV moved the royal residence there. Buda then became known as Óbuda (Old Buda) and began to develop separately. Óbuda was a separate town until its formal union with Buda and Pest in 1872.

Today Óbuda and neighbouring *Aquincum* are a mixture of the oldest and newest aspects of Budapest. A rewarding morning (most of the attractions tend to close early) may be spent seeking out, from under flyovers, behind schools and between tower blocks, the remains of the earliest settlements. Starting in **Óbuda**, and at the southern end of Pacsirtamezo utca, are the remains of one of the largest Roman amphitheatres (larger than the Colosseum in Rome). The remains are now rather pitiful, but the amphitheatre once held 16,000 spectators. Dating from AD160, it was unearthed in 1937 during the demolition of eighteenth-century residences. It is believed that during the ninth century it was used as a fortress by the invading Magyar tribes.

At the northern end of Pacsirtameso utca, at number 63, there is the **Roman Camp Museum** (Római Tábor Múzeum) displaying the ruins of a small Roman bathhouse together with various other relics. The remains of the public baths can actually be found underneath the Flórián tér flyover. This is the actual site of the Roman military camp, which during its heyday in the second and third centuries, played host to 6,000 garrisoned soldiers. Leave the underpass to the north-west, pass the tastefully arrayed column stumps and walk for 15 minutes to 19-21 Meggyfa utca. Behind the school is the **Hercules Villa**, so-called because of the three beautiful mosaic floors which illustrate scenes from the legend of Hercules. These date from the third century and are thought to have been arranged in Alexandria before being shipped to Hungary.

Just to the east of Flórián tér is Fő tér, traditionally the centre of Óbuda. At Szentélek tér 1, just on the south-east corner of the square, is the eighteenth-century Baroque **Zichy Mansion**, which now houses a collection of paintings by Viktor Vásárhely, all of which were donated by the artist to the state in 1982. To the north-east of Fő tér, at Laktanya utca 7 is the gallery devoted to the works of the sculptor, Imre Varga. The statue of the three large women with umbrellas in Hajógyár utca provide a 'taster' for the exhibition. Árpád híd HÉV station lies just along the bank of the Danube. From here, one can take the journey north to *Aquincum*.

If approaching *Aquincum* by HÉV train, or by road along Szentendrei utca, it is possible to see the remains of a Roman aqueduct that runs alongside the road. Note also the second century AD civilian amphitheatre tucked away behind *Aquincum* HÉV station, built to hold 8,000. The excavations of the remains of the civilian town of *Aquincum* are much more substantial than those in Óbuda, principally because when excavations began in the 1870s, this area was still only a field. Upon entry to the site, to the left can be seen the sad remains of the Basilica. Further on in front of the museum are the public baths, followed by the market place. Behind and beyond the museum are various private dwellings, workshops and some smaller baths. Various aspects of the water supply system, including sewerage and heating provision, can be seen. The small museum in the centre exhibits coins, statues, pottery, jewellery and, more unusually, a third-century organ, actually still playable. The site can be found at Szentendre utca 139, close to *Aquincum* HÉV station (trains from Batthyány tér in Buda).

The Buda Hills

The Buda Hills lie within the metropolitan area of Budapest, but are, in character, many times removed from the city. They are situated on the western fringes of the city, in Budapest's XII and II districts. An area of elegant villas and apartments which lies to the west of Moszkva tér gradually gives way to wooded hills and open countryside, crossed by well-marked paths and the Pioneer Railway, which is run entirely by children. Hill-top look out towers, a game reserve, small skiing grounds and limestone caves complete the picture, for this is Budapest's main area of extensive open space, where it is possible to shun the crowds entirely, yet still be within the city boundaries. In summer this is the perfect area to get away from the heat of the city. At any time, a visit to the Hills provides the perfect break from the bustle of the capital. All the walking tracks and paths mentioned here, and the various railways, look-out towers and caves, can be found on any city map of Budapest, or in the *Budapest Atlasz*.

The Rack Railway, Pioneer Railway And János-Hegy

Moszkva tér, just west of Castle Hill, is an important (and not particularly pretty) transport interchange, where many bus and tram routes converge. It is served by Moszkva tér metro station (metro line 2). A short walk (or tram or bus ride) from here, west along Szilágyi E. fasor street, brings one to the lower terminal of the **rack railway**, which is part of Budapest's municipal transport system. From here, trains running on a rack-and-pinion system carry passengers up the hill, through the wealthiest suburbs of Budapest, where there are ornate villas secluded in large gardens, and tree-lined avenues curving up the hillside alongside the tracks.

From the top station, Széchenyi-hegy, it is a short walk to the southern terminus of the **Pioneer Railway**, a Budapest oddity and a unique hangover from Communist days. In theory it is now known as the Children's

Railway, although the old name still seems to be in use a lot. It was built by youth brigades in 1948, and was run by the (now disbanded) Young Pioneers, the youth groups that became the Communist equivalent of Western Scout and Guide associations. It is still run by children, who act as ticket collectors and guards, and who man the stations. Adults drive the trains and do most of the maintenance work, but do their best to keep a low profile. The 13- and 14-year-old boys and girls who work on the line remain tight-lipped and exude an air of brisk efficiency which does not quite match that of the trains themselves, which clank and shudder alarmingly as they meander through the woodland on ancient and bumpy rails. The railway runs every day except Monday. Trains leave at intervals of roughly 40 minutes and take 45 minutes to complete the journey, stopping at various isolated halts en route where a uniformed youth will salute the train as it arrives and leaves.

The first stop on the line in Normafa, a modest little resort with a few skiing facilties, from where there is a bus connection down into the city. But most people travel on the train to János-Hegy station, from where it is a 15 minute climb up the hill to the Erzsébet lookout tower on the summit of **János-hegy** (512m/1,679ft), the highest point in Budapest. There is a fabulous view from here, encompassing the whole of the capital and the countryside beyond. The lookout tower is also the terminus of a city bus route. Just below the lookout tower is the top station of a chairlift down to Zugliget, from where there are more bus connections back to the city centre.

János-hegy is not the end of the line, however, and the trains continue beyond it to Hűvösvölgy, linked by tram and bus to Moszkva tér. There is a small amusement park by the station, but otherwise there is little to see here. The main attraction of taking the train up to here is the quiet walking in the Nagy-hárs-hegy area, a low forested hill (surmounted by another lookout tower) which the train encircles.

Another attraction in this part of Budapest is the **Budakeszi Game Reserve**. Frequent buses (number 22) run there from Moszkva tér (and call outside the Szépjuhászné station on the Pioneer Railway). Get off the bus at the 'Vadazpark' sign and walk for 10 minutes to the entrance. Fenced in just beyond the entrance are some of the animals one is likely to encounter in the park, but the distant sighting through the trees of a wild boar or pig or roe deer can be much more rewarding than a closer sighting behind wire. There are various shelters and feeding points scattered through the reserve, where animals are more likely to be found. Either way, this is a very pleasant place to stroll, with numerous benches situated alongside the, slightly confusing, maze of trails.

Limestone Caves And Hármashatár-Hegy

The other part of the Buda Hills worth visiting, which offers a different set of attractions, lies to the east of the Pioneer Railway. Here, two underground caves in the Buda Hills have been formed (uniquely) not by infiltrating rain water but rather by thermal waters which bubble up through the ground. Bus 65 from Kolósy tér, by the Danube (served by Szépvölgyi station on the HÉV line from Batthyány tér), takes one out to Szépvölgyi utca and the **Pál-völgyi Stalactite Caves**. The tour of the caves lasts 40 minutes and take place hourly; it takes in 500m (1,640ft) of the 6 ½km (4 miles) circuit of caves that have been discovered, and goes down 30m (98ft) below the ground surface. Both this cave, and the very different **Szemlőhegy Caves**, 20 minutes walk away at Pusztaszeri utca 35, are well worth visiting. Hourly guided tours take about half an hour. Also in this part of Budapest is the **Kiscelli Museum** at Kiscelli utca 108, which includes various collections of furnishings and antique printing presses housed in an old monastery.

Bus 65 runs on from the Pál-völgyi Caves to the summit of Hármashatár-hegy (495m, 1,624ft), where there is a café and another lookout tower. Hang-gliders take advantage of rising thermal air currents here, mushroom-hunters try to sort out the toxic from the non-toxic fungi that grow throughout these forests, while walkers merely follow the clearly signposted trails that run across the countryside here.

Additional Information

This section contains details about the addresses and opening times of museums, galleries and other places of interest in Budapest.

For information relating to entertainments in Budapest, see Chapter 8 'What To Do In Hungary'. For information on practical matters such as accommodation, where to find information or how to use the public transport system, see the Fact File section at the end of this book.

Places To Visit
Pest
City Zoo
In the Városliget (City Park)
Open: daily 9am-6pm (4pm October to March).

Vidámpark
In the Városliget
Open: daily 10am-8pm.

Parliament Building
Tours arranged by Budapest Tourist
Roosevelt tér 5
☎ 117 3555

Buda
Gül Baba Tomb
Mecset utca
Open: May to October only, 10am-6pm daily except Monday.

Labyrinth of Caves
Úri utca 9
Open: daily except Tuesday, 10am-6pm.

Pál-völgyi Stalactite Caves
Szépvölgyi utca 162
Open: April to October, daily except Monday, 10am-6pm.

Szemlőhegy Caves
Pusztaszeri utca 35
Open: daily except Tuesday, 9am-4pm.

Matthias Church
Church crypt open: daily April to September, 8.30am-8pm, October to March 9am-7pm. Main body of church open during daylight but no visitors allowed during services.

Museums
Buda Castle
Budapest Museum of History
Open: 10am-6pm daily except Monday.

Hungarian National Gallery
Open: daily 10am-6pm (4pm December to March).

Ludwig Collection
Open: daily 10am-6pm, closed November to February.

Elsewhere in Buda
Arany Sas Pharmacy Museum
Tárnok utca 18
Open: daily except Monday, 10.30am-5.30pm.

Foundry Museum
Bem József utca 20
Open: daily except Monday, 10am-5pm.

Hungarian Museum of Commerce & Catering
Fortuna utca 4
Open: daily except Monday 10am-6pm.

Jewish Museum
Táncsics Mihály utca 26
Open: May to October; Tuesday to Friday 10am-2pm, Saturday & Sunday 10am-6pm.

Kiscelli Museum
Kiscelli utca 108
Open: 10am-6pm (4pm November to March) daily except Monday.

Military History Museum
Entrance from Tóth Árpád sétány
Open: 10am-6pm, daily except Monday.

Museum of the History of Music
Táncsics Mihály utca 7
Open: Monday, 4-9pm; Wednesday to Sunday 9am-6pm; closed Tuesday.

Semmelweis Museum of the History of Medicine
Apród utca 1-3
Open: daily except Monday, 10am-6pm.

In Obuda and Aquincum
Hercules Villa
Behind 19-21 Meggyfa utca
Open: May to October only, 10am-2pm (6pm weekends) daily except Monday.

Roman Camp Museum
Pacsirtameso utca 63
Open: as above.

Ruins at Aquincum
Entrance at Szentendre utca 139
Open: as above.

Vásárhely Museum
Zichy Mansion
Szentélek tér 1
Open: Tuesday to Sunday 10am-6pm.

In Pest
Agricultural Museum
In the castle in the Városliget City Park
Open: daily except Monday 10am-5pm (6pm Sundays).

Ethnographic Museum
Kossuth tér 12
Open: Tuesday to Sunday 10am-6pm.

Hungarian National Museum
Múzeum körút 14-16
Open: daily except Monday, 10am-6pm.

Liszt Memorial Museum
Vörösmarty utca 35
Open: Monday to Friday 12noon-5pm. Saturday 9am-1pm.

Museum of Fine Arts and Műcsarnok Art Gallery
Both on Hősök tere
Open: 10am-6pm, daily except Monday.

National Jewish Museum
Next to the Central Synagogue off Károly körút
Open: May to October only, Monday and Thursday 2-6pm, Tuesday, Wednesday, Friday and Sunday 10am-1pm.

National Lutheran Museum
Deák tér
Open: 10am-6pm daily except Monday.

Petőfi Literary Museum
Károly Mihály utca 16
Open: daily except Monday, 10am-6pm.

Postal Museum
Andrássy utca 3
Open: daily except Monday, 10am-6pm.

Transport Museum
At Hermina utca (main site) and also in the Petőfi Csarnok (aviation exhibition) nearby, in the City Park
Open: 10am-6pm, daily except Monday.

Underground Railway Museum
Deák tér Metro
Open: daily except Monday 10am-6pm.

2
THE DANUBE BEND

The River Danube (known to Hungarians as the Duna) is the great river of central and south-eastern Europe. In fact, Napoleon gave the Danube a higher status than the Rhône and the Rhein (or even the Loire) by calling it 'the king of the rivers of Europe'. Rising in the mountains of the Black Forest and Bavaria, the 2,737km (1,700 mile) course of the Danube takes the river through eight countries and four capital cities including, of course, Budapest. It finally drains into the Black Sea, forming an enormous delta that covers a large area of Romania. Popular culture, at least, often portrays the Danube as romantic. This is the river of idle river cruising, of Vienna, Budapest and the dozens of other medieval cities that lie along its length. But another part of the Danube's attraction is the fabulous scenery that the river often passes through, and the area known as the Danube Bend — where the river cuts through the Pilis and Börzsöny Hills, and swings round in a great curve, as it flows between the towns of Esztergom and Szentendre — is undoubtedly one of the most beautiful stretches of the entire length of the river. Added to the attractions of the hills and the river are a number of charming towns and historical sites, especially in Visegrád, once the site of one of Hungary's largest and most impregnable castles, and at Esztergom, which for nearly a thousand years has been the ecclesiastical centre of the whole of Hungary. The fact that the places to visit here are all relatively close to one another, and that nowhere on the Danube Bend is much more than an hours drive from Budapest, means that the area is one of the most popular places for visitors in the country. But although Esztergom, Visegrád and Szentendre are often crowded in summer, it is easy to escape into virtual solitude in the good hiking and walking country of the Pilis and Börzsöny Hills.

Many people visit the Danube Bend on day-trips from Budapest, but staying in the area, even for only a day or two, gives one a good chance to get away from the city heat and polluted air of Budapest for a while. There are hotels in Esztergom, Szentendre and in smaller settlements on the bend such as Visegrád. Accommodation in private homes is also plentiful and for those who wish to see a lot of this area, the most convenient place

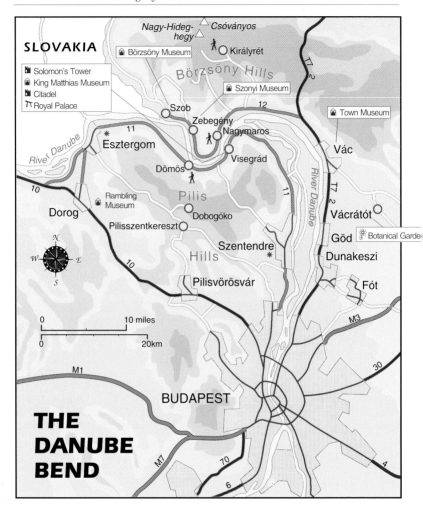

SLOVAKIA

Nagy-Hideg-hegy
Csóványos
Börzsöny Museum
Királyrét

Börzsöny Hills

Szonyi Museum

- 🏰 Solomon's Tower
- 🏛 King Matthias Museum
- 🏰 Citadel
- 🏛 Royal Palace

Szob
Zebegény
Nagymaros
12
Town Museum

11
Esztergom
Visegrád

River Danube
Dömös

10
Rambling Museum
Pilis
Dobogóko
Dorog
Pilisszentkereszt
Vácrátót
River Danube
Göd 🌿 Botanical Garden

N
W — E
S
10
Szentendre
Hills
Dunakeszi

Pilisvörösvár
Fót

0   10 miles
0   20km

M1

M3

30

BUDAPEST

THE DANUBE BEND

M7
70
6
4

to stay is probably Visegrád, which is on the central part of the bend and which has good connections, by road or public transport, with the other places of interest. The car and passenger ferry across the river here also makes it a convenient place to stay.

The Danube Bend is a very easy area to travel around, whether by car or by public transport. There are main roads on both sides of the river, running north from Budapest. The most scenic stretches are around Nagymaros (on the north side) and Visegrád (on the south side). There are no bridges across the Danube. However, there are a number of ferries, which are marked on maps. Some are only for pedestrians, and operate seasonally, but most take cars. These ferries operate at very regular intervals and rarely entail waiting for more than a few minutes. There is a railway on the left bank of the river, with trains from Nyugati station in

Budapest to Vác and Nagymaros. The service is regular and usually reliable. Some of the trains along this line are fast express trains heading for Slovakia and beyond. Buses from Budapest serve Esztergom, Vác and Visegrád, and many other settlements on the bend. Most services are hourly, as is the service along the main road linking Szentendre, Visegrád and Esztergom, and the villages between them. The most entertaining way to travel between Budapest and the Danube Bend settlements is by boat. The passenger terminal in Budapest is at Vigadó tér, on the East Bank of the Danube alongside the Duna Intercontinental Hotel. Here information can be obtained about services from Budapest to Vác, Visegrád, Szentendre and Esztergom (see Additional Information at the end of this chapter for further details). The first part of the journey is fairly dull — undoubtedly the best part is between Kismaros and Szob or Esztergom. It is best to book tickets for these sailings a couple of days in advance, though some may still be available on the day. Of course, journeys do not have to begin or end in Budapest, and it is perfectly possible to travel between the Danube settlements themselves, since boats stop off at a number of landing stages along the route. More details on reaching Esztergom and settlements in the Pilis range are given below, in sections relating to these areas.

The charming old centre of Szentendre

The West Bank

❈ **Szentendre** (St Andrew), 19km (12 miles) to the north of Budapest, is a town of considerable charm and character on the West Bank of the Danube, whose winding streets lined with pastel-coloured houses, many art galleries and pretty hilltop churches draws hordes of day trippers from Budapest. It is accessible by road 11, or by the HÉV train service from Batthyány tér in Budapest (40 minute journey, trains departing every 10 minutes). A separate ticket must be bought for this journey as the HÉV line goes outside the city limits. There are also frequent buses from Erzsébet tér in the centre of Budapest (metro: Deák tér), and there are a number of boat services from Vidagó tér in Budapest.

The site has been inhabited since the Stone Age, and was settled by the Romans who knew it as *Ulcisia Castra*. During the fifteenth century a community of Serbian merchants settled here after their homelands were overrun by the Turks. Szentendre itself succumbed to the Turkish forces during the sixteenth century but following their expulsion in 1690 many Serbs returned to the town along with Bosnians, Albanians and Greeks, whose homelands were still under threat. Consequently the town derives much of its character from these people, although today Szentendre only contains a small minority of Serbs, and much of the present flavour of the town comes from the artist's colony established here at the beginning of the twentieth century.

From the HÉV terminal, and adjacent bus station, it is about a 10 minute walk to the centre along Kossuth utca (though a slight detour along Duna Kanyar körút, takes one to a small open-air display of Roman stonework, situated on the site of the former Roman military camp). Just before
 Kossuth utca crosses the Bükkös stream, one passes the Serbian Požarevačka Church dating from the 1740s. Continue over the bridge and along Dumtsa Jenő utca and to your left at number 10 there is the Barcsay Collection of drawings and paintings by the Transylvanian artist Jenő Barcsay, who joined the artist's colony here in 1928. Further on, turn left down Péter-Pál utca where one finds the Peter-Paul Church (1753). Unfortunately the interior furnishings were taken back to Yugoslavia at the end of the Great War, but the exterior is original and a history of the church in English may be found inside the porch.

From here it is a short walk north to the main square, Fő tér (which is linked to the Danube quayside by another pretty street, Görög utca). The merchant cross in the centre was erected in 1763 by Serbian merchants to celebrate the town's escape from plague that year. The square gets very busy in summer, but relief may be found in some of the numerous surrounding galleries and museums. To the east, numbers 2 to 5 on the square, are eighteenth-century Serbian merchants' houses which today display the work of contemporary artists working in the town. Behind these buildings, away from the square, on Vastagh György utca, is the Margit Kovács Museum, the best gallery in Szentendre, which displays

the work of Hungary's most famed ceramist. Even the most jaded of
travellers, worn out by the eternal ducking between the T-shirt stands and
menu boards, will not fail to be charmed by the simplicity and grace of her
work. Back in the square, the Baroque Serbian Blagoveštenska Church,
built in the 1750s (also known as the Greek Church, because of a tomb-
stone of a Greek merchant found to the left of the entrance) boasts beautiful rococo windows and exquisite icon paintings by Mihailo Živkovič
dating from the early years of the nineteenth century. Next to the church,
at number 6, in a former Serbian school, is the Ferenczy Museum dedicated to the works of the Ferenczy family, foremost amongst whom was
the impressionist painter Károly Ferenczy (1862-1917), who spent his
youth in the town. There are smaller rooms devoted to his eldest son
Valér, an expressionist painter, and to the twins Noémi and Béni who
dabbled in tapestry and bronzeware respectively. Back across Fő tér at
number 21 there is a collection of bleak canvases by János Kmetty (1889-
1975).

Continue up the incline along Rákóczi utca, briefly note the crumbling
Baroque Town Hall but pay more attention to the small Museum of
Childhood (at number 1) which contains a fascinating collection of toys,
cribs, and childhood memorabilia. From here, one can ascend the hill
which rises above the town via one of a number of steep paths, to
Templom tér, home to a number of craft stalls, which sell various folk
souvenirs around the Catholic Parish Church. The church is of medieval
origin, the first stone building in the town, whose many reconstructions
have resulted in the incorporations of elements of Romanesque, Gothic
and Baroque styles. The frescoes in the sanctuary are the collective work
of the town's artistic community during the early years of the twentieth
century. Nearby, the Béla Czóbel Museum features the work of yet another local artist. A short walk away, along Alkotmány utca stands the
Belgrade Church (1764). From the mid-eighteenth century, Szentendre
was the ecclesiastical centre of Hungary's Serbian community, and the
remains of several Serbian Orthodox bishops can be seen in the crypt
which is open to anyone who can persuade one of the reluctant priests to
find the key. It is much easier to gain admission to the adjoining Museum
of Ecclesiastical Art. This contains a variety of treasures, dating from the
sixteenth to the nineteenth centuries, gathered from Serbian churches
across the country after the Serbs gradually returned home following the
Turkish withdrawal from their land.

From here, it is a short walk down the hill to Bogdányi utca. Anyone
whose artistic appetite has not been satiated may want to drop into the
Imre Ámos-Margit Anna collection at number 12 on this street. Alternatively, continue on to the small square doubling as a car park which
features the Tsar Lázár memorial cross. Lázár was a Serbian ruler, be-
headed by the Turks in 1389 in response to the killing of Sultan Murad
during the Battle of Kosovo, by which the Turks occupied the Kingdom
of Serbia. Further on along the road is the Preobraženska Church, built by

the Serbian Tanners' Guild in the 1740s and at number 51 is the Szentendre Gallery, which exhibits more works by past and present members of the famous colony. One may follow the road on to the small, but worthwhile, sculpture park.

Four kilometres (2½ miles) away from the town along road 11 is the Szentendre Village Museum (Skansen) the largest, oldest and best of Hungary's village museums. The purpose of the museum is to reconstruct rural villages from ten regions of Hungary, and in doing so to give visitors a feel of what life was like in Hungary in previous centuries. Although the Skansen was started in 1968, only two of the ten regions have been completed, although these are more than large enough to make a visit worthwhile. The two completed units are of the Upper Tisza region and the Kisalföld. There is also one completed building from Western Transdanubia. On view are various peasant dwellings, small churches and craft workshops populated by guides in traditional dress who dispense information (though not usually in English). During the summer months there are also displays of traditional crafts such as baking, basket weaving, and pottery making. Further information in English is available at the entrance.

Twenty kilometres (12 miles) beyond Szentendre the road along the Danube follows the river round in a broad U-shape, for a time heading in a southerly direction, back towards Budapest, rather than taking the more direct route, which would involve crossing over part of the Pilis range which comes right down to the river here. This is one of the most impres-

White-washed thatched-roofed cottages at Szentendre Village Museum

A reconstruction of the Lion's Fountain in the Royal Palace at Visegrád

The Danube Bend; a view of Visegrád from the hills above Nagymaros

✳ sive stretches of scenery in the bend, where the hills fall steeply down to the river on both sides, and which is overlooked on the south side by the impressive citadel high above **Visegrád**, a small town, and busy tourist centre, which occupies a narrow ledge between the river and the steep hillsides.

The Romans were the first to notice the defensive potential of the high cliffs above the river, with their commanding view over the surrounding countryside. They built a fort here which was still in use in the tenth century, when the area was inhabited by Slavs who gave the place its name — Visegrád means 'High Castle'. In the mid-thirteenth century, King Béla IV chose this location to build an impregnable fortress. But subsequent kings of Hungary, realising that the threat of a Mongol invasion from the east had subsided, changed the castle's role from a defensive site to one of a Royal Palace, news of whose riches and splendour spread throughout Europe in the Middle Ages. In 1335 the Visegrád Congress was held here, when delegates from all over Europe failed to agree how to respond to the growing power of the Habsburgs but managed to consume 10,000 litres of wine in the process, during a 2-month bout of feasting, jousting and debating. Contemporary accounts tell of wine flowing from the fountains in the palace's hanging gardens. In 1483 the palace was described to Pope Sixtus IV as a *paradiso terresti* — paradise on earth. This was at the time of King Matthias Corvinus, who enlarged the castle and rebuilt it in Gothic, then Renaissance, style and who presided over the most glorious (and decadent) period of the castle's history. It was abandoned at the time of the Turkish invasion in 1543, and when German settlers turned up in the mid-seventeenth century they used stone from the palace to build their houses. German is still the first language of many of the people who live in Visegrád and other settlements along the Danube here. After that, what was left of the palace was eventually buried by landslides from the steep slope immediately behind it. At one time the palace buildings occupied a site of 44 acres (18 hectares), but despite descriptions of life there by numerous medieval travellers, many historians considered the castle a myth until the 1930s, when the archaeologist János Schluek unearthed part of it. Archaeological investigations are still continuing, but those parts of the castle which are now visible, which constitute only a small part of what was once one of the most fabulous buildings in central Europe, give an indication of its former splendour.

Π The entrance to the Royal Palace is at Fő utca 27, a little further on along the main road from the Danube landing stages. Some parts of the palace have been reconstructed, in a somewhat crude manner but one which allows visitors to tell which bits are original and which are modern. The former rooms, courtyards and terraces of the palace are all clearly discernible, and a plan of the site is available from the ticket office at the entrance for those who want to identify properly what they are looking at. On the top level of the site is a perfect copy of the marble Lion's Fountain, from the original of which wine reputedly once flowed. The terrace on which it sits was once the garden, one of the most beautiful parts of the medieval palace.

The palace was once encircled by high walls, which stretched from the banks of the Danube right up to the citadel on the top of the hill. By the river, close to the landing stages, is the Water Bastion, which was an observation post. Above this on the hillside is Solomon's Tower (Salamon tornya), a very solid-looking (and heavily reconstructed) bastion that is the only remaining part of the old defensive system. Behind the 8m (26ft) thick walls is the King Matthias Museum, named after the great fifteenth- century king of Hungary, who held court at the Royal Palace during its most glorious era. The museum displays archaeological finds from the palace, including the red marble *Visegrád Madonna* carved by Tomaso Fiamberti in the fifteenth century. Just above the tower, on Sibrik Hill, are the very insubstantial remains of a small castle.

The most distinctive and dramatic feature of Visegrád, especially im- pressive to those who arrive in the town by boat, is the Citadel, perched on steep cliffs high above the town and surrounded by thick forests. The Citadel was built in the mid-thirteenth century, at the same time as the castle, and was once considered impregnable enough to be the repository for the Hungarian crown jewels. Like the castle, it has been restored rather crudely in places, but it is nonetheless an impressive building, its rooms housing exhibitions relating to the history of Visegrád. The real reason to come up here, however, is for the fantastic views over the Danube which it provides. Beyond the Hotel Silvanus is the Nagy-Villám observation tower, which does likewise. It is possible to walk up the steep paths from the town to the citadel (look for the signs to the *fellegvár*). There is also a bus up there which runs from the Matthias Statue on Salamán-torony utca in the town.

There is a car and passenger ferry from Visegrád across to Nagymaros, from where a number of excursions into the Börzsöny Hills can be made (see under 'East Bank'). The next village after Visegrád is Dömös, the best base from which to explore the Pilis Hills. Beyond Dömös the Danube valley broadens, and the road runs through lush farmland for 15km (9 miles) before reaching Esztergom.

Esztergom

Two ranges of low hills fall gently down to the shores of the Danube at Esztergom, the point where the river narrows and turns as it flows off the flat lands of Northern Hungary and begins to cut through the mountains of the Danube Bend. Here, the river forms the international frontier between Hungary and Slovakia, and the forlorn-looking Slovak port of Štúrovo glares grimly across the water at Esztergom, with its clutch of historic sites, elegant squares and beautiful churches. The historical sig- nificance of Esztergom rests on its being the centre of Hungarian Catholi- cism for nearly a thousand years. Nowadays, it is as much a tourist as a religious centre, with hordes of day-trippers from Budapest coming each day to look at the Basilica, the dome of which dominates the skyline for

❋

The Nagymaros Dam

Anyone travelling west along the Danube from Visegrád or Nagymaros (on the opposite bank) will see evidence of the Gabčikovo-Nagymaros Dam, in the form of earthworks, makeshift loading bays and moored dredging ships. In Communist days, this was to have been the site of what would have been one of the biggest environmental disasters in Europe. The governments of Hungary, Czechoslovakia (as it was then) and Austria had agreed to build a dam here, in which turbines producing hydroelectricity would have been installed. Although the government of Czechoslovakia had already done a lot of construction work on their side of the Danube, further upstream (abandoned after the Communists were ousted from power), the more liberal Communist regime in Hungary found itself under intense pressure from environmental groups within the country, which were not suppressed as easily as the ones in Czechoslovakia had been. They complained that: the still water in the lake behind the dam would create the right conditions for water-borne diseases to thrive, which would affect the health of the inhabitants of Esztergom and other towns; that the natural beauty of the region would be wrecked; that if the dam ever burst or came under enemy attack, there would be disastrous consequences for Budapest, which would be hit by massive tidal waves and floods; and that Austria, which was to have provided finance and technology for the dam in return for energy produced from it, but which would not have been affected by these problems, was exploiting the weaknesses of Hungary and Czechoslovakia, and behaving like an old colonial power. As a result of these pressures, the government of Hungary dithered as to whether the dam should go ahead, and just before the fall from power of the Communists the project was abandoned, though it may still be completed in a much smaller version. As a result of this climbdown, the natural beauty of the Danube Bend — and, more importantly, the safety and welfare of the people who live by the river — has been retained, in a rare but welcome triumph for environmental campaigners.

miles around, and also at the other churches, museums and galleries which have been established around the town centre. Despite the number of people here, Esztergom is well worth visiting, either as the culmination to a tour of the Danube Bend settlements or as a separate day excursion from the capital. Two roads lead from Budapest to Esztergom. The quickest is via Pilisvörösvár and Dorog (road 10 then road 111, distance: 45km/ 28 miles) but the more scenic route is via Pomáz and Piliszentkereszt, which gives one a chance to visit Dobogókő, one of the main centres of the Pilis Hills. The most scenic, and longest, route is the one already described

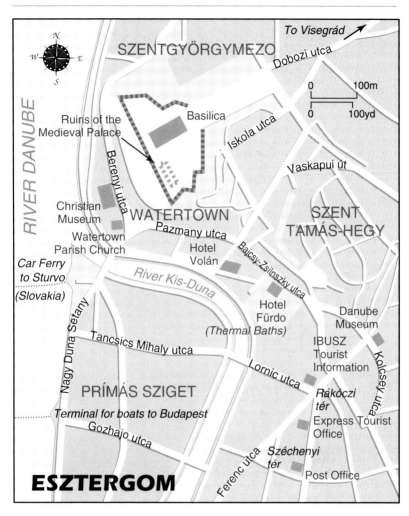

in this chapter, via Szentendre and Visegrád. Buses between Esztergom and Budapest are frequent and the fastest take just over an hour (some run via Visegrád and take much longer). They drop one off very close to the Basilica, making the less frequent train services — which stop at the railway station, a little way from the town centre — much less convenient. Travellers with a lot of time on their hands might wish to take one of the boats which run up the Danube from Budapest, taking a leisurely 5 hours to cover the distance. There are a number of hotels in the town, and one of the tourist offices around Kossuth Lajos utca, in the centre of town (a short walk from the Basilica) will help travellers find a hotel or private room. However many choose to visit Esztergom on a day excursion from somewhere else. The bridge across the Danube at Esztergom was never rebuilt after the World War II, so a decrepit ferry takes cars and passengers over to Štúrovo every hour provided, of course, travellers have adequate documentation to visit Slovakia.

On Christmas Day in AD1000, Stephen I, the country's patron saint and widely regarded as the founder of the modern state, was crowned the first king of Hungary in Esztergom, the place of his birth. The town was chosen as the first capital of Hungary, and remained so until the thirteenth century, when the threat of the Mongol invasion forced the royal court to decamp to Buda. Esztergom, however, remained the centre of Hungarian Catholicism, and a number of churches and monasteries were built here, culminating in the construction of the fantastic **Basilica**, which dominates the town, in the nineteenth century. It is the most recent church to have been built on this site, and incorporates some parts of older churches in its construction. In the year 1010 Stephen I chose the steep hill which rises above the Danube as the site for the first cathedral of Esztergom. Two Anglo-Saxon princes, Edmund and Edward (both sons of Edmund Ironside) sought refuge in the building soon after its construction, and Edward actually married Stephen's daughter. The cathedral was rebuilt and destroyed several times, and construction of the present Basilica was begun in 1822. When it was completed, over 30 years later, it was the largest church in Hungary — 118m (387ft) long, 40m (131ft) high with a dome over 70m (230ft) high. Liszt composed a special piece of music, the *Esztergom Festival Mass*, to celebrate the completion of the building, and this was performed at the dedication ceremony in 1856. The massive size of the church and the overbearing decorations inside — marble and ornate mosaics cover the walls, roof and the inside of the dome — confirm the strength of the Roman Catholic Church in Hungary. It still exerts a great influence over the people of this country, despite the efforts of the Stalinist President Rákosi, who in the 1950s jailed hundreds of priests to try to reduce the power of the Church. By the 1970s, however, the outlook of the State had changed, and in 1988, Hungary's liberal laws on foreign travel allowed over 60,000 Hungarians to attend the Pope's Mass for Eastern Europe in Vienna, and 2 years later millions of Hungarians welcomed the Pope when he visited their own country.

The main entrance to the Basilica is usually through the southern doorway. This passes the door for the stairway up to the cupola before leading one into the interior of the Basilica, which is large, airy and overwhelming. The red marble chapel on the left, named after Archbishop Tamás Bakócz who commissioned it, was built by Florentine craftsmen in the early sixteenth century, as part of the cathedral that stood here until it was ransacked by the Turks. When the current Basilica was constructed, the chapel was dismantled and the 1600 numbered pieces were reassembled in the new position chosen for it. The chapel is one of the most beautiful parts of the cathedral. Opposite, on the North Wall, is the plainer Chapel of St Stephen, where a cabinet contains a bodily relic of the English saint, Thomas à Becket, who was murdered in Canterbury Cathedral in 1170 on the instructions of Henry II. Becket had once studied with a former Archbishop of Esztergom, who brought the relic here. Above the main altar, on the West Wall, is one of the world's biggest oil-on-canvas paintings, the work of the nineteenth-century Italian painter Michelangelo Grigoletti but based on the Titian painting *Assumption* which hangs in the Frari Church, Venice. On the wall of the right (north) transept are some more holy relics, this time of the three Martyrs of Kassa (then in Hungary; now Košice, Slovakia) who were executed in 1619 for their religious beliefs. The painting above the altar here shows Stephen offering his crown to the Virgin Mary. This is a common theme in Hungarian painting as Stephen had no son to inherit his crown, thereby causing many years of conflict in Hungary as different groups tried to control the succession, seriously weakening the newly-founded State.

A door in the wall of the north transept gives access to the treasury of the Basilica, where many religious items dating from the Middle Ages, including some beautifully decorated medieval chalices, and the gold Calvary of King Matthias, which dates from the fifteenth century, are on display to the public. By the main entrance door to the church there are steps down to the predictably gloomy crypt, where the bodies of the cathedral's former prelates are buried and where parts of the original church started by Stephen have been found. Next to the entrance to the crypt are the stairs up to the top of the dome, from where the fantastic view from the outside gallery of the cupola more than makes up for the steep climb, and often horrendously long queues, that visitors will encounter on the way up.

To one side of the Basilica is the **Medieval Palace**, in which King Stephen was born, and which in the Middle Ages was home to various kings of Hungary and Archbishops of Esztergom (and, for 200 years, the Royal Mint) until it was wrecked by the Turks in 1543. Like the palace at Visegrád, the building was eventually abandoned and became submerged in earth until it was excavated (and partially restored) in the 1930s. The rooms of the palace now house a museum, with displays relating to the history of the castle and the cathedral. The vaulting in a couple of the rooms is original. Visitors can also see a copy of the twelfth-century marble throne used by Béla III, and parts of the original churches that once stood on the site of the present Basilica. The highlight of the palace is probably the chapel, built by French architects in the twelfth century, which has remnants of twelfth and fourteenth-century frescoes on the walls, preserved under the earth that gradually filled all the rooms of the chapel when parts of the castle collapsed after the Turkish invasion. In the Hall of Virtues there are fifteenth-century wall paintings depicting Intelligence, Temperance, Fortitude and Justice, with signs of the zodiac painted across the great arch.

Down from the Medieval Palace, and across the road, a path leads up from Batthyány Lajos utca to **St Thomas' Hill** (Szent-Tamás Hegy). The name of the Hill honours Thomas à Becket, after the chapel that was established here by one of Henry II's daughters-in-law, Margaret Capet, who strongly disagreed with the king's decision to have Becket murdered. She later married King Béla III and came to Hungary. The chapel on the hill dates from 1823 and is usually locked. The Stations of the Cross along the path to the summit look a bit decrepit now, but there are good views from the top across to the Medieval Palace and the Basilica.

Between the Cathedral Hill and the Danube is the **Watertown** (Víziváros) district. Some of the buildings here are associated with the cathedral, including the Theological College and Cathedral Library. On the little square where Bajcsy-Zsilinszky utca and Berényi Zsigmond utca meet is the **Watertown Parish Church** (Vízivárosi plébániatemplom), is a richly decorated Baroque church dating from the 1720s, built in Italian Baroque style. A little way up Berényi Zsigmond utca is the entrance to what was once the Archbishop's Palace, which is now the **Christian Museum** (Keresztény Múzeum), one of the finest provincial museums in Hungary where many dazzling pieces of medieval religious art, including paintings, tapestries and altarpieces from Italy, Germany, the Low Countries, Austria and Hungary are displayed.

A bridge nearby allows one to cross to **Prímás Sziget**, a pleasant island where visitors and the town's citizens take strolls along the tree-lined avenues and paths. The island is separated from the rest of the town by an arm of the Danube called the Kis-Duna, and the paths which run along this narrow stretch of water also make for pleasant evening strolls. The centre of Esztergom is **Széchenyi tér**, an elegant, triangular-shaped square lined

Esztergom, the ecclesiastical centre of Hungary, is dominated by the great domed Basilica

with eighteenth-century buildings, the most imposing of which is the town hall, with its rococo decorations, which occupies the whole of the south side of the square. Busier, and uglier, is Rákóczi tér to the north, where IBUSZ and other tourist offices can be found. Just up from the square, on Zalka Máté utca, there is an open-air street market. Rákóczi tér is linked to the cathedral by Bajcsy-Zsilinszky utca, a functional street along which many of the town's hotels, shops and restaurants can be found, while on Kölcsey utca is the **Danube Museum** (Magyar Vízügyi Múzeum), which includes displays relating to the now abandoned Dam a little way upstream at Nagymaros (see Feature Box). On Bajcsy-Zsilinszky utca, behind the Hotel Fürdő, there are some thermal baths.

The Pilis Hills
The Pilis Hills, which fall steeply down to the Danube at Visegrád, form the closest area to Budapest for hiking and walking. Although no peaks rise much above 750m (2,460ft), there are some dramatic walks, peaceful valleys and good views to be enjoyed in these hills. Once, the Pilis formed an important hunting reserve, used by the court at Visegrád. Later on a monk from Esztergom turned many of the hunting lodges into small monasteries, which became inhabited by hermits. Anyone planning to walk in these hills should buy the walking map *A Pilis és a Visegrádi-Hegység Túristatérképe* from bookshops and tourist information centres, which shows the paths through the forest. There are dozens of possibilities for walks in these hills besides the ones described here. There are two main starting-points for walks: the small, overgrown village of Dömös, beside the Danube, on the main road between Visegrád and Esztergom; and the resort of Dobogókő, which can be reached by road from the south (ie Budapest) via Pomáz and Piliszentkereszt, or from the north-west (ie from Esztergom) via Pilisszentlélek. There are infrequent buses to Dobogókő from Pomáz, which is on the HÉV line from Budapest to Szentendre. More frequent buses running along road 11 between Esztergom, Visegrád, Szentendre and Budapest call at Dömös. **Dobogókő** itself is one of the highest points of the hills, and though it is a fairly featureless sort of place it boasts a small Rambling Museum in a wooden building that was Hungary's first tourist hostel, and, behind that, a concrete platform with panoramic views all the way over to the Danube. Other than this, Dobogókő has only a TV transmitter and a plush hotel to recommend it.

From the church in the centre of **Dömös** it is a 30 minute walk along the red/yellow/green-marked path to a junction in the forest, where a steep and difficult path marked with red triangles takes walkers up past the Vadalló Rocks and then up to Predikaloszek, a towering crag (total walking time from Dömös: 2 hours, 10 minutes). A path marked with green markers runs from the junction in the forest up through the Ram-Szakadek, a narrow, steep-walled precipice which is also difficult to get through and must be ascended in some places by means of ladders and chains. Those who successfully manage to reach the top can carry on along the yellow-marked path to Dobogókő (total time from Dömös to Dobogókő: 2 hours 50 minutes). Doing this walk in reverse, from Dobogókő to Dömös, and down the Ram-Szakadek rather than up it, involves far less climbing and takes a shorter time.

The East Bank

For historical reasons, the East Bank of the Danube has fewer points of interest than the West Bank. Defensive settlements such as Visegrád were built on the West Bank of the Danube to repel invaders who were coming, for the main part, from the east. Alone amidst a succession of towns along the East Bank, Vác is the only settlement of any interest, and really the main reason for heading across the Danube at all is to reach the wild and deserted Börzsöny Hills, which occupy the area between the North Bank of the Danube at Nagymaros, and the Slovak border at Parassapuszta.

✳   Though fairly unprepossessing **Vác** is not an unpleasant town, surprisingly steeped in history and easily accessible by boat, bus or train from Budapest, a mere 35km (22 miles) away. The earliest settlement here dates from the Bronze Age, though the town was situated on the wrong side of the Danube to have been encompassed by the Roman Empire. During the eleventh century Vác became one of the ten episcopies founded by King Stephen I, and Géza I built a fortress and cathedral here. The town suffered badly at the hands of the Mongol forces in 1241 and had to be completely rebuilt by Béla IV. Between 1544 and 1686 Vács changed hands approximately 30 times between Turkish and Habsburg masters and as a consequence by the close of the seventeenth century lay once more in ruins. The present day Baroque town centre, embankment and Triumphal Arch date from the reconstruction of the eighteenth century. The tower blocks and industry on the outskirts of the town were added during the Communist era.

The triangular Március 15 tér, 10 minutes walk from the railway station, stands at the heart of modern day Vác. On the west of the square at number 11 stands the Baroque Town Hall erected by Bishop Kristóf Migazzi and completed for the visit of Empress Maria Theresa in 1764. The town's coat of arms is featured on the arch of the gable. Opposite, at number 6, is the former Bishop's Palace which in 1802 became the country's first institute for the deaf and dumb. Admire the façade of the imposing rococo Dominican church and then leave the square down Köztársaság út. Along this road one passes a Holy Trinity statue dating from the 1750s and, opposite, a Baroque Piarist church (eighteenth century) on the way to Konstantin tér upon which stands the town's neo-Classical cathedral, built from 1763 to 1777. It is worth a wander through the enormous Corinthian columns to view the impressive murals of Franz Anton Maulbertsch. His painting of the meeting of Mary and Elizabeth behind the altar was only discovered in the 1940s after it had been bricked over by Bishop Migazzi. Off Konstantin tér at number 4 Múzeum utca is the Town Museum named after Vak Bottyán, one of the rebel leaders during the War of Independence (1703-11). Follow the street to Géza Király tér which was the eleventh-century centre of Vác. The cathedral once situated here was reduced to dust back in 1241, so present day visitors must make do with the eighteenth-century Baroque Franciscan church.

The only surviving remnant of medieval Vác is the Round Tower situated at the northern end of the promenade which runs the length of the town and from where one may catch a ferry to Szentendrei Island. Hungary's only Triumphal Arch is situated 1km (½ mile) to the north of Március 15 tér along Köztársaság út. It was built by the ubiquitous Bishop Migazzi in honour of the 1764 visit of Maria Theresa. The architect Isidore Canevale also designed the cathedral. The bleak, windowless building nearby is the state prison. It was built in 1777 and converted from a barracks into a prison in 1855. Its rather infamous past is commemorated by two memorial plaques. The first relates to two Communist prisoners bludgeoned to death while on hunger strike during the Horthy era. The second relates to victims tortured here during the Stalinist period of the early 1950s and to the mass escape during the 1956 Uprising.

Leaving Vác, road 2 to the south at the Gombás stream boasts an unusual stone bridge dating from the 1750s with six baroque statues. Meanwhile **Vácrátót**, 10km (6 miles) away, is famed for its 69 acre (28 hectare) botanical gardens boasting 23,000 different kinds of flowers, trees and assorted plants. Unfortunately there is no information in English available and if visiting from Vác it is advisable to take the bus as the railway station is a good 50 minute walk from the entrance. Inside there is a small lake and water-mill but the gardens are not especially pretty and one would have to be a fairly keen botanist to derive total satisfaction from a visit.

The Börzsöny Hills

Wilder and bleaker than the Pilis range on the opposite side of the Danube, the Börzsöny is an area of eerily silent forest watched by circling eagles, and tiny mountain villages where the pace of life is as unhurried and traditional as one could find. Soon after Vác the valley of the Danube begins to close in, and at Nagymaros, with its splendid views over to the Citadel above Visegrád, on the opposite bank, the Danube is almost flowing through a gorge, cutting through the hills in a narrow U-shape. There are three possible starting points for treks and walks in the Börzsöny: Nagymaros on the river itself; Királyrét, inland from the river; and Diósjenő or Nagybörzsöny, over to the east and west of the range respectively. The possibilities from each settlement are described below in turn. Anyone wishing to see more of this area should buy the map *A Börzsöny* from bookshops and tourist information centres, published by Cartographia, which shows dozens of possibilities for walks in these hills besides those described here and also the locations of *túristáháza*, hostels in the hills which can be used by travellers (though those wishing to stay in them should try to book in advance at tourist offices in the region).

Twelve kilometres (7 miles) beyond Vác, a right-turning in the village of Kismaros takes one up through a pleasant valley through Szokolya to the small hamlet of **Királyrét**, from where there are many possibilities for walking. There are buses to Királyrét from Kismaros, and the narrow gauge railway from Verőce via Kismaros to Királyrét may reopen one day. From Királyrét (or the car park a mile or so beyond it along the road) there are a number of ways of walking up to the hostel at Nagy-Hideg-hegy (where there is food and a passable view) or to the enormously high cylindrical lookout tower at the summit of **Mount Csóványos**, at an altitude of 938m (3,076ft) the highest point in the Börzsöny. The view here is worth it for those who can brave the steep step-ladders that run up inside the tower (which is itself a real blot on the landscape). Walking times really depend on the route taken (careful examination of the map is needed before setting off), but as a guide it takes about 3 hours to walk from Királyrét to Nagy-Hideg-hegy, and another hour or so to get to Csóványos from the hostel there. To walk from Királyrét to Csóványos directly may take over 3 hours (the last part is *steep*). Csóványos can also be reached from the east, where it takes 3 to 4 hours to reach the summit from the town of **Diósjenő**, from where many walks into the northern part of the range can be made.

Finally, anyone who makes it all the way over to **Nagybörzsöny** in the western part of the range should look out for the thirteenth-century Romanesque village church there which, uniquely, survived the Mongol and Turkish invasions more or less intact. It is the sole reminder that this village was once a very prosperous mining community, reduced to a humdrum existence when the gold, iron and copper deposits on which its medieval prosperity rested, were worked out.

An obvious excursion for anyone staying in or visiting Visegrád is to take the car and passenger ferry from there over to **Nagymaros**, a nondescript town which, like Visegrád, is built on a narrow shelf of land between the steep hillsides and the river, with houses splayed unevenly up the higher ground. Apart from the superlative views over towards the Citadel, and the regular train services from Nagymaros to Nyugati Station in Budapest, the main reason for coming here is to walk. From the ferry landing-stages or railway station at Nagymaros, take the route marked with blue crosses *steeply* up through the houses to the car park at the end of the Panorama autóút road (which is a turning off the road between Kismaros and Kóspallag — a long way round from Nagymaros!) From here, take the blue-marked path which forks left, up to the lookout tower at the summit of Hegyes-tető (482m/1,581ft), from where there is a superb view of the Danube Bend and over into Slovakia. The last part of this walk is again *steep*. The walk up from Nagymaros takes a good couple of hours. From the top it is possible to drop down to the railway station at Dömösi atkeles v.m. for a train back to Nagymaros (but check the timetable before you set out — few trains stop here). The station serves the village of Dömös, on the other side of the Danube, in theory reachable by a small passenger ferry. Workings associated with the proposed Nagymaros Dam (see Feature Box) are clearly visible here. Another longer option from the summit at Hegyes-tető is to walk down to the village of **Zebegény**, where there is also a railway station, and a museum and gallery devoted to the life and work of the artist István Szőnyi, who was born here, and who depicted the life and landscape of the region in his paintings.

Those who walk, drive to or otherwise manage to reach **Szob** the next village beyond Zebegény where the railway crosses into Slovakia (there is no road crossing here, though), might want to visit the Börzsöny Museum, at Hámán Kató utca 14. It has displays relating to peasant life in these hills, and also to the archaeological finds from the Ipoly Valley, nearby. But apart from these minor attractions there is really little reason to head west from Nagymaros apart from crossing into Slovakia.

Additional Information

Boats On The River Danube
The main booking and information office for boat services on the Danube is in Budapest at the departure point, Vidagó tér, on the East Bank of the Danube.

Services run all year but are reduced in winter. All are for passengers only. No hydrofoils operate on these routes. The following is intended as a general guide. Most settlements along the Danube have a landing pier at which boats call.

Timings and frequencies (summer only): **Budapest** to Esztergom (3 daily, 5 hours); Szentendre (5 daily; 1 hour 30 min); Vác (1 daily, no winter service; 2 hours 45 min); Visegrád (4 daily, 3 hours). **Esztergom** to Budapest (3 daily; 4 hours); Szentendre (3 daily, 2 hours 45 min); Vác (1 daily, 2 hours); Visegrád (3 daily, 1 hour 30 min). **Visegrád** to Nagymaros (every hour throughout the day — car ferry); Budapest (3 daily, 2 hours 30 min); Esztergom (3 daily, 1 hour 45 min); Vác (1 daily, 45 min).

Places To Visit
Dobogókő
Rambling Museum
Open: Thursday to Sunday 10am-4pm.

Esztergom
Basilica
Centre of town overlooking Danube, main steps up from Iskola utca
Open: 9am-5pm, March to December; 9am-3pm, daily except Mondays in January and February.

Christian Museum
Berényi utca 2
Open: 10am-5.30pm, daily except Monday.

Danube Museum
Kölcsey utca 2
Open: 10am-5.30pm, daily except Monday, March to October only.

Medieval Palace (Housing Castle Museum)
Next to basilica
Open: 9am-5pm, April to October; 10am-4pm, November to March; closed Mondays throughout the year.

Szentendre
Barcsay Collection
Dumtsa Jenő utca
Open: 10am-6pm, April to September; 9am-7pm, October to March; closed Mondays throughout the year.

Béla Czóbel Museum
Templom tér
Open: 10am-6pm, April to October; 9am-5pm, November to March; closed Mondays throughout the year.

Ferenczy Museum
Fő tér 6
Open: 10am-6pm, April to October;
9am-5pm, November to March; closed
Mondays throughout the year.

Imre Ámos-Margit
Bogdányi utca 12
Open: Tuesday to Sunday; April to
October 10am-6pm, November to
March 9am-5pm.

Kmetty Museum
Fő tér
Open: as Ferenczy Museum.

Margit Kovács Museum
Corner of Görög utca and Vastagh
    György utca
Open: 9am-7pm, daily.

Museum of Childhood
Rákóczi utca 1
Open: 10am-5.30pm, daily except
Monday.

Museum of Ecclesiastical Art
Engels utca 5
Open: 10am-5.30pm, Wednesday to
Sunday.

Szentendre Gallery
Bogdányi utca 51
Open: mid-March to end October,
10am-6pm, closed Mondays.

Szentendre Picture Gallery
Fő tér
Work by local artists
Open: 10am-6pm, April to October;
9am-5pm, November to March.

Szentendre Village Museum (Skansen)
On road 11 north-west of Szentendre
Open: April to October, 9am-5pm,
closed Mondays.

Szob
Börzsöny Museum
Hámán kató utca 14
Open: 10am-5pm daily except Monday.

Vác
Town Museum
Múzeum utca
Open: 10am-12noon, 1-5pm, daily
except Monday.

Vácrátót
Botanical Gardens
Open: April to October only, 8am-6pm

(4pm Saturdays) and for concerts in the
evenings (for details consult Dunatours
in Vác).

Visegrád
Royal Palace
Entrance to ruins at Fő utca 27
Open: 9am-5pm, April to October; 8am-
4pm, November to March; closed
Mondays throughout the year.

Solomon's Tower (Matthias Museum)
Salamán Torony utca
Open: May to October, 9am-5pm, closed
Mondays.

Citadel
Above Visegrád
Open: daily, 9am-5pm.

Zebegény
Szőnyi Museum
Bartóky utca 7
Open: March to November, 9am-5pm,
December to February, 10am-6pm,
closed Mondays throughout the year.

Tourist Information Centres
Esztergom
IBUSZ
Rákóczi tér
☎ 33-12-152

Gran tours
Rákóczi tér
☎ 33-13-756

Szentendre
Dunatours
Bogdányi utca 1
☎ 26-11-311

Vác
Dunatours
Széchenyi utca 1
☎ 27-10-940

Visegrád
Dunatours Fő utca 3a
☎ 26-28-330

Fanny Reisen Travel Agency
Fő utca 46
☎ 26-28-303

Svada Tourist Office
Rev utca 6
☎ 26-28-160

3
THE KISALFÖLD

The Kisalföld (Little Plain) stretches west from Budapest as far as Vienna, and as such is the first glimpse of Hungary that many visitors will see as they travel by train or car from the Austrian border to Budapest. As flat and monotonous as the Great Plain, the Kisalföld is more densely populated, with many towns and industrial areas, particularly along the River Danube, which marks the northern borders of Hungary and divides the Kisalföld from the plains of Slovakia to the north. Despite the uninspiring countryside and the presence of large clumps of tall industrial chimneys which break up the flat horizon in many places, especially around the horribly polluted city of Tatabánya, there is great charm to be discovered in this region — in the old towns along the Austrian border such as Sopron, Szombathely and Kőszeg, or in the regions of the Örség or Vértes, where the flat plains give way briefly to low, rolling hill country. Sopron, in the north-western corner of Hungary, is one of the most visited and interesting cities in the country, and is certainly a highlight of this region. It is also a good base from which to see many of the attractions described in this chapter. These include the Eszterházy Palace at Fertőd, and, further afield, the towns of Győr, Kőszeg, Szombathely, the huge Benedictine monastery at Pannonhalma, and the Romanesque church in the tiny village of Ják, one of the most noted buildings of its kind in Europe. The region also yields some surprises: the oldest known footprint in the world (which is preserved under glass at the archaeological site at Vértesszőlős); a working narrow-gauge steam railway at Nagycenk; and at Fertőrákos, a quarry once used by the Romans to extract rock for their tombs and buildings. There is certainly a lot to see and do here, and those who are tempted to bypass this region entirely and head straight for Budapest may well be encouraged to linger for a while instead.

The Kisalföld is an easy area to travel in. A motorway links Budapest with Győr, passing close to Zsámbék, Vértesszőlős and Tata. The main line from Budapest to Vienna takes the same route. After Győr, routes divide, with main road and railway lines heading west to Sopron (from where there are easy road and rail links to Vienna), and north-west to Vienna (the

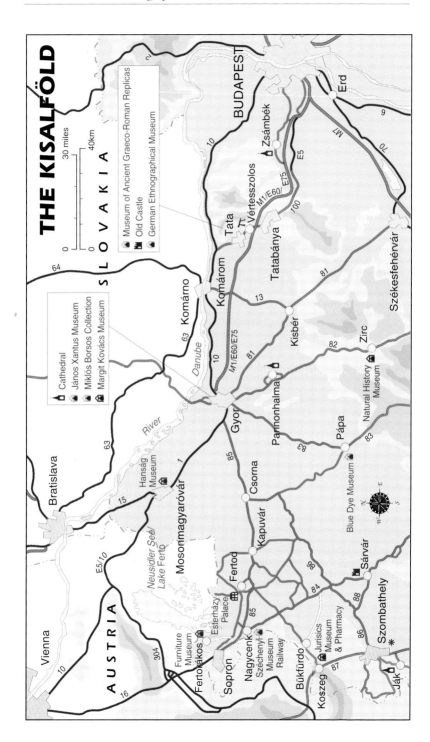

THE KISALFÖLD

S L O V A K I A

30 miles

40km

Museum of Ancient Graeco-Roman Replicas
Old Castle
German Ethnographical Museum

BUDAPEST

Zsámbék

Erd

Vértesszolos

M7

E5

E75

Tata

M1/E60/

Tatabánya

Komárom

100

Székesfehérvár

64

Komárno

13

Kisbér

81

Zirc

63

Danube

M1/E60/E75

81

82

Cathedral
János Xantus Museum
Miklós Borsos Collection
Margit Kovács Museum

Pannonhalma

Natural History Museum

River

83

Pápa

83

63

Győr

85

Csorna

Bratislava

Hanság Museum

Mosonmagyaróvár

1

Kapuvár

Blue Dye Museum

15

Sárvár

Neusiedler See/ Lake Fertő

Fertőd

98

Szombathely

E5/10

84

Esterházy Palace

88

Furniture Museum

85

Jurisics Museum & Pharmacy

86

Vienna

Fertőrákos

Nagycenk Széchenyi Museum Railway

Bükfürdő

Köszeg

87

Ják

A U S T R I A

304

Sopron

16

10

faster way) and Bratislava. Hydrofoils and slower, more relaxing cruise ships also ply the Danube between Budapest, Bratislava and Vienna, giving travellers a different view of the Kisalföld. Many visitors to Hungary will cross into the country at Hegyeshalom, north-west of Győr, which is the frontier post on the main road and railway routes between Budapest and Vienna. There are many other crossing points into Austria, though fewer into Slovakia, since this requires one to cross over the Danube.

Budapest To Sopron

Between Budapest And Győr

Thirty kilometres (20 miles) west of Budapest, a short distance from the motorway junction at Herceghalom, is the village of **Zsámbék**, the site of a hauntingly beautiful ruined hill-top church. Built between 1220 and 1258 for the Premonstratensian Order, it stands today as one of the most important examples of Romanesque architecture to survive in Hungary. Gothic additions came courtesy of the Pauline Order which took over the church in 1475. In the sixteenth century the church was plundered and damaged by Turkish troops and subsequently fell into disuse. In 1763 it was almost totally destroyed by earthquake and today only one lateral wall remains. Some of the poetry of the place has been lost by the decision to smooth off the crumbling Romanesque edges with red brick, but the church still manages to retain its sad dignity and most of the dead echoes of its former grandeur. There is a small exhibition of photographs and masonry in a subterranean museum next door.

Further on along the motorway, 56km (35 miles) from the centre of Budapest, is **Tatabánya**, a huge industrial and coal mining centre which greets travellers with polluted air, endless lines of concrete residential blocks, and several power plants belching sunset-coloured smoke over the plains. The town's only sight lies just outside it. Sitting on a mountain-top overlooking the city is the Turul Statue, a giant bronze effigy of an eagle, which clutches the sword of the ancient Magyar tribal chieftain, Árpád, in its talons. It was erected in 1896 to commemorate the thousandth anniversary of the foundation of the Hungarian State. Understandably though, Tatabánya is not a place to linger. The only reasons for doing so are the jazz festival (in summer) and the attraction of walking in the hills to the north and south of the city, the only high ground in the Kisalföld. Of the two ranges, the Vértes, to the south, probably offer the most possibilities. Accessible on foot from Vértessomló, south of Tatabánya, is the ruined castle of Vitányvár which sits on a crag overlooking the plains. To the north of the city, the Gerecse range also offers hiking possibilities, but it must be said that there are nicer and more interesting areas to walk in Hungary than these.

Just beyond Tatabánya, along the road to Tata, is **Vértesszőlős**, an uninspiring village where, in the 1960s, some of the most important archaeological discoveries in Europe were made. There is a sign on the main road through the village which points the way to the digs, which are situated on a low ridge overlooking the valley. The archaeologist who led the digs was Dr László Vértes, whose work is commemorated on a plaque at the site. He discovered that the people who once lived here were some of the earliest humans. A skull found on the site showed that men who lived here were not far evolved from apes, and Vértesszőlős Man, as these people were christened, is an even earlier stage of human evolutionary development than Neanderthal man. Five hundred thousand years ago, early man was attracted to this site by the mineral springs (long since vanished) which provided fresh water, and which also attracted animals, who were trapped and eaten. The remains of these animals, and of the fires over which they were cooked, have all been discovered here. The digs can be viewed behind glass. Also on display are some of the tools used by early man, reconstructed skulls of the people who once lived in the caves here, and, on one rock, an impression which is thought to be the earliest human footprint in the world.

A little way beyond Vértesszőlős, the main road passes through **Tata**. The focus of the town is not Ady Endre utca, the main street, but a large lake called Öreg-tó (Old Lake), on the shores of which is a castle, Öregvár, which began life as a medieval fortress but underwent the usual reconstruction work by the Turks and Habsburgs before undergoing its most recent transformation, into a fish farm, restaurant and museum. The latter has displays relating to the history of the town, including many fine pieces of Roman and medieval stone carving, and also displays of work by local craftsmen, the most noted of which are the decorous ceramics made by Domokos Kuny. The lake is beautifully situated, surrounded by trees and parkland, but swimming is forbidden. However, in summer, there are usually boats and other small craft for hire. Near the castle there are two museums worth seeing. On Rákóczi utca, just up from the castle, there is the Museum of Ancient Graeco-Roman Replicas (Antik Másolatuk), a bizarre collection of life-size plaster copies of old Roman and Greek statuary, including a copy of the Elgin marbles, housed in an old synagogue. The plaster copies have been made from originals housed in the museums of Paris, London, Rome and elsewhere. At Alkotmány 2, between the castle and Tata's main street, there is the German Ethnographical Museum (Német Nemzetiségi Néprajzi Múzeum) devoted to the lives and culture of the German speaking people who once lived in the Kisalföld. They were brought here after the Turkish invasion, when the area was considered underpopulated and was in need of defending. The building which houses the museum was once a mill, one of dozens in the town which utilised the power of water flowing out of Öreg-tó, which is slightly higher than the main part of the town. Like other mills in the town the building has been well restored, though water no longer flows past it. A square in the centre of the town, Országgyűles tér, boasts a wooden clock tower with four clock faces, which dates from 1763. On the other side of the main street is a smaller lake, Cseke-tó, which is surrounded by parkland including a ruined church — a folly, but one built from original Roman and medieval stonework.

Beyond Tata the road runs through **Komárom**, a dull town sliced in half by the River Danube, the northern part of the town, called Komárno, is in Slovakia. The two parts of the town are linked by a steel road bridge, one of only two crossing points on the river between Budapest and Bratislava. Komárno, over the river, is an important Slovak port, with many grimy-looking docks, warehouses and factories. The motorway runs well to the south of Komárom, so the town is easily avoided, in fact there is really nothing of any note beyond Tata before Győr is reached.

The places of interest mentioned here can easily be reached by public transport. Buses run from Moszkva tér in Budapest to Zsámbék. It is difficult to approach this village from other directions using public transport. Tatabánya, Vértesszőlős, Tata, and Komárom are all on the main line between Budapest and Győr, though only a few trains stop at the smaller places — check timetables carefully. The museum at Vértesszőlős is a 15 minute walk up the hill from the station (cross over the main road first). There are two stations at Tata (Tóvároskert, and the main station, Vasútállomás), both of which are a fair distance from the town centre. The station at Komárom, an important rail junction, is right next to an unattractive stretch of the Danube.

Situated on the main highway between Budapest and Vienna, **Győr** is easily accessible by car, bus or train from the capital. The city stands in the middle of the Kisalföld at the junction of the Danube, Rába and Rábca rivers and is actually the major industrial centre of western Hungary, though fortunately the attractively pedestrianised and respectfully preserved historical core of the town does not even begin to hint at this to the casual visitor. There is certainly a more than adequate supply of museums and monuments around the centre and though not as beautiful as Sopron it is more of a town and does tend to absorb its large number of visitors rather more comfortably. It is also the perfect base for a highly recommended visit to Pannonhalma Abbey.

Archaeological evidence suggests that the area was inhabited by the Celts as far back as the third century BC. The Romans built a settlement here (calling it *Arrabona*) and in the eleventh century King Stephen established an episcopal see here. During the Middle Ages Győr developed as an important commercial centre. The town was frequently devastated by Tukish raids throughout the sixteenth century though it was only actually occupied for 4 years during the 1590s. Under Habsburg control the town took the name of Raab, which is how it is referred to on the Arc de Triomphe in Paris. Napoleon spent a night here on his way from Italy in 1809.

If arriving by train, walk across the park towards Ciklámen Tourist to the centre. The bus station is situated behind the railway station. The imposing building opposite Ciklámen Tourist is the neo-Baroque town hall dating from the late 1890s. During the 1956 uprising the building was occupied by the rebel Provisional National Council. The large modern building directly opposite this across the main Vienna-Budapest road on Szabadság tér contains the offices of the county council and local water authority. From Szabadság tér walk to your left up Aradi Vértanúk utca

The town hall at Gyor, one of many fine buildings in the city

to the early eighteenth-century Baroque Carmelite church. The order's coat of arms can be seen above the double-gate. Inside, the ornate carved benches, pulpit and altarpiece are all original. The hotel next door is the former Carmelite monastery, and was once used as a military prison.

The Carmelite church faces onto Köztársaság tér which is reputed to have escaped flooding in the eighteenth century due to the miraculous powers of the statue of *Mary of the Foam* situated in the small chapel next door to the church. In the middle of Köztársaság tér is a statue of the poet Károly Kisfaludy (1788-1830). Moving around the square: number 13 was built for Ferenc Zichy who was the Bishop of Győr from 1778 to 1782; number 12 dates from 1620 though the gate is some 100 years younger. Around the corner at number 4 Alkotmány utca is the house where Napoleon slept on 31 August 1809. It houses the picture gallery of the János Xantus Museum. Back into the square, across at number 5 is an exhibition of Roman stonework housed in sixteenth-century underground fortifications, part of the old castle of Győr.

From here take the short walk up to the top of Chapter Hill (Káptalandomb) to the cathedral, the foundations of which are thought to date from the time of King Stephen. The chancel is Romanesque and dates from the twelfth century. The church suffered severe damage during the Mongol invasion in 1241 and was almost completely rebuilt in Gothic style in the 1480s. Baroque elements were introduced in the seventeenth century and the final bout of reconstruction occurred during the 1820s when the main façade was reconstructed. Pride of place amongst its treasures is the reliquary bust of St Ladislas which is situated in a small Gothic chapel near the entrance. The piece dates from around 1400 and contains a piece of the monarch's skull. The frescoes in the cathedral are the work of Austrian painter Franz Anton Maulbertsch and date from the late eighteenth century.

Opposite the main façade of the cathedral is the Bishop's Palace, and moving anti-clockwise around the cathedral one finds some foundation stones of an eleventh-century chapel crowned by a statue of St Michael. On the wall of the cathedral is a relief dedicated to the town's casualties during World War I. At number 2 on the square is a museum dedicated to the twentieth-century painter and sculptor Miklós Borsos. From here take a walk down Káptalandomb utca to the Ark of the Covenant, constructed in 1731 at the command of Emperor King Charles III to appease the local community after two Habsburg soldiers had accidentally knocked the monstrance from a priest's hand during a Corpus Christi procession while in pursuit of a fugitive.

To the north of here is Duna-Kapu tér. A food market is still held in the square every Wednesday and Saturday. In the middle of the square there is a well on top of which is an iron weathercock, one of the symbols of Győr; the Turks affixed a weathercock above the town's gate and vowed they would never leave until it crowed. From here one could cross the river and a 20 minute walk north-east would bring you to the attractive Bishop's Wood which boasts wild deer, or one could spend a relaxing afternoon in the leisure complex (which includes thermal baths) clearly visible, and audible, from the bridge.

All those who remain untempted by all this should walk back along Rózsa Ferenc utca. At number 1 is the highly recommended Margit Kovács Museum similar to the one in Szentendre. Ceramist Kóvacs (1902-

77) was born in Győr. Next continue south into Széchenyi tér, Győr's main square. Along the northern side at number 4 is the 'Iron-Beam house' built in the seventeenth century which derives its curious name from the wooden beam at the corner of the building placed here in the early nineteenth century. Travelling Viennese businessmen would, as a custom, knock nails into the beam to show that they had stayed there. The building now contains a display of African art. At number 5 is the János Xantus Museum named after a local archaeologist which covers local history and has a fantastic collection of stamps. The building itself is a former Benedictine theological academy and dates from 1742.

The Column of the Virgin Mary standing in the centre of the square was erected in 1686 by the Bishop of Győr in celebration of the recapture from the Turks of Buda Castle. Along the south side of the square is the church of St Ignatius which was originally built for the Jesuits in the early seventeenth century and which later passed to the Benedictines. Standing next to the church is the former Jesuit monastery built between 1651 and 1667. The Széchenyi Pharmacy next door is both a museum and a working chemist. Originally founded by the Jesuits, it is well worth a look inside at the beautiful seventeenth-century internal furnishings.

Twenty kilometres (12 miles) south-east of Győr along road 82 stands **Pannonhalma Monastery**. If relying on public transport from Győr, buses are cheaper and more frequent (hourly) than trains, and they also drop you off nearer to your destination. The monastery is a beautiful and quite breathtaking sight, atop the 280m (918ft) high St Martin's Hill which overlooks the small town. In order to look round the monastery one is required to join one of the guided tours which are organised at the gate. Tours in French and German are quite frequent and reasonably easy to follow. A tour in English would have to be pre-arranged ☎ 96-70-191.

Pannonhalma is a Benedictine monastery founded in AD996 by Prince Géza, the first Magyar leader to embrace Christianity. The original building was completed by his son King Stephen though the first major constructions were not until the early thirteenth century. The Gothic cloisters date from this time. Serious damage was sustained courtesy of the Turks and between 1786 and 1802 with the Benedictine Order temporarily dissolved the building functioned as a prison. Much of the restoration came in the nineteenth century. In the 1820s a 55m (180ft) high neo-Classical tower was erected and in the back-end of the century the interior of the abbey church was redecorated in a neo-Romanesque style by Ferenc Storno. In the 1940s a secondary school was added and both the monastery and the school managed to survive the anti-religious measures of the early 1950s largely unscathed.

Amongst the treasures of Pannonhalma is the Latin deed founding the abbey at Tihany (on Lake Balaton) which dates from 1055 and contains the oldest surviving record of the Hungarian language. The library, founded by King Ladislas is the oldest in the country and retains over 300,000 volumes. It is the fifth largest collection of books in Hungary and the largest Benedictine library in the world. There is also a small but worthwhile art gallery consisting of various Italian, German and Dutch masters. The most famous work on display is *Fête in Brussels* by David Teniers, unusual because of the rather secular nature of its subject matter. One final priceless treasure the monastery can boast is a quite magnificent view of the surrounding countryside; a wonderful aid to contemplation.

Between Győr And Lake Balaton

Road 82 runs south from Győr, skirting Pannonhalma and then running through the Bakony highlands to Veszprém and Balatonfüred, at the north-eastern end of Lake Balaton (see Chapter 4). Twenty kilometres (12 miles) north of Veszprém, the road passes through **Zirc**, a fairly ordinary sort of place but one which may be worth a stopover on the journey south. The former Cistercian abbey church, dating from the first half of the eighteenth century, rises above the centre of the town. Natural history buffs will enjoy the collections of stuffed and live animals, housed in the old abbey buildings, as well as the arboretum nearby, where many rare species of trees and plants are preserved.

By taking road 83 from Győr motorists can reach the western end of Lake Balaton (see Chapter 4 for entries on Tapolca, Sümeg and Keszthely). Those travelling along this route will pass through **Pápa**, which, like Zirc, is dominated by a large eighteenth-century parish church, the interior of which is decorated with frescoes and other Baroque decoration. At Fő utca 6 is a former protestant church, now a museum displaying religious and other relics. Another museum in the town is the Blue Dye Museum (Kékfestő múzeum), housed in a building once used as a cloth-dyeing factory, which is now given over to exhibits relating to long-forgotten dyeing processes and also displays of the folk costumes that were made using them.

Heading West From Győr

Most people travelling west from Győr will be heading for Sopron along road 83. The road passes close to Fertőd (just west of Kapuvár) and, closer to Sopron, near to Nagycenk (for entries on both places, see in the section 'Near Sopron').

A more important road, the E60/E75, runs north-west from Győr to Mosonmagyaróvár, where it divides, with the E75 heading towards Bratislava, and the E60 towards Vienna. **Mosonmagyaróvár** may be worth a brief halt for anyone travelling this route. Since medieval times, the town has been an important industrial and commercial centre on the trading routes between Budapest and Vienna. On the main street is the Hanság Museum, with displays relating to the local history of the region, and in another building along the street is a good display of Hungarian sculpture and painting from the seventeenth to the nineteenth centuries. All this is overshadowed, however, by the bloody events which took place here in 1956, during the Hungarian Uprising. On Friday 26 October, soldiers from the ÁVH secret police fired on unarmed demonstrators here, killing about eighty and wounding many more. After the massacre,

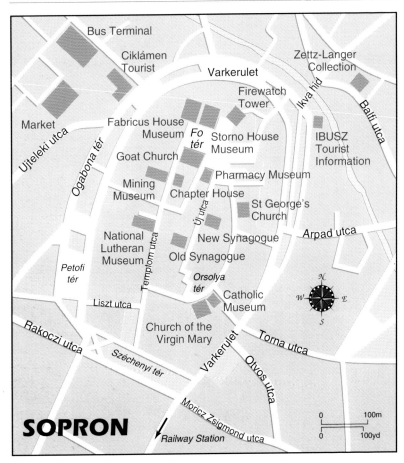

Bus Terminal
Ciklámen Tourist
Varkerulet
Zettz-Langer Collection
Firewatch Tower
Ikva hid
Balfi utca
Market
Fabricus House Museum
Fo tér
Storno House Museum
IBUSZ Tourist Information
Ujteleki utca
Ogabona tér
Goat Church
Mining Museum
Chapter House
Pharmacy Museum
St George's Church
Uj utca
National Lutheran Museum
Templom utca
New Synagogue
Old Synagogue
Arpad utca
Petofi tér
Orsolya tér
Catholic Museum
Liszt utca
Rakoczi utca
Church of the Virgin Mary
Varkerulet
Torna utca
Otvos utca
Széchenyi tér
Moricz Zsigmond utca
Railway Station
SOPRON
0   100m
0   100yd

the mob reassembled and routed the ÁVH headquarters in the town, killing several of the ÁVH leaders who had ordered the attack to take place. It is only since the end of the Communist era in Hungary that the town has been allowed to remember these tragic events, one of the most poignant reminders anywhere in the country of a past that should never be forgotten.

❋ **Sopron**
Sopron is possibly the most beautiful town in Hungary. Situated at the foot of the 400m (1,312ft) high Lövér hills near the Austrian border, it possesses more listed buildings (240) and historical monuments (115) than any other Hungarian settlement outside the capital. Sopron is actually three-parts surrounded by Austria and being such a small town (it has only 57,000 occupants) it does have a tendency to become swamped with visitors from across the border, especially during weekends in the summer months. Much of the town has become geared specifically towards serving these visitors and consequently when they have departed and the

numerous cafés, restaurants and ice-cream parlours have closed the town tends to have a rather hollow feel to it.

Archaeological evidence suggests that the area has been inhabited since neolithic times. Under Roman rule it took the name *Scarbantia*. It was situated on the north-south trade route. The town developed quickly following Magyar occupation in the tenth century and in 1277 it was raised to the rank of city. Neither Turks nor Mongols got as far as Sopron

Views of the old centre of Sopron, one of Hungary's most visited towns

though the city suffered badly in Allied bombing raids and had to be substantially rebuilt in the 1960s. The town serves as a good base for visits to the Esterházy Palace at Fertőd, the Lake Fertő nature reserve and the steam railway at Nagycenk. Arriving by train, the centre is a mere 10 minute walk along Mátyás Kiraly utca. The bus station is 5 minutes from the centre along Lackner Kristóf utca.

Probably Sopron's most famous landmark is the **Firewatch Tower** (Tűztorony), the former purpose of which is rather given away by its name. Sentries standing watch would also signal the hours with their trumpets. The tower is 61m (200ft) high and its base dates back to the

Middle Ages having been built on the remains of the Roman city gate, part of which may be viewed inside. The middle section dates from the sixteenth century and the Baroque upper level was added in the 1680s. It is possible to ascend the tower for a view of the city. At the base of the tower stands the Gate of Loyalty (Hűség-Kapu) erected to commemorate the 1921 vote by the city's population to return to Hungarian control, the town having been ceded to Austria under the 1920 Treaty of Trianon.

Every house standing on Fő tér is a listed building. To the left as you enter the square from the Gate of Loyalty stands the Eclectic Town Hall (Városkáz) which dates from 1895. In the middle of the square one finds the Baroque Trinity Column erected by Cardinal Kollonich in 1701, much to the chagrin of the local Protestant community. On the south side of Fő tér at number 2 there is a small **Pharmacy Museum** (Patika Múzeum) with a display of various documents and potions. Opposite this at number 8 is the **Storno House Museum** which largely dates from the eighteenth century. Plaques on the wall record the building's casual acquaintances with both King Matthias and Ferenc Liszt. Inside there are two museums. One is devoted to the history of the town and the other to the large and impressive collection of paintings, furniture and fittings gathered by painter and architect Ferenc Storno and his family who occupied the premises from 1872. It is Storno who was largely responsible for the restoration work on the monastery at Pannonhalma at the end of the nineteenth century.

Next door to the Storno House at number 7 is the Lackner House which once belonged to the seventeenth-century mayor whose name adorns the premises and who bequeathed the house to the town. At number 6 is the **Fabricius House Museum** the upstairs of which houses a small archaeological exhibition. The cellar contains three large Roman statues. Opposite this is the **Goat Church** (Kecske templom) which derives its name, according to legend, from a goatherd who paid for its construction after finding treasure in a field. Supposed evidence for this theory are the carved goat crests that appear on the interior walls of the church, though these are just as likely, if not more, to have formed part of the coat of arms of the family that commissioned the church. The church was originally built for the Franciscans and was completed in 1300. The interior is mainly Baroque and rococo. Three coronations and five Diet sessions took place here during the seventeenth century.

Moving away from the square down Templom utca, to the left at number 1 is the fourteenth-century **Chapter House** (Káptalan terem) which contains some superb representations of the deadly sins, all explained in English on a free information sheet. Across the street at number 2 is the former Esterházy mansion which presently houses a **Mining Museum** (Központi Bányászati Múzeum) which is slightly more interesting than it sounds. Further along Templom utca one finds a late-Baroque Lutheran church which dates from 1783. The tower of the church was added some 80 years later because at the time of the original construction it had been decreed by Emperor Joseph II that Lutheran churches were not to be allowed towers, a situation explained, illustrated and embellished by the **National Lutheran Museum** (Evangélikus Országos Múzeum Soproni Gyűteménye) at number 12.

A left turning off Templom utca down Fegyvertár utca leads one to Orsolya tér, the former site of a salt market. Situated on the square is the neo-Gothic Church of the Virgin Mary which was built in 1864. Next door at number 2 is a **Catholic Museum** (Soproni Katolikus Egyházművészeti Gyűtemény) housed in a former school. The square contains a small, arid fountain dedicated to the Virgin Mary. At number 5 there is a small **Guild Museum** (Lábas-ház) displaying local craft skills. Leave Orsolya tér via Új utca which in the Middle Ages was the Jewish quarter. Indented at number 22 is a **Synagogue** dating from the first quarter of the fourteenth century. Following the expulsion of the Jews from the city in 1526 the building was converted into a house and the building's original function only came to light in 1967. It has since been restored and comprehensive information in English is available. Further up across the street at number 11 is another synagogue of similar age. Jews were only allowed back into the town in the nineteenth century.

Új utca leads once again to Fő tér. Swing right down Szent György utca upon which is situated the Gothic **St George's Church** (Szent György templom). The church originally dates from the fourteenth century but it was substantially rebuilt in the late seventeenth century. Next turn left down Hátsó kapu utca. At number 2 is Caesar House which gives access to the medieval town walls.

To the north of the town centre, past IBUSZ and over the Ikva bridge at number 11 Balfi utca is the **Zettl-Langer Collection**, a private collection of porcelain and weaponry assembled by the nineteenth-century business-man after whom the collection is named. Further on up Pozsonyi utca on the way to the Gothic Church of St Michael one passes the House of the Two Moors, so called after the statues flanking its gate. Behind the church is the oldest architectural monument of Sopron, the remains of the thir-teenth-century Chapel of St Jacob. Beyond this, a walk to the top of Vienna Hill will reward those with enough energy not only with an outstanding view but also the ruins of a Roman amphitheatre.

Sopron's other main attraction is the Lövérek Hills to the south of the town. Buses 1 and 2 go by the Lövér hotel where hiking trails begin. For those with limited ambitions in this direction there is a simple short walk to the Károly Lookout Tower (23m/75ft high) which provides a good view of the surrounding area.

Near Sopron
Eight kilometres (5 miles) north of Sopron, easily accessible by an hourly bus, is the town of **Fertőrákos** which boasts a limestone quarry whose use dates back to Roman times and which only came to an end in 1945. The impressive complex of huge, hollow chambers plays host to a series of concerts during the Sopron Festival held from mid-June to mid-July. St Stephen's Cathedral in Vienna was constructed from stone hewn from

this quarry. During World War II the site was used by the Germans as an underground aircraft factory. Meanwhile back in the town, anyone waiting for a bus could pay a visit to a small Furniture Museum housed in a former Bishop's Palace at 153 Fő utca.

Once, the Iron Curtain, the border between Hungary and Austria, passed through **Lake Fertő**, and it was a strictly controlled no-go area. Austrians know the same lake as the Neusiedler See. Now the border defences have been scaled down and the lake is open to all those who want to swim, go boating or have picnics. The alkaline water in the lake attracts many species of waterfowl, and fresh fish is served up, usually fried, in stalls along the shore.

Twenty-seven kilometres (17 miles) east of Sopron, accessible by hourly bus, stands the highly popular Esterházy Palace at **Fertőd**. The palace is situated at the far end of the settlement on the main road, easily identifiable behind the huge rococo wrought-iron gates. It was constructed in the 1760s and owes its origin to one Prince Miklós Esterházy whose loyal family had acquired vast wealth from the Habsburgs at the end of the 1703-11 War of Independence. Miklós deliberately set out to rival the grandeur of Versailles and the palace became the celebrated host to numerous gala balls, concerts and hunting parties. Yet within a decade of the prince's death in 1790 the palace was well on its road to ruin and decay. The picture gallery, puppet theatre, hermitage and music house all disappeared and the main building fell into a state of neglect. Sheep were even kept in some of the downstairs rooms. War damage and large scale theft during the 1940s proved to be the nadir. In the 1950s a botanical experimentation centre and part of the agricultural technical school were transferred to the palace and serious restoration at last began. Work, however, progresses slowly. Most rooms are quite bare and what furniture is on display is unlikely to be original.

The entrance to the palace is at the far end of the ochre courtyard. Guided tours are available or one is free to escape the poison of the crowd and wander at one's own speed in the company of an information booklet available in English. Only part of the 126 room complex is open to the public. The highlight of the ground floor is the Sala Terrena which has been almost completely restored and which boasts impressive ceiling frescoes by Joseph Ignaz Milldorfer and a floor of white marble. Meanwhile, on the upper floor, the Banqueting Hall features a superb fresco by J.B. Grundemann entitled *Apollo on the Chariots of the Sun* and the two original fireplaces. The palace also features a small Haydn Memorial Room. Haydn was originally taken into service by Prince Miklós as *Kapellmeister* in 1761, and subsequently took charge of the palace orchestra, opera house and theatre. During the period 1770-90 at least one new opera performance was given every month. At the back of the palace the French gardens descend into wild undergrowth all too quickly. They are being replanned, slowly.

Another Eszterházy mansion lies 11km (7 miles) south-east of Sopron at **Nagycenk**, on road 85 immediately east of its junction with road 84. The house here, however, is a far more modest affair than Fertőd, with none of the latter's rococo splendour. Nagycenk was once the home of Count István Széchenyi, who was a patron of some of Hungary's most noted nineteenth-century engineers and inventors. He brought Hungary's first gaslights, running-water baths and flush toilets to this house. Széchenyi was known to be a keen Anglophile. The gaslights were originally brought from England, and he organised the construction of the Buda-pest-Vác railway (the second to be built in Hungary, and supervised by British engineers) after travelling on the Liverpool-Manchester railway in England. British engineers were also responsible for the Chain Bridge in Budapest, another of the large engineering projects which he sponsored. His house is now a museum dedicated to nineteenth-century science and technology. Another part of it is a plush hotel. Opposite the house is the Széchenyi Museum Railway, where narrow-gauge steam-engines haul trains for a couple of miles through the fields every weekend in summer from April to October. The other terminus is a little way back along the road to Sopron.

South From Sopron

Between Sopron And Szombathely

Fifty-one kilometres (32 miles) south of Sopron is **Kőszeg**, whose position on the frontier between Austria and Hungary has shaped its history. In 1532 the Kőszeg garrison, numbering about 400, defended the town's castle against a Turkish army numbering 100,000. Astonishingly, the Hungarian garrison held out for 3 weeks, and in doing so they saved Vienna from being captured by the Turks. After nineteen attempts at destroying the town, Sultan Suleiman withdrew, and when the campaign resumed the next year the defences around Vienna had been strengthened to such a degree that the Turks knew that an attack would be futile. Kőszeg is now a small, friendly provincial town, nestling in the first foothills of the Austrian Alps, proud of its history and of its hero, Captain Miklós Jurisics, who defended the castle against the Turks and whose name and memory is recalled time and time again in the town's monuments. Its central part comprises well-preserved burghers' houses and mansions lining gently winding streets and squares. The town is very picturesque and has a distinctive German or Austrian flavour, enhanced by the deluge of Ger-man-speaking tourists that come here from across the border (there is a frontier crossing 2km/1 mile outside the town) and Kőszeg was once known to its former German-speaking inhabitants as Güns. The Strucc Hotel, at Várkör 124, is reputedly the oldest hotel in Hungary, and there are a number of restaurants and bars in the town which try to recreate a 'medieval' atmosphere for tourists.

A road called the Várkör encircles the old town, following what was once the route of the old city walls. In Fő tér, the main square, is the Church of the Sacred Heart. From the square it is possible to walk down a narrow passage, past the IBUSZ office and under Heroes' Tower (Hősi Kapu), a fake medieval gateway erected in 1932 to commemorate the 400th anniversary of the siege. Beyond the gateway is the pretty and well-preserved old square, Jurisics tér. The most interesting buildings lining the square are the town hall at number 7, with its religious frescoes and heraldry, an old Pharmacy (now a museum) at number 11, and the Jurisics Museum, at number 6 by the gateway, with historical displays in what was once the General's house. In the square, beyond a Baroque column to St Mary, there are two churches, the Baroque Church of St Emerich, and the Gothic Church of St James, built in 1403 and containing the tomb of Miklós Jurisics. The castle, not the most impressive of buildings, despite its history, is just beyond the square, along Rajnis utca, its rooms given over to a historical exhibition mainly consisting of old weapons, a tourist hostel and a café. Medieval pageants and shows are staged here in summer. There are traces of the moat visible, but most of the castle has undergone heavy bouts of rebuilding through the centuries, and was heavily restored in the 1950s and 1960s.

To the west of Kőszeg is a low range of hills, **Kőszeg-hegy**, in which it is possible to go hiking. The hills straddle the border; Austrians and Hungarians can use the paths that cross the border, but foreigners cannot. Those walking in this region should always carry their passports, as this is a border region. Once closed because of its sensitivity, most of the region is now open to hikers and there are maps available which show the walking tracks in the hills. The highest peak is Irottko 882m (2,893ft), right on the border, where those who show their passports to the guards can climb the lookout tower for a view over the surrounding countryside.

Sixteen kilometres (10 miles) east of Kőszeg is **Bükfürdő**, a modern spa town specifically designed to attract rich westerners from over the border. The facilities here are well-developed and expensive to use, with many pricey hotels and a large golf-course and other sporting facilities. The water comes out of the ground at 58°C (136°F) and is used in the treatment of digestive ailments. The spa was discovered after World War II during prospective oil exploration work. If the place appeals, there are cheaper hotels, pensions and campsites in Bük, less than a mile from the spa but much less expensive.

Szombathely is 23km (14 miles) south of Kőszeg. Regular trains take 30 minutes to run between the two towns. It is the largest town in western Transdanubia and claims to be the oldest town in the country. It is a busy commercial centre and some may find it rather lacking in charm. However, it does contain the best collection of Roman remains in Hungary after *Gorsium* and *Aquincum*. The town of *Savaria* was founded here in AD43 by the Emperor Claudius. Situated on the 'Amber' trade road that stretched from *Constantinople* to the Baltic, Savaria quickly prospered and in AD107 it became the capital of the Roman province of *Upper Pannonia*. In AD455 the town was destroyed by an earthquake but was rebuilt to prosper again under Frankish rule in the eighth century through its trade links with

Germany. The town was destroyed once more in 1241 by the Mongol invaders and almost descended into a terminal decline. The modern day settlement principally dates back to the eighteenth century. In 1777 an episcopal see was established here. At the end of World War II the city was flattened once again, this time by United States bombers. Major reconstruction took place in the 1950s.

The town's railway station is situated some 15 minutes walk from the town centre. The bus station is more central and overlooks the Romkert or Garden of Ruins, the entrance to which is actually behind the cathedral. Among the garden's attractions are the topsy-turvy remains of a Roman road and the ruins of *Pannonia's* largest Christian church, the Basilica of St Quirinus, which features some beautiful floor mosaics. The Cathedral next door is neo-Classical in style and was originally built between 1791 and 1815. It was substantially rebuilt in the 1950s following war damage. Turn right from the cathedral into Berszenyi Dániel tér and walk past the huge eighteenth-century town hall to the Smidt Museum which occupies one wing of the eighteenth-century Bishop's Palace. The museum houses the private collection of one Lajos Smidt, a local doctor, and contains an idiosyncratic assembly of art, weaponry, furniture and what can only be described as 'odds and ends' collected by Smidt on the battlefields of the Great War.

From here walk east into Köztársaság tér, an elongated triangular square and the main shopping area of the town, walk directly south out of the square along Rákóczi utca until you reach the Temple of Isis. Dating from the second century AD, the temple only came to light during construction work in 1955. The main exhibits are a sacrificial altar illuminated by the rising sun and various reliefs depicting the gods Isis, Victoria, Fortuna-Abundantia and Mars-Harpokrates. Concerts are often staged against the backdrop of the temple during the summer months. Situated just to the south of the temple is the Szombathely Art Gallery featuring a collection of socialist art from the 1920s and 1930s. Most interesting among them are the works of Gyula Derkovits (1894-1934) and István Dési Huber (1895-1945), both local artists. Opposite the museum is a former synagogue which now houses a music college and concert hall.

Szombathely contains a number of places of interest a little way from the centre of the town. At number 9 Kisfaludy utca, on the way to the railway station, is the Savaria Museum which houses a large and interesting display of Roman stonework and a substantial collection of Hungarian paintings. North-west of the town centre there is a boating lake and fishing pond situated opposite a large outdoor thermal bath complex. Beyond the fishing pond is an outdoor Village Museum which is well worth a visit. The museum complex contains a number of eighteenth- and nineteenth-century farmsteads (chronologically arranged) which have been reconstructed from various sites in the Örség region. In the northern suburbs of the town accessible by bus number 2 from Petőfi utca is the Kámoni Arboretum which displays over 2,500 types of trees, shrubs and

The ornate carvings around the doorway of the cathedral at Ják are admired as Hungary's greatest Romanesque stonework

Koszeg, a small picturesque town near the Austrian border

flowers. Further along the road, the Gotthárd Astrophysics Observatory houses an exhibition on cosmology.

Near Szombathely

Bükfürdő, Kőszeg and the Kőszeg-hegy hills are all within easy reach of Szombathely, by train, bus or car. The other obvious excursions from the city are Ják and Sárvár.

Ják is 13km (8 miles) south-west of Szombathely, reached by a turning off the E65/Road 86 at Balogunyom. Ják is a tiny village surrounded by flat fields, its sole point of interest being the magnificent Benedictine abbey church, situated on a small mound in the centre of the village. Despite heavy reconstruction at the beginning of the twentieth century, this church is the best preserved piece of Romanesque architecture in Hungary. It was built between 1220 and 1256, and commissioned by a local aristocratic family who would during services occupy the galleries inside the church, built especially for them. The founder allegedly whipped any of his serfs who did not attend services here on a Sunday. The most obvious architectural embellishment is above the exterior of the main doorway, a Norman-style semi-circular archway with two ascending rows of statues depicting the apostles above it, and a figure of Christ at the top. The original heads of the statues were lost during Turkish times. Most are now copies of the originals made during various reconstructions of the church. It is thought that the Hungarian stone-carvers who made the statues copied the styles found in churches in Austria and Germany, such as that at Regensburg, from where Norman-style architecture spread into Central Europe. The other distinctive feature of the church is its twin towers, with their Baroque spires. Initially seemingly identical, there are differences between the towers — only the north tower, for instance, has a rose window carved into it. Inside the church there is more rich ornamentation, including faded frescoes, one of which depicts the legend of St George and the Dragon. Opposite the main church is the thirteenth-century chapel of St James, a tall white building topped by an onion dome, and which is usually locked.

The other excursion from Szombathely is to **Sárvár**, a town 27km (17 miles) to the east. While not being much of a destination in its own right the town may merit a brief halt on the way to somewhere else. Pride of place is a castle which has been so modified over the centuries that it now looks more like an odd pentagonal family manor. Much of the credit for this must go to Tomás Nádasdy who transformed the building into its present day structure, and turned it into an important humanist centre, in the sixteenth century. It was here in 1541 that the first Hungarian version of the New Testament was printed. There is a museum contained within the complex dedicated primarily to Tomás and Ferenc Nádasdy, whose battle exploits against the Turks are reproduced along the walls of the Festival Hall. Sárvár also boasts Hungary's youngest spa, its waters only being discovered in the 1960s, and a large and peaceful botanical garden. All the above are in easy reach of the town's bus and train stations.

Additional Information

Places To Visit

Fertőrákos

Quarry
Open: May to September, 8am-7pm
(9am-5pm), daily except Monday.

Furniture Museum
Fő utca 153
Open: May to September, 9am-3pm
(5pm weekends), daily except Monday.

Fertőd

Esterházy Palace
Open: Guided tours from 8am-12noon, 1-
5pm (4pm winter), daily except Monday.

Győr

Miklós Borsos Collection
Martinovics tér
Open: April to September, 10am-6pm;
October to March 9.30am-4.30pm;
closed Mondays throughout the year.

Margit Kovács Museum
Rózsa Ferenc utca 1
Open: 10am-6pm (5pm October to
March), daily except Monday.

Xantus János Museum
Széchenyi tér
Open: as immediately above.

Pannonhalma Monastery
In village of same name, south-east of
Győr
Guided tours on the hour, every hour
(except midday), 9am-4pm, daily except
Monday.

Ják

Abbey Church
In centre of village
Open: daily, April to October, 8am-
6pm, November to March, 10am-2pm.

Kőszeg

Jurisics Museum and Pharmacy
Both on Jurisics tér
Open: 10am-6pm, daily except Monday.

Castle
Rajnis utca
Open: 10am-6pm, daily except Monday.

Mosonmagyaróvár

Hanság Museum
135 Fő utca
Open: April to October, 10am-6pm.
November to March, 10am-5pm. Closed
Monday.

Nagycenk

Széchenyi Mansion
On road 85 north of Nagycenk village
Open: April to October, 10am-6pm
(2pm November to March), daily except
Monday.

Sárvár

Castle
Open: 10am-6pm, daily except Monday.

Sopron

Catholic Museum
2 Orsolya tér
Open: summer months, Monday and
Thursday 10am-4pm. Sunday 11am-4pm.

Fabricius House Museum
Fő tér 6
Open: 10am-6pm daily except Monday.

Firewatch Tower
Fő tér
Open: 10am-6pm (4pm November to
March), daily except Monday.

Mining Museum
Templom utca 2
Open: 10am-6pm (4pm winter), daily
except Wednesday.

National Lutheran Museum
Templom utca 12
Open: April to September, Monday to
Thursday, Saturday and Sunday, 10am-
1pm.

Pharmacy Museum
Open: April to October, 10am-6pm.
November to March, 9am-5pm.

Storno House Museum
Fő tér 8
Open: 10am-6pm (4.30pm winter), daily
except Monday.

Synagogue
22 új utca
Open: April to October 10am-5pm.
November to March 10am-4pm. Closed
Tuesdays.

Szombathely
Astrophysics Observatory
Szent Imre Herceg utca
Open: Monday to Friday 9am-4pm.

Kámoni Arboretum
Szent Imre Herceg utca 102
Open: 9am-6pm, daily.

Romkert (Garden of Ruins)
Behind Cathedral
On Berzsenyi Dániel tér
Open: May to October, 10am-6pm, daily
except Monday.

Savaria Museum
Kisfaludy utca 9
Open: 10am-6pm, daily except Monday.

Smidt Museum
In Bishop's Palace on Berszenyi Dániel tér
Open: 10am-6pm, daily except Monday.

Szombathely Art Gallery
Corner of Batthyany tér and Rákóczi utca
Open: daily except Monday, 10am-6pm.

Temple of Isis
Rákóczi utca
Open: May to October, 8am-6pm, daily
except Monday.

Village Museum
By the Horgásztó lake
Open: April to October, 10am-6pm,
daily except Monday.

Tata
Museum
In Castle,
By Öreg-tó lake
Open: 10am-6pm, daily except Monday.

Museum of Ancient Graeco-Roman Replicas
Rákóczi utca
Open: 10am-6pm (May to October),
2pm (weekdays in winter), 4pm (weekends in winter); closed Mondays
throughout the year.

German Ethnographical Museum
Alkotmány utca 1
Open: as immediately above.

Vértesszőlős
Museum and Archaeological Site
Above main road (signposted)
Open: April to October, 10am-3pm
(6pm weekends), daily except Monday.

Zirc
Natural History Museum
Next to Abbey Church
Open: April to October, 9am-5pm (until
1pm winter), daily except Monday.

Tourist Information Centres
Győr
Ciklámen Tourist
Aradi Vértanúk útja 22 ☎ 96-11-557

Kőszeg
IBUSZ
Varosház utca 3 ☎ 94-60-376

Mosonmagyaróvár
Ciklámen Tourist
Fő utca 8 ☎ 98-11-078

Pannonhalma
Pax Tourist
Vár utca 1 ☎ 96-70-191

Sárvár
Savaria Tourist
Várkör 33 ☎ 96-94-578

Savaria Tourist
Várkör 57 ☎ 94-60-195

Sopron
Ciklámen Tourist
Ógabona tér 8 ☎ 99-12-040

IBUSZ
At Várkerület körút 41
☎ 99-13-28

Lokomotiv Tourist
Várkerület körút 90 ☎ 99-11-111

Szombathely
Savaria Tourist
Mártírok tere 1 ☎ 94-12-348

IBUSZ
Széll utca 3 ☎ 94-14-141

Tata
Komturist
Ady Endre utca 9 ☎ 34-81-805

Tatabánya
Komturist
Győri utca 8 ☎ 34-11-936

Zalaegerszeg
Zalatour
Kovács Károly tér 1 ☎ 92-11-443

4
LAKE BALATON AND THE BAKONY HIGHLANDS

A way from Budapest, promoters of Hungary's burgeoning holiday industry point to **Lake Balaton** as the most popular place in provincial Hungary visited by both foreign and domestic tourists, and every summer the resorts along the shores of central Europe's largest lake become packed out by a polyglot collection of visitors, speaking every central European language but all after much the same things — watersports, swimming, sun and a good time. The trouble really comes with the last of these expectations one person's good time is the next person's loud noise or dull afternoon. The brochures like to promote Balaton, the 'nation's playground', as catering to all needs. If they are to be believed, then it would seem that glitzy, all-night disco-goers rub shoulders in the same resorts with those who prefer an afternoon stroll by the lake or an evening at a concert. To some extent, these contradictions hold true, and this is the reason why Balaton leaves many people dissatisfied or disappointed. But there probably is something here for everyone, provided that you are prepared to overlook what does not appeal, and to make an effort to seek out the best examples of what you are looking for in a visit to Balaton.

The lake covers an area slightly larger than Lake Geneva, and is in the form of an oblong, 80km (50 miles) in length but with an average width of only 14km (9 miles), narrowing to a width of 1½ km (1 mile) opposite the Tihany peninsula. The total length of the shoreline is just under 200km (124 miles), but not all of this is built up. The sprawl of resorts along the southern shore provides a contrast to the silent, muddy reed beds which characterise the area around Keszthely in the south, or the steep, rocky hillsides which fall down into the lake at the edge of the Tihany peninsula. Despite its size, the lake is very shallow, with an average depth of only 3m (10ft), with the deepest point, 12m (39ft), again reached around the Tihany peninsula. This shallowness, combined with long stretches of fine, hot weather in summer, means that the temperature of the water in the lake in summer is often above 25 degrees. But it also means that the lake freezes over very quickly in winter, when the tourists have gone and the people who live in the villages around the lake shore cut holes in the ice and fish

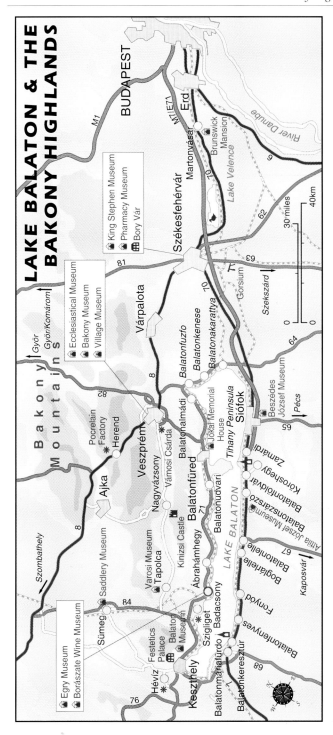

LAKE BALATON & THE BAKONY HIGHLANDS

BUDAPEST

M1

Győr/Komárom

Győr

Bakony Mountains

Szombathely

M1/E71

Erd

River Danube

Martonvásár

Brunswick Mansion

Lake Velence

70

9

62

63

Székesfehérvár

81

Várpalota

8

82

Pocelain Factory

Herend

Ajka

Veszprém

Nagyvázsony

Vámosi Csárda

Balatonalmádi

Balatonfüred

71

Balatonfuzfo

Balatonkenese

Balatonakarattya

70

Tihany Peninsula

Jókai Memorial House

Siófok

Beszédes József Museum

Pécs

65

Gorsium

Szekszárd

64

Zamárdi

Kőröshegy

Balatonföldvár

Balatonszárszó

Attila József Museum

67

Balatonlelle

Boglárlelle

Fonyod

Balatonszemes

Kaposvár

Balatonudvari

LAKE BALATON

Ábrahámhegy

Badacsony

Szigliget

Balaton Múzeum

Festetics Palace

Keszthely

Balatonmáriafürdő

Balatonkeresztúr

68

Hévíz

76

Sümeg

84

Kinizsi Castle

Tapolca

Varosi Museum

Saddlery Museum

King Stephen Museum
Pharmacy Museum
Bory Vár

Ecclesiastical Museum
Bakony Museum
Village Museum

Egry Museum
Borászate Wine Museum

0   30 miles
0   40km

through them, or else glide around on the lake surface on skates. The shallow waters, however, can be deceptive, and in windy conditions the water can become very choppy or even rough, causing ferries to be cancelled and warning flares to be fired which order boats to stay close to the shore (yellow flares) or, rarely, order all boats and swimmers to leave the open water (red flares). In summer, boats and jetties groan under the combined weight of people fishing. Pike-perch and carp are the most common varieties caught, and there are many stalls along the lake shore which sell the day's catch to hungry swimmers, the fish usually fried and drenched in batter. The lake is unpolluted, speed boats are not even allowed, for fear of fuel leaking into the lake, and the water, rich in minerals such as calcium and magnesium, is usually beautifully clear, making any swimming or water-sports enjoyable. A range of low hills behind the lake's northern shore, the Bakony Highlands, are home to typically Hungarian villages, quiet stretches of woodland, acres of scorching vineyards and wheatfields and smaller collections of orchards, fruit trees or market gardens, which rise up slopes packed tightly together, and peppered with small groups of whitewashed farm buildings. The Bakony Highlands form one of Hungary's most important wine-making areas. Vine-growing was first introduced to the area by the Romans. A number of varieties of bottled mineral water also come from the region.

Balaton is a recently formed lake (less than 20,000 years old) so its benefits were not known at all to Stone Age man. The Romans, however, developed some of the medicinal spas around the lake, some of which are still used today. Resorts started developing in the early decades of the twentieth century, and in the early part of the Communist era trade unions (through whom most workers were obliged to arrange their holidays) bought up or developed many hotels and recreation complexes along the shores of the lake. By the 1970s Balaton was seeing more tourists from abroad, particularly from West and East Germany, where families formerly divided by the Berlin Wall could meet for holidays, since travel to Hungary for citizens of both nations was comparatively easy. Poles and Czechs came here for a water-and-sun holiday if they could not make it down to Bulgaria (formerly the favourite summer holiday area for many East Europeans), and people from Western Europe, particularly Italy and Austria, also began to come to Balaton, attracted by the cheap prices and an opportunity to see life behind the 'Iron Curtain'. At the same time restrictions on the lives led by Hungarians were eased, and many city dwellers bought second homes by the lake, which they would use at weekends or rent out through agencies, as the government began to look more favourably towards individuals amassing private capital. This led to the growth of faceless resorts, with the southern shore around Siófok and Boglárlelle in particular becoming little more than a seamless string of villas and lakeside hotels, bars and water-sports facilities. Thankfully, building has been very carefully controlled around other parts of the lake, most notably in the Tihany peninsula, most of which is a nature reserve;

the immediate impression of Balaton is one of a formless built-up sprawl, but areas of character are there to be found — mainly along the western or northern shores of the lake.

Nowadays, people come to the Balaton for a variety of different holiday activities. Around the lake are a number of resorts and towns, some with more character than others; generally, the resorts on the southern shore offer a holiday atmosphere while those on the northern shore strive to cater for those who prefer a more sedate pace to things. At Balatonfüred and Hévíz (near the western end of the lake) there are important spa facilities, where people bathe in or drink the reputedly therapeutic waters. Swimmers congregate at beaches along the length of the lake, though principally at resorts such as Siófok or Balatonfüred. Swimming is best on the southern shore, where the lake is very shallow for a long way out, and where the lake floor is usually sandy. A small entrance fee is charged to use virtually all the beaches; they are usually crowded, and are in any case not beaches at all, but consist of a strip of grass for sunbathing, flanked by the lake on one side and a motley collection of bars, shops and restaurants on the other. At nearly all these places there are opportunities for boating and water-sports, and tennis, horse-riding or even flights over the lake can be arranged by hotels or tourist offices. Nightlife and discos spring up in many hotels after nightfall, and in the northern resorts and towns (particularly Tihany or Balatonfüred) there may be more cultural offerings such as concerts or plays in the evening. Walks along the lake are usually impossible, because of the number of private villas which have gardens sloping down to the shore, so walkers should head for the beautiful scenery of the Tihany peninsula, with good views over the lake, or for the Bakony Highlands, particularly in the area around Tapolca and Badacsony in the south-west part of the lake. Historical sites are few and far between on the southern shore — which is given over to more hedonistic pleasures — but there are a number of points of interest along the northern shore, particularly around Balatonfüred, the Tihany peninsula, Keszthely, or around the 'inland' towns of Veszprém, Sümeg or Székesfehérvár.

It is fairly easy to travel to and around Lake Balaton. People visit Balaton on day or weekend trips from Budapest, and it is unwise to travel to Balaton on a Friday evening or to return on a Sunday evening. The M7 motorway runs from Budapest to Siófok on the southern shore, after which a main road links all the resorts. The junctions at Balatonaliga or Polgárdi allow motorists to leave the motorway and head along road 71 which runs along the northern shore. There are frequent trains from Déli station in Budapest to Siófok, Boglárlelle and other places on the southern shore, which run there via Székesfehérvár. Services from Budapest to the northern shore also pass through Székesfehérvár and then on through Balatonfüred to Tapolca (for connections to Keszthely). Both lines offer good views of the lake, but unfortunately the punctuality of the train services (particularly on the line along the southern shore) can be very poor. There are steam-train services along the lakeside routes in summer (look out for leaflets or information posted up at stations). With the frequency of railway services, the bus services that link Budapest with towns such as Siófok, Balatonfüred, Veszprém, Tapolca, Keszthely and the smaller resorts along both sides of the lake are probably less convenient. Most services run several times a day, mostly using the Erzsébet tér bus terminal in the capital, although a few use the Népstadion. In summer, passenger ferries link many of the resorts, but there is only one car ferry in operation, running from the southern end of the Tihany peninsula over to the opposite side and which operates all year.

Fierce competition is keeping the prices for accommodation lower than they might otherwise be, but hotels and private rooms cost a lot more than elsewhere in provincial Hungary. Any tourist office (such as Siótour, Balatontourist or IBUSZ) will find a room in a hotel, although it may be advisable to book in advance, either in Budapest or before coming to Hungary. Finding a private room is easy, either through a tourist office or private accommodation agency (which are easy to spot) or simply by calling at any of the thousands (literally) of homes around the Balaton which hang a sign saying 'Zimmer frei' outside their front gates. There are dozens of campsites around the shore, which are more expensive than anywhere else in Hungary and which are also usually very crowded. Most campsites are open from May to September inclusive. For more information try to get hold of a map or leaflet detailing all of Hungary's campsites, available from most tourist offices in the country.

Between Budapest And Lake Balaton

There are a number of places of interest between Budapest and Lake Balaton, which could be visited by anyone travelling between these two places, or alternatively as day excursions from the capital or from towns in the eastern part of Lake Balaton, such as Siófok, Balatonfüred or Veszprém.

Beethoven is supposed to have composed his *Moonlight* and *Appassionata* piano sonatas while staying as a guest of the Brunswick family in their large whitewashed nineteenth-century villa in the small village of **Martonvásár**, just a short distance beyond Budapest's outermost suburbs. The former estate grounds are now agricultural research facilities belonging to the Hungarian Academy of Sciences, which have planted copious numbers of trees, flowers and lawns throughout the estate. Part of the main building, however, is given over to a museum where various musical instruments, letters and musical scores belonging to Beethoven are displayed. Beethoven gave piano lessons to Theresa and Josephine Brunswick and ended up falling in love with Josephine, whom he wrote to as his 'immortal beloved'. One part of the grounds left untamed by the plant scientists is the island in the small lake, where,

Sunset over Lake Balaton

Bory Vár, a bizarre folly in the outskirts of Székesfehérvár

surrounded by rambling beech trees, open-air concerts are given on summer evenings under a stern-looking bust of the composer. Tickets and information about concerts are available on the spot or from the Philharmonia ticket office at Vörösmarty tér 1 in Budapest, which also organises coach transport to the house. To reach the house, turn off the motorway at the junction near Martonvásár (the house is on Dózsa GyÎrgy utca, very close to the crossroads in the centre of the village) or take a stopping train from Budapest to Martonvásár, and walk 5 minutes up the road which leads diagonally away from Martonvásár station. The house is 5 minutes' walk away up this road, on the right. Those who do not welcome the company of buzzing things while they are listening to music should remember to bring some insect repellent.

Lake Velence (Velenci-tó) is 14km (9 miles) beyond Martonvásár, and 46km (28½ miles) from Budapest. The lake has an area of 26sq km (10sq miles), although half the lake is covered by reed beds, and the whole of the south-west corner has been spared from development by being declared a nature reserve, annually attracting over 30,000 nesting birds. Like Balaton, Velence is very shallow (never more than 2m/6½ ft deep), which means it warms up quickly in summer and occasionally freezes over in winter. Along the southern shore, tourist facilities are burgeoning, with private beaches which one must pay to use, holiday villas mushrooming in clusters and a general growth of tourist paraphernalia, with Lake Velence seemingly determined to emulate its much larger neighbour to the west. The main resorts, Velence, Gárdony and Agárd, actually merge into one another, and there are excellent opportunities for sailing, windsurfing and angling. The northern part of the lake is less built-up. Accessible by ferry from Velence or Agárd is the small fishing village of Pákozd, from where it is possible to take walks in the Velence Hills. At the summit of Mészeg Hegy 351m (1,151ft), the highest point in the hills, from where there is a fine view over the lake, a stone obelisk commemorates the first victorious battle of the 1848-9 War of Independence, while nearby some abandoned military equipment from World War II recalls more struggles here nearly a hundred years later.

The largest settlement lying between Budapest and Lake Balaton is **Székesfehérvár**, now an industrial town encircled by the usual rows of high-rise residential suburbs, but which 900 years ago was one of the most important towns in Hungary, where King Stephen built a palace and a cathedral and declared it the centre of his mission to bring Christianity to Hungary. Stephen's father, Prince Géza, built the first cathedral here in AD997, and was buried in it when he died 3 years later. The church was built of brilliant white limestone and stood on a hill surrounded by marshland, which is why Székesfehérvár is named thus — the word means, in Hungarian, 'Seat of the White Castle'. King Stephen's cathedral, which superseded his father's, was even more splendid, with marble floors, gold-encrusted altars and walls and columns made from lime-stone, all designed by Italian architects and master craftsmen. Stephen was buried in it when he died in 1038. For over 500 years, Hungarian kings and queens were crowned in this cathedral, and held court at the royal palace that Stephen built. But by 1688, after a century of Turkish rule had ended, the place was a ruin. Rebuilding of the city took place in the eighteenth century, when the town once again assumed an important religious role. However, there is no longer anything to rival the splendid buildings that stood here during the Middle Ages, and the attractions of the town rest on its museums, ruins, and, more unusually, the presence of an eccentric folly built in the suburbs of the town during the nineteenth century.

The centre of the town is a quiet, unevenly-shaped square, Városház tér. The town hall occupies an elegant mansion built along the south side of the square. Part of the ground floor of the building is now a tourist office. The square is also home to an eighteenth-century Bishop's Palace, built with stones from the ruined basilica, and also an eighteenth-century Franciscan church. Behind the Bishop's Palace are the ruins of the basilica (Romkert) really only foundations of a church which was built initially to rival St Mark's in Venice. St Stephen's sarcophagus is displayed near the entrance to the ruins, as are other pieces of stonework from the cathedral that once stood here. Some of the tombs excavated from the church were moved to Budapest in the nineteenth century.

Fő utca, lined with handsomely-restored eighteenth-century houses, leads off Városház tér from next to the Bishop's Palace. Along here, on the left, is the shabby-looking Church of St John of Nepomuk, with some nice Baroque decoration inside. Just beyond it, on the same side of the street, is the King Stephen Museum (István Király Múzeum) which is the main museum detailing the history of the town. Opposite the museum is the Black Eagle Pharmacy Museum (Fekete Sas). The building operated as a pharmacy from 1745 until 1971 and now displays various pills, potions and medical devices from the eighteenth and nineteenth centuries. The road ends at Gagarin tér, where there is a striking floral clock and, over to the right, in the corner of the square, a building which houses travelling art exhibitions.

Arany János utca runs south from Városház tér. A little way along here is St Stephen's Cathedral, originally founded in the thirteenth century but which has been altered and rebuilt through the centuries to leave it in a Baroque style. Most of the decoration inside dates from the eighteenth century. The paving in front of the church marks the outline of a church that once stood here in the tenth century. Next to it is the tiny St Anne's Chapel, the only remaining medieval building in the town, built in the 1470s and used, during the Turkish occupation, as a mosque. Inside there are some remains of Turkish wall paintings. The statue in front depicts Domonkos Kálmáncsehi, Provost of the town when the chapel was founded, looking up at the cathedral. In one hand he holds the foundation deeds of the chapel, while his other hand rests on a model of the chapel. The street runs on down to Szent István tér, around the corner from which a Carmelite church boasts particularly elaborate rococo decorations, including some fine wall-paintings by the Austrian artist Franz Maulbertsch. In the middle of the square is a statue of King Stephen on horseback. Behind the buildings to the right of the square, which include the neo-Classical County Hall, is the bus station.

The information office at the bus station will inform visitors which number bus to take out to Bory Vár, arguably the best, certainly the oddest, sight in the town. This elaborate folly is situated in Székesfehérvár's eastern suburbs, near large factories producing televisions and radios — the town's most important industries. It was built over a period of 40 years by Jenő Bory, a professor at the Academy of Fine Arts in Budapest, to honour his wife, Ilona Komocsin. The place deliberately combines elements of Renaissance, Romanesque and Gothic architecture, and was built in the form of a castle with turrets, mock battlements and courtyards, and an interesting terraced garden. Most of the rooms now contain paintings by Bory and his wife. Ilona was Bory's favourite subject and appears in a lot of his paintings. Aside from this, it is an absorbing building to wander round, and the garden, and views from the turrets, are lovely.

Most trains running between Budapest and the Balaton stop at Székesfehérvár. The town is a short distance off the main Budapest-Siófok motorway. Székesfehérvár is an easy day excursion from either centre, but those who want to stay should be able to find accommodation through the tourist offices or at one of the city's three hotels.

Twelve kilometres (7 miles) to the south of Székesfehérvár, situated down a left turning just before the village of Tác, are situated the largest and best Roman ruins in Hungary. Accessible by hourly bus from Székesfehérvár, the remains of the town of **Gorsium** may not be spectacular but the site is expansive, covering over 2sq km (1sq mile) and does offer a quite seductive serenity. The sort of fertile silence that a place like this really requires and deserves. The original Roman settlement dates from AD46 when a military camp was established with the capacity to hold around 500 men. By the beginning of the following century *Gorsium* had developed into the major religious centre of the province of *Pannonia Inferior* and its inhabitants numbered some 8,000. The settlement was twice laid to waste. In AD178 by the Sarmatians and then again in AD260, after which it was refounded in AD295 by the Emperor Diocletian who renamed it Herculia. Herculia remained occupied long after the Roman withdrawal and the Avar cemetery here dates from around the sixth century. At the beginning of the eleventh century much of the town's masonry was used in the construction of Székesfehérvár, the last inhabitants disappeared at the beginning of the Turkish occupation. Excavations of the area date from only 1934 and are still in progress. Among the ruins are a palace, a Christian basilica, a cemetery and various dwellings, shops and civic buildings. An information booklet is available in English

Boating on Lake Balaton

at the entrance and various artefacts from the site may be found in the King Stephen Museum in Székesfehérvár.

The Southern Shore

Virtually the whole of the 70km (43 miles) of the southern shore of Lake Balaton has been developed into one long concrete and grass strand. All the settlements are linked by road 7 and the railway line running parallel to it. The construction of the railway during the 1860s is where we can date the modern development of the lake as a holiday centre from. Most of the holiday apartments are situated by the strand. What town there is will be situated beyond the main road. Holiday homes bridge the gap between settlements. Approaching from Budapest, the first resort on the southern shore is **Balatonvilágos**, actually one of the most exclusive and least commercialised of the resorts, it being the former preserve of Party officials.

Balatonvilágos then merges imperceptibly with **Siófok**, the largest resort on the southern shore covering a 16km (10 mile) stretch of strand, every inch of it full to bursting point during the summer months. With a plethora of food stalls, night-clubs and topless bars lining the route to the string of lakeside highrise hotels, this is by far the resort with the liveliest nightlife. Anyone searching for anything more edifying is left with little choice than to pay a visit to the Beszédes József Museum at Sió utca 2. Beszédes was a hydraulic engineer and the museum is devoted to the history of water supply management but it is not quite as dull as one might fear. The first canal in the area dates back to Roman times. The museum also includes a brief history of the lake; under Turkish occupation a fleet of some 10,000 men was stationed in Siófok. The only other building worth a brief flirtation is the very obvious Balaton Meteorological Tower in the centre of town which offers a view of the surrounding area.

Zamárdi, the next resort along, offers the usual strand and watersport attractions on a smaller scale. Anyone in need of an idiosyncracy should take a 20 minute signposted walk up the hill to Szamárkő, a large stone believed to be an ancient Magyar sacrificial site. Legend has it that the rock bears the impression of a hoof made by Christ's donkey. On the way, at Fő utca 83, is the Tájház, a small folk museum based in an old peasant house. A car ferry to Tihany is Szántód's only real point of interest though a little further inland at **Szántódpuszta** there are a number of eighteenth- and nineteenth-century farm buildings which have been transformed into a museum complex with various exhibitions covering everything from local flora and fauna to the history of the Szántód ferry. The complex also includes two inns, a café and a wine bar.

The resort of **Balatonföldvár** only came into existence at the end of the nineteenth century. Highly recommended is a 4km (2 mile) walk (or bus ride) to the fifteenth-century Gothic Catholic church at **Kőröshegy**, originally built for the Franciscans. Look out for details of the chamber music concerts that are held here in summer. **Balatonszárszó** is most famed as the place where poet Attila József flung himself under the wheels of a freight train on 3 December 1937. He was 32. He spent his last days in a pension at József utca 7 in what one presumes to have been an unsuccessful attempt to recover from a bout of depression. The building now houses a memorial museum from where a booklet containing a brief life of this unfortunate being along with translations of some of his verse is available in English. His body rests in an unkempt cemetery at the edge of town along Kossuth utca.

Balatonszemes is actually a medieval settlement which was only transformed into a resort at the end of the nineteenth century. Ten minutes up the hill from the railway station there is a small Postal Museum housed in a nineteenth-century mail-coach station. During the late nineteenth century the small bathing resort of **Balatonlelle** gradually expanded itself into the older town of Balatonboglár to form the hybrid **Boglárlelle**. Today the resort has a very strong German presence. Younger Balatonlelle's only point of interest is the former mansion at Kossuth utca 2 dating from 1838 which boasts colourful and energetic displays of folk-dancing during the summer months. **Balatonboglár**'s most obvious attraction is the spherical lookout tower on top of Castle Hill. Situated upon Cemetery Hill next door are Catholic and Lutheran chapels which house temporary art exhibitions.

Fonyód is the second largest resort after Siófok and similarly ultra-modern. There is a passenger ferry from here to Badacsony on the northern shore. From Fonyód onwards the resorts are much smaller and more sparsely populated. **Balatonfenyves** is in itself unremarkable but it does serve as the base for a journey through the 10 acres (4 hectares) of surrounding marshland via a narrow gauge railway which runs to Csisztapuszta. The marsh is now considered a valuable conservation area as the nesting ground for a wide variety of birdlife. At **Csisztapuszta** there are some thermal baths, discovered accidentally in 1956 during oil drilling.

The last stretch of the southern shore is largely covered by reeds and is still largely virgin territory as far as tourism goes. **Balatonmáriafürdő** has only been developed as a bathing resort since 1967. One may catch a passenger ferry from here to Balatongyörok. Inland, **Balatonkeresztúr** boasts a Baroque church dating from the 1750s which is well worth a visit for its vivid and comprehensively decorated interior. The wall frescoes include portraits of members of the Festetics family who owned land around Keszthely. A former Festetics manor house at Ady utca 26 is now used as a hostel. The final coastal settlement on the southern shore is **Balatonberény** which features a nudist beach.

At the south-western tip of the lake is 8,645 acres (3,500 hectares) of marshland known as the **Kis-Balaton** (Little-Balaton). In 1949 about half of the area was declared a nature reserve. Today over one hundred breeds

Lake Balaton, a popular venue for tourists and watersport enthusiasts

of bird are found here including the white egret, the grey spoonbill and the black-headed gull. Anyone wishing to visit the area requires permission from the National Office for Nature Conservation in Budapest (V, Arany utca 25 ☎ 132 7371).

The Northern Shore And The Bakony Highlands

Lake Balaton is a playground for children

Whereas the southern shore of Lake Balaton is a string of largely faceless resorts, the northern shore has more character and has a number of historic and natural sites worth visiting. On the eastern part of the lake's northern shore is Balatonfüred, perhaps the liveliest and most interesting resort on the lake, and nearby is the Tihany peninsula, an area of largely unspoiled beauty where the town of Tihany is a major draw for visitors. Inland, the larger town of Veszprém boasts a number of historical attractions. On the western edge of Lake Balaton are the resort towns of Keszthely and, a little way inland, the large spa town of Hévíz, while the Bakony Highlands stretch right down to the lake around Badacsony, and as they stretch inland provide numerous opportunities for walking. A railway line, with trains from Budapest (via Székesfehérvár) runs all along the northern shore, linking most of the places mentioned in this section including Balatonfüred, Badacsony, Tapolca (the main centre for the Bakony Highlands), and Keszthely. Other towns are no more than a short bus ride away from the nearest station. Road connections are good, too, with the main road 71 running the length of the northern shore, along which there are frequent buses. In the introduction to this chapter details of the various ferry and passenger ships which link the northern with the southern shore are given.

The North-Eastern Shore To Balatonfüred

Motorists will come off the motorway at Balatonaglia and follow the shore northwards to **Balatonakarattya**, through which the railway also passes. Here, the Rákóczi fa is a dead tree trunk where the freedom fighter Ferenc Rákóczi is alleged to have tied his horse during the War of Independence in the early eighteenth century. The next village, **Balatonkenese**, has only a little more to offer, in the form of a Baroque church and preserved peasant dwellings along its main street. Around the north-eastern corner of the lake, **Balatonalmádi** is the first real Balaton resort on this shore. It claims to have the largest beach on the northern shore, and this together with its modern new shopping complexes do not really conspire to encourage one to linger. The medieval Chapel of St Job was transplanted to the Catholic church here during the nineteenth century. Inland, **Vörösberény**, boasts a tastefully decorated Catholic church dating from the 1770s and, further on up the hill, a thirteenth-century fortress church, a squat little building nestling behind its intact defensive wall by the side of the road. Next along the lake from Balatonalmádi is **Alsóörs**, with a beach and more campsites and hotels. In the park there is a monument to Soviet pilots who crashed here during World War II, while a little way up the hill at Petőfi köz 7 is a sixteenth-century building known as the Turkish House, so named because the chimney is meant to resemble a turbanned head. It was once inhabited by a Turkish tax collector. In **Felsőörs**, further inland, there is a well-preserved Romanesque church built of dark red sandstone, with eighteenth-century furnishings inside. Details about the history of the church can be read in English. The next resort beyond Alsóörs, Csopak, is hardly worth stopping for before **Balatonfüred** is reached.

In 1846 the first steamship ever to set sail on Lake Balaton was launched from Balatonfüred . Now, ferries, passenger cruise ships (there are frequent sailings across to Siófok) and sailing boats crowd towards this resort, as do most visitors who come to the northern shore. Balatonfüred gets busy but somehow never manages to lose the degree of refinement common to all spa towns. Its lakeside promenade, decked out in summer with trees, flowers and impromptu musicians (inevitably of the Classical variety), offers the opportunities for gentle strolling that cannot be found on the southern shore. The town has a strong cultural life, and in summer there are frequent concerts staged in the town's churches and other venues. Tourist offices should be able to provide details of these events. There are many hotels here, some of which cater solely for spa patients, and other accommodation possibilities include many pensions and private rooms to rent. The town affords easy access to the Tihany peninsula and other places on the lake, which makes staying here an attractive possibility. The centre of town is immediately up from the harbour where boats dock. The railway station is a little inconveniently situated in the northern part of town, inland from the lake.

The Romans probably knew about the curative properties of the spring waters here. In the eighteenth century, the Benedictine monks who lived on the Tihany peninsula rediscovered the medicinal properties of the waters. The town grew into a fashionable spa during the nineteenth century, popular with the Hungarian nobility. In the nineteenth century the waters were mixed with goat's whey and used for curing lung diseases. Now 30,000 people come to the spa every year for treatment, making the resort busy all year round and swelling the number of summer visitors. The waters that gurgle from the ground here are now thought to be especially beneficial to heart patients, and many noted and distinguished visitors to the Balatonfüred Heart Hospital have planted trees along the shore of the lake. In the small park near the harbour and piers, behind the twin statues of *The Fisherman* and *The Ferryman* is a statue of the Indian Nobel-prize winning poet Rabindranath Tagore, who planted a lime tree here when he stayed in 1926 and began the tradition of tree-planting. The statue carries an inscription of the poem he wrote about his stay. The area of parkland and trees continues eastwards from here, along the shore of the lake, for 1km (½ mile).

Just up from the harbour and the park is the Round Church (Kerek Templom) on Blaha Lujza utca. The church is neo-Classical in design and dates from the 1840s. Opposite the church, across the main road, is the old summer residence of the nineteenth-century novelist Mór Jókai, sometimes described as the Hungarian Dickens, now a memorial museum celebrating his life and works. The street is named after the popular nineteenth-century singer and actress Lujza Blaha, who was known as the 'nation's nightingale' and who lived in the house at number 4. Opposite the villa is Balatontourist, the local tourist office (at number 5), and further along is the square Gyógy tér (Health Square), the centre of the old spa area. The spa's medicinal spring waters can be sampled from the columned Kossuth Well, built in 1800, for free. Elegant nineteenth-century spa sanitoria line the square. The most imposing building is the Heart Hospital, through which 10,000 patients pass every year. In 1831 the first Hungarian Language Theatre anywhere in the country was constructed on the square. Six columns still remain, standing in their original location, but the theatre has long since gone. A park stretches down from the square to the lake. By the lake, there is a statue of the nineteenth-century engineer

István Széchenyi. The inscription tells that 'if a man tired of work sees the waters of lake Balaton, he will feel new blood in his veins', and people have been coming to the lake in great numbers to relax and unwind for over a century.

The Tihany Peninsula

The Tihany is a rocky, picturesque peninsula which stretches out into Lake Balaton south-west of Balatonfüred. From its southern tip it is only a few kilometres across the water to the southern shore. This is where the lake is at its narrowest. The Tihany is a small area of great contrast. Tihany-rév, the southernmost tip, is a garish holiday resort and ferry port. The town of Tihany is beautiful but overrun by tourists, while the rest of the peninsula is genuinely unspoiled countryside, stretching across the western half of the peninsula to the high cliffs along the western side. Here it is possible to walk and escape the crowds that descend on Tihany town and on Balatonfüred. The area was declared Hungary's first National Park, in 1952, and is probably the single most popular area along the shores of Lake Balaton. Tihany is reached by a turning off

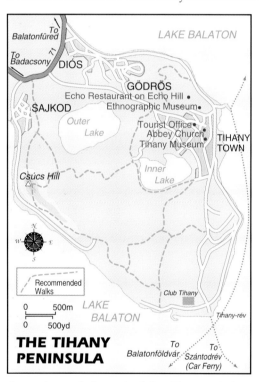

the main road along the lake. This road skirts Dios and Gödrös before entering the town of Tihany, and then heads south to the ferry terminal at Tihany-rév, from where the Balaton's only car ferry operates all year round across to Szántód. Boats from Balatonfüred dock at Tihany town, from where it is a walk up to the abbey complex on the hill top above the lake. There are no rail connections (the nearest station, at Aszofo, is a fair way inland) but there are plenty of buses from Tihany and Tihany-rév to Balatonfüred and other places along the northern shore. One has to pay to use the beach at Tihany town and Tihany-rév. The beaches near Dios, Gödrös and Sajkod are free, though are liable to be muddy and reedy in places.

The map of the Tihany peninsula must be studied in detail by anyone wishing to walk in the area. There are two lakes on the peninsula. The Inner Lake, just to the west of Tihany town, and visible from the Abbey Church, is the smaller of the two. It is surrounded by vineyards and orchards. A path runs from its southern tip to the Aranyház Geyser cones, where a number of rock funnels have been forced open by (now defunct) geysers. The lake itself is a product of former volcanic activity; it fills a fossilised volcano crater. The Outer Lake, to the north-west, is bigger. It was drained at the start of the nineteenth century, and refilled in 1975. It is now a marshy swamp, where reeds grow and are harvested (in winter, when the reeds stand above the frozen waters of the lake), and where there are numerous species of birds and waterfowl, protected by stringent conservation regulations. A red-marked trail runs along the west coast of the peninsula, from the main road west of Dios all the way round to Tihany-rév. It takes 2 to 3 hours to walk the whole length. Some of the path is high up above the lake, affording incredible views over it. The lookout tower on the summit of Csúcs Hill, halfway along, offers the best panorama. It is possible to cut across from Csúcs Hill east to the Inner Lake and Tihany town. Those who continue south and make it down to Tihany-rév will find the huge holiday complex and marina there closed to visitors. There are frequent buses from Tihany-rév up to Tihany (and on to Balatonfüred).

Tihany town is a pretty but expensive and touristy resort, stretching up from the pier, where boats to Balatonfüred dock, to the Abbey Church on the summit high above the lake. Many houses in the town are built of grey basalt, a volcanic rock, with whitewashed terraces or porticoes. The thatched roofs are made from reeds which grow along the shores of the Balaton and the lakes on the peninsula. The distinctive twin-towered Abbey Church is visible from all over the peninsula (and from the southern shore of the lake), its white towers rising above the red roofs of the surrounding houses. The Benedictine abbey was founded here by King Andrew I in 1055. The foundation deed, preserved at Pannonhalma Abbey near Győr, is the oldest document in existence to include words written in the Hungarian language. King Andrew is buried in a marble-covered tomb in the cool crypt beneath the church he founded — although virtually all the present building dates from Baroque times, the original churches built on this spot having fallen down or been destroyed. The interior of the church is famed for its rich decorations. There are incredible eighteenth-century wood carvings by Sebestyén Stuhlhoff, who preserved the face of his dead fiancée in the angel kneeling to the right of the first altar on the left of the church, and beautiful nineteenth-century frescoes adorn the walls. Organ concerts are held in the church in summer. The modern sculpture in the square outside the church depicts King Andrew, in stone and aluminium. In the old priory, next door, is the Tihany Museum, which besides the predictable collection of paintings and other artefacts from around the Balaton has a display of costumes, musical instruments and tools from communities east of the Ural Mountains in Russia, from where the Magyar people are said to have originated. Roman remains are displayed in the basement of the museum, including a shrine to Hercules dating from the second or third century AD. The rest of the collection here is of more mundane mosaic floors, and parts of columns or buildings.

Other points of interest in Tihany are the open-air Ethnographic Museum, near the abbey, where the former cottages of a smallholder and a fisherman have been preserved and beyond it the Óvár, the old castle, which lies to the north of Tihany village. Nothing of the castle exists any more. It was built on a rocky volcanic outcrop, in which the remains of cells carved by Russian Orthodox monks in the eleventh century can be seen.

Fifteen kilometres (9 miles) to the north of Balatonfüred along road 73 stands the town of **Veszprém** whose pleasant Baroque old town and proximity to Lake Balaton make it an attractive and popular destination. Prince Géza established one of Hungary's first episcopal sees here. A cathedral and royal palace were built on the town's highest hill and in AD997 King Stephen defeated a major pagan rebellion here. During medieval times it became the seat of the queen's household and the site of her coronation, consequently it became known as the 'Queen's Town'. In the 1530s Veszprém became the battleground between two rival claimants for the Hungarian throne, Ferdinand of Habsburg and János Szapolyai, and the town was utterly destroyed. In 1538 Bishop Márton Kecsethy reported only thirty-eight houses of mud and straw standing. The Turkish wars saw further destruction as Veszprém became disputed territory between the Turks and the Habsburgs. The town fared little better during the 1703-11 War of Independence. In 1702 the castle was demolished on the orders of the Habsburgs. As with many Hungarian towns much of the centre today dates from the reconstruction of the mid-eighteenth century.

The railway station is some 2km (1 mile) from the centre of the town (connected by bus number 1) and the bus station is some 10 minutes walk to the east. Triangular Óváros tér flanked by pretty pink and blue eighteenth-century Baroque and rococo houses is an ideal place to begin a tour of the town. Rising beyond numbers 7 and 8 on the square is the Fire Tower whose medieval base actually formed part of the town's castle. It was severely damaged by an earthquake in 1810 but rebuilt soon after. Entrance to the tower is via a small alley just inside the Heroes' Gate. The gate itself was erected in 1936 on the site of one of the gates of the medieval castle, to commemorate the dead of World War I. Contained within one wing is a small military exhibition, the curator of which may assume that you have walked in more by accident than design and direct you up along Vár utca.

At number 12 Vár utca stands the former Piarist monastery, and next door to this is the Piarist church built between 1828 and 1836. The Greek letters on the façade translate as 'Mary, Mother, God'. Today the church is used to house temporary exhibitions of a religious or artistic nature. Further along, at number 16 is the late eighteenth-century Baroque Bishop's Palace. During its construction, using the stones of the royal palace which had stood on the site since the days of King Stephen, part of the medieval Queen's Palace was unearthed. It has since been named the Gizella Chapel after King Stephen's wife. Its north wall is decorated with frescoes of the Apostles which date back to the thirteenth century. A little further along Vár utca stands St Michael's Cathedral, the crypt of which survives from 1400. The rest of the building originally dates from 1723 but was substantially altered during major restoration work at the beginning of the twentieth century which has produced its present neo-Romanesque appearance. A glass dome behind the cathedral houses the remains of the St George's Chapel built in 1016. It is said to have once housed a relic of St George brought here by King Stephen. Opposite, at number 35, is an eighteenth-century canon's house which now plays host to a collection of Roman Catholic ecclesiastical treasures. Vár utca then ends abruptly with noble white statues of Stephen and Gizella erected in 1938 on the 900th anniversary of Stephen's death. From the parapet there is a good view of Séd Valley and the Bakony Forest. To the left note Valley Bridge (constructed in 1936) and on the right are the white rocks and cross of Benedict Hill.

Return back down Castle Hill and walk through Óváros tér to Szabadság tér. At number 1 is the town hall dating from 1793. It was originally a private construction for the Kapuváry family whose coat of arms still adorn the building even though it passed into civic hands back in 1885. A short way down Ovári Ferenc utca is the very modern Petőfi Theatre which was the first building in Hungary to be constructed from reinforced concrete! The circular stained glass window at the front is the work of Sándor Nagy and is entitled *The Magic of Folk Art*. It features various symbolic representations of Hungarian society. The final attractions to be found around the centre of town are situated on Megyehaz tér, a short walk south-east from here. The Bakony Museum illustrates the general history of the region; pride of place belonging to Roman mosaics from nearby Balácapuszta and a wide array of folk costumes. Next door to this is the Bakony House built in 1935, a replica of a traditional homestead suitably furnished. About 1km (½ mile) west of the centre off Kittenbeger utca lies the town zoo and botanical gardens named after the nineteenth-century zoologist Kálmán Kittenbeger. There is a small Village Museum south of the gardens in the Fejes Valley.

Excursions From Veszprém

Twelve kilometres (7 miles) to the north-west of Veszprém along road 8 stands the small village of **Herend** which has achieved world fame through its porcelain factory. The factory opened in 1839 and gained its first taste of international approval at the 1851 Great Exhibition when

The old centre of Veszprém, in the Bakony Highlands

Queen Victoria ordered a Chinoiserie dinner service. Other famous admirers include Tsar Alexander II, Kaiser Wilhelm I and the Shah of Iran. The factory museum on Kossuth utca has an exhibition of the porcelain and a display of porcelain-making techniques. There is plenty of opportunity to purchase the wares of the factory throughout the town. All major credit cards are accepted.

Three kilometres (2 miles) to the south-west of Veszprém, **Balácapuszta** (situated by the village of Nemesvámos) is the earliest and largest Roman site of the Balaton region containing the remains of several farm buildings and a villa with reconstructed frescoes. This is really only of interest to antiquarians, and most will prefer to continue on along the main road for a further 2km (1 mile) to one of Hungary's most famous highwayman's inns, the **Vámosi Csárda**, said to be the haunt of one of Hungary's most famous folk heroes, Jóska Savanyú. The inn itself is a two-storey Baroque building with courtyard and outbuildings typical of the eighteenth century. Displays of folk music and dancing occasionally take place in the courtyard.

Twenty-three kilometres (14 miles) south-west of Veszprém, the town of **Nagyvázsony**'s main attraction is the Kinizsi Castle dating from the fifteenth century. In 1472 King Mátyás Corvinus presented it to one of his favourite generals, Pál Kinizsi, said to have been a lowly miller's assistant who attracted the king's attention through his great courage and strength on the battlefield. Kinizsi's main claim to fame is to have danced triumphantly holding three dead Turks (one between his teeth) after the battle of Kenyérmezo in 1479. During the Turkish occupation the castle became one of the border fortresses between Turkish and Habsburg ruled territory. During the War of Independence it was used as a rebel base yet inexplicably it managed to escape complete decimation for its sins and is relatively well preserved today. Its 30m (98ft) high keep displays an exhibition of furniture, weaponry and shackles (in the eighteenth century the keep was used as a prison). The restored chapel contains the cover of Kinizsi's red marble sarcophagus. In the immediate vicinity of the castle is a Postal Museum and a small Ethnographical Museum.

Between Tihany And The Badacsony

Heading west from Tihany and Balatonfüred along the northern shore of the lake, there is a string of characterless resorts and towns, each with similar collections of hotels, campsites, holiday homes and fee-paying, crowded beaches. There is very little to detain one at any of these places, bar the usual Balaton pleasures of watersports, swimming and rudimentary nightlife. At **Örvényes**, just beyond the junction for the Tihany, an eighteenth-century watermill is still in operation. There is a small collection here of peasant artefacts, wood-carvings and pottery. On the small hill above the mill there are the ruins of a small Romanesque chapel. The churchyard at **Balatonudvari**, the next village along the road, boasts unusual gravestones, made of white limestone and fashioned into heart shapes. The motif was popular around 1800 and is also seen in Germany and Austria. Further on, **Balatonakali** is famous for its *akali muskotály* white wine. At **Ábrahámhegy** there is an arboretum containing species of cedar and pine trees from all over the world. But all this can safely be avoided as one travels to the second major clutch of attractions on the north shore: the Badacsony peninsula, which juts out into the lake just beyond Badacsonytomaj; inland, the town of Tapolca and the Bakony Highlands; at the western extremity of the lake, the resort of Keszthely and the Festetics Palace, and close by, the spa resort of Hévíz, with the northern hemisphere's largest thermal lake.

Badacsony And The Western Bakony Highlands

The Badacsony is a flat-topped mountain which juts out abruptly into the lake, its steep basalt cliffs rising to a height of 438m (1,437ft). To the north, stretching between the lake and the inland town of Tapolca, there are similar hills rising out of the flat landscape, all with precipitous slopes crammed with vineyards, which culminate in flat, windy summits. These are ancient, long-extinct volcanic cones, and their presence gives a strange and surreal air to the landscape of this part of the Balaton region. Their fertile volcanic soils support some of the most extensive areas of vineyards in Hungary, and wine has been made here since the sixth century AD. The hills form the western, and most interesting part of the Bakony Highlands.

Walking in the Bakony is rewarding but can be difficult. The hills are universally steep, even if they are not particularly high; this is no place for gentle strolling. The weather can be hot and the vineyards that are built up most of the slopes offer little shade, although the higher and steeper parts of some of the hills are forested. Many vineyards are guarded by large and ferocious dogs, which are usually kept tethered to the tiny villas and shacks that pepper the mountainside. A few of these buildings have been converted by their enterprising owners into makeshift cafés, which are pretty rudimentary but which do at least sell cold drinks, and, of course, some of the product of the vineyards which surround them. Anyone planning to walk in the Bakony should buy the large-scale map of the region.

The village of **Badacsony**, on the southern tip of the peninsula, is an important resort, with ferry links across to Fonyód and round to other places on the northern shore. The railway station is close to the beach and harbour. The slopes of the mountain rise almost immediately from the lake shore. A museum very close to the railway station displays the work of József Egry (1883-1951), a local locksmith who became an artist and whose paintings depict the scenery and people of the Balaton region. From the railway station, it is possible to follow the yellow-marked trail up the hill a fair way to the Róza Szegedy House, a picturesque hillside villa which is dedicated to the memory of the poet Sándor Kisfaludy, married to Róza Szegedy. The Kisfaludy Ház restaurant, situated nearby in a building which was once a wine press, is well-known locally. Further on along the path marked with yellow + symbols is the Borászate Wine Museum, with displays relating to the region's long tradition of viticulture.

From the museums it is possible to explore the Badacsony Mountain itself. From the Róza Szegedy House the yellow-marked track runs steeply up the hillside to the Rózsa-kő (the Rose Rock), where it is said that if a man and woman sit with their backs to the Balaton, they will be married within the year. Using the map it is then possible to follow any number of trails up to the Kisfaludy lookout tower on the summit, a rickety wooden construction that gives a superlative view over the Balaton. From here the trail continues on to the northern flank of the mountain, and the Kökapu (Stone Gate), two precipitous basaltic pillars which are a reminder of the volcanic activity which once formed this region. From here it is possible to follow a blue-marked track all the way down through the forest, crossing the road at the bottom of the valley and then heading up another volcanic peak, Gulács (393m/1,289ft). From here it is possible to drop down to the village of Nemesgulács and the railway station beyond it, from where there are trains back to Badacsony. The walk from Badacsony station via the Róza Szegedy House, the Kisfaludy lookout tower and Gulács to the railway station at Nemesgulács will take a good 4 to 5 hours and is strenuous in places.

The dull, functional inland town of **Tapolca** is a good base for seeing some more of the western part of the Bakony, and is also a convenient place from where the castle at Sümeg can be visited. Tapolca is an important railway junction, and the railway along the northern shore of the

Balaton curves northwards to pass through it before heading back to the lake at Keszthely. Roads from Tapolca run east to Nagyvázsony and Veszprém and north-west to Sümeg and then to Sárvár, Szombathely and Kőszeg (see Chapter 3) and then Austria. Tapolca is an important centre for the processing of the mineral bauxite, which is mined in the surrounding hills. At the end of the town's main street are the Tavas Caves, some fairly ordinary limestone grottoes where mining activities have caused the stream that formed them to disappear. In the other direction, near the Hotel Gabriella, there is a fifteenth-century Catholic church and the Varosi Museum, with an interesting mock-up of a nineteenth-century schoolroom. Apart from these two minor attractions, however, there is nothing to keep one away from the surrounding hills and countryside.

Two of the best climbs in the Bakony can be approached easily from Tapolca. To the south-east of the town is **Csobánk**, a bare hill surrounded by vineyard-covered slopes, on whose summit are the ruins of a castle and a fabulous view. There are a number of paths up. The easiest and shortest way up is to follow the green-marked track running up from the church in Gyulakezi, then branching off to the right and taking a path marked with green L symbols for the last bit of the way steeply up to the summit. This walk takes about 1½ hours. There are also paths up from the villages of Diszel and Kaptalantoti. South of Tapolca is a very obvious and steep-sided hill, **Szent-György-hegy**, whose upper slopes are thickly forested. Again, there are a number of paths up to the summit (there is a look-out point at the highest point). The shortest way is probably from the village of Kisapati, to the east, but access can also be gained from villages on the west side. Either way, it is a steep, tough climb taking a good couple of hours. The vineyards on this hill reputedly produce the region's finest wines.

The dullness of Tapolca is certainly not replicated in the town of **Sümeg**, along the road and railway line heading north-west. Here, the impressive ruins of a castle sit on top of a conical limestone (not volcanic) hill, overlooking a picturesque old town whose Baroque mansions date back to the time when this place was the seat of the bishops of Veszprém. At the end of Deák Ferenc utca (number 14) is a parish church whose interior is covered with beautiful eighteenth-century frescoes, considered the finest in Hungary, painted by Franz Anton Maulbertsch in 1757-8. Most show Biblical scenes. The back wall shows Maulberstch's patron, Bishop Biró, and the man kneeling before him is said to represent the artist himself. The first castle at Sümeg was built in the thirteenth century. The walls and other fortifications are later additions of the Middle Ages. The castle kept out the Turks but was destroyed by the Habsburgs and burned down in 1713, when it was abandoned. It has been undergoing restoration since the 1960s. Small exhibitions have been set up in its rooms, and there are displays of jousting and other medieval-style entertainments and pageants in the castle courtyard in summer. The views from the ramparts are superb. Below the steps up to the castle, the former Bishop's Stables now house a Saddlery Museum.

Situated on the northern shore of Lake Balaton where roads 84 and 71 meet, the town of **Szigliget** once used to be an island and today is surrounded on three sides by water and reeds. The picturesque village of thatch-roofed white houses is crowned by the ruins of a thirteenth-century castle which successfully managed to resist the attentions of the Turks due to the steepness of the hill it is situated upon and the marshy nature of the surrounding land. Unfortunately it was demolished in 1702 on the orders of the Vienna Council of War who feared that it might be used in a nationalist rebellion. Along Fő tér in the village below is the Esterházy Summer Mansion, built around 1780, which now serves as a rest home for writers. The 25 acres (10 hectares) of botanical gardens attached to the mansion may only be visited with permission. Nearby characterful Kossuth Lajos utca contains many of the former outbuildings of the Esterházy estate.

Thirteen kilometres (8 miles) east of Szigliget along road 71 stands **Keszthely**, whose main street follows the path of a Roman road which led to the fortified town of *Valcum* (present day Fenékpuszta) 7km (4 miles) south of Keszthely. The first settlement here dates back to the thirteenth century. The town remained largely immune from the Turkish threat and from 1739 until its 'liberation' in 1945 was the property of the Festetics family, most notable amongst whom is György Festetics (1755-1819) who founded the large, and originally public, library in the family mansion, established Europe's first agricultural institute (the present day University of Agricultural Sciences) and developed Hévíz as a spa resort. Keszthely was connected to the railway built on the southern shore of the lake in 1866 only by a small branch line and consequently it has been much less developed as a resort. All the pleasures of the *strand* (beach) are available in Keszthely but the town has managed to retain a sense of its own history and much of its character as a cultural and educational centre.

The bus and rail stations are situated opposite each other near the lake. To get to the town centre walk away from the railway station along Martirok utca to Kossuth Lajos utca. To your immediate left is the Balaton Museum with a familiar mixed bag covering the geological and ethnographic history of the region. From here walk north up Kossuth Lajos utca to Fő tér, the main town square, on which is situated a Gothic parish church originally built for the Franciscans in the 1380s. The church was fortified against a possible Turkish assault in 1550 and rebuilt in Baroque style in 1747. In 1878 the present tower was erected. Inside, on the walls of the chancel may be seen some impressive fourteenth-century frescoes which were only discovered in 1974. On the south side of the church are the foundation walls of an earlier Romanesque church. The remainder of Kossuth Lajos utca is pedestrianised and leads to the Festetics Palace. The palace originally dates from the mid-eighteenth century but was substantially rebuilt in the late nineteenth century. Highlights of a tour of the

The Festetics Palace at Keszthely, one of Hungary's most important Baroque monuments

palace include the Mirrored Ballroom, in which chamber music concerts are held, and the Helikon Library which was founded in the 1790s and which contains some 80,000 volumes and some beautifully carved oak furniture by local craftsman János Kerbl. The gardens are beautifully tended and well worth a wander in. Concerts are occasionally held outdoors in front of the palace during the summer months. The agricultural institute established by György Festetics may be found nearby down Bercsényi utca. Today it houses a display of various agricultural devices, the institute having transferred itself down Széchenyi utca. Also of interest is the town cemetery at the base of Kossuth Lajos utca, not far from the museum, which houses the Festetics family vault built in the style of a Greek temple.

Seven kilometres (4 miles) south of Keszthely, accessible by a painfully infrequent bus and train service, is the village of **Fenékpuszta**, site of the Roman settlement of *Valcum*. One would require a passion in things Roman bordering on the perverse for a visit here to be merited, nevertheless for anyone so disposed the ruins may be found just in from the main road in what could loosely be described as a park. To your immediate left as you enter are the remains of a storehouse while over to the right, past the bent goalpost and beyond the rusted fence, is a Christian basilica which, if it were any more ruinous, would be entirely non-existent.

Eight kilometres (5 miles) to the north of Keszthely is situated one of the oldest of Hungary's spas. In use since medieval times, the thermal lake at **Hévíz**, at 50,000sq m (54,000sq ft), is the largest in Europe and the second largest in the world (the largest is in New Zealand). Sixty million litres of water a day gush from springs 1km (½ mile) underground to completely renew the lake every 28 hours. The temperature, even in winter, does not fall below 30°C (86°F) which in slightly cold weather produces an interesting steaming effect. The waters are said to be good for rheumatic, inflammatory and articular diseases though prolonged immersion is not recommended due to their slightly radioactive qualities. The mud at the bottom of the lake is dried and exported for use as mud-packs. From April to October bathers must bob between the pretty red Indian water lilies that bloom on the surface of the lake. Buses to and from Keszthely leave every hour and take about 25 minutes. The bus drops you off at the T-shirt and hot dog stands next to the lake which one may enter either via the strand running around it or the health complex built on top of it which looks, and smells, like a hospital. Indeed the atmosphere of the resort does rather tend toward that of a large and expensive hospital. The crown princes of the Habsburg empire who patronised the resort at the end of the nineteenth century have been largely replaced by their ailing Germanic descendents. For anyone wishing to stay, there is no shortage of accommodation. Most of the large hotels in the vicinity have their own private supply of the medicinal waters.

Additional Information

Places to Visit

Badacsony
Egry Museum
Near station
Open: May to September, 10am-6pm,
daily except Monday.

Borászate Wine Museum
On hillside above town (road leads
there from Kisfaludy Ház restaurant);
open: mid-May to mid-October, 10am-
6pm, daily except Monday.

Balatonszárszó
Attila József Museum
József utca 7
Open: April to October, 10am-6pm,
November to March, 10am-2pm, daily
except Monday.

Balatonfüred
Jókai Memorial House
Jókai utca
Open: April to October, 9am-6pm, daily
except Monday.

Balatonszemes
Postal Museum
Open: June to September, 10am-6pm,
daily except Monday.

Gorsium
Ruins
Open: May to October, 9am-6pm;
November to April, 10am-5pm, closed
Mondays throughout the year.

Herend
Factory Museum
Open: April to October, Tuesday to
Sunday 8.30am-4.30pm. November to
March, Monday to Saturday 8am-4pm.

Balaton Museum
Kossuth Lajos utca
Open: Tuesday to Sunday 10am-6pm.

Keszthely
Festetics Palace
Sopron utca
Open: April to September, 10am-6pm
(7pm June, July, August); October to
March, 9am-4.30pm. Closed Mondays
throughout the year.

Martonvásár
Brunswick Mansion
Park open: daily, 10am-4pm; Beethoven
Museum in Park open: 10am-12noon,
2-4pm, daily except Monday.

Nagyvázsony
Kinizsi Castle
Open: April to October, 9am-dusk.

Örvényes
Preserved watermill
Turn right off main road just before
village sign; open: daily all year,
8am-5pm (4pm winter).

Siófok
Beszédes József Museum
Sió utca 2
Open: daily except Monday, 9am-1pm
and 2-5pm.

Sümeg
Castle
Above town
Open: daily, 8am-dusk.

Saddlery Museum
Vak Bottyán utca
Open: daily 8-11.30am and 2-5pm.

Szántódpuszta
Open: Summer daily 9am-5pm. Winter
Tuesday to Saturday 8am-4.30pm and
Sunday 8am-12noon.

Székesfehérvár
Romkert
Vár körút
Open: April to October, 9am-6pm, daily
except Monday.

King Stephen Museum
Fő utca
Open: 10am-6pm, daily except Monday.

Pharmacy Museum
Fő utca
Open: 10am-6pm, daily except Monday.

Bory Vár
Mariavolgy utca
Open: weekdays, 9am-5pm, weekends,
10am-12noon and 3-5pm.

Tapolca
Varosi Museum
Templom domb 2
Open: 10am-4pm, daily except Monday
and Sunday.

Tihany
Abbey Church
Open: 10am-6pm daily, closed during
services.

Tihany Museum
Next door to Abbey
Open: 10am-6pm, daily except Monday.

Veszprém
Ecclesiastical Museum
Paták tér
Open: May to October, 9am-5pm, daily
except Monday.

Bakony Museum
Megyeház tér
Open: March to October, 10am-6pm,
November to February, 10am-4pm,
closed Tuesdays throughout the year.

Village Museum
Fejes Valley
Open: May to October, daily except
Monday, 10am-6pm.

Zamárdi
Folk Museum
Fő utca 38
Open: 10am-5pm daily except Monday

Tourist Information Centres
Virtually every resort along the Balaton
has its own small tourist and/or accommodation office. Only the main ones in
the region are listed here. Some smaller
offices are only open during the summer.

Agárd
On southern shore of Lake Velence
Gárdonyi utca 18
☎ 22-55-148

Badacsony
Balatontourist
Park utca 10 ☎ 87-31-249

Balatonföldvár
Siótour
Hősök utja 9-11 ☎ 84-40-099

Express Utazasi Iroda
József Attila utca 9 ☎ 84-40-371

Balatonfüred
Balatontourist
Blaha Lujza utca 5 ☎ 86-42-8230

IBUSZ
Petőfi utca 4a ☎ 86-42-251

Balatonkeresztúr
Siótour
Ady Endre utca 26 ☎ 84-76-180

Boglárlelle
Siótour
Dózsa György utca 1 ☎ 84-50-665

Fonyód
IBUSZ
Szent István utca 4 ☎ 85-61-816

Hévíz
Zalatour
Rákóczi utca 8 ☎ 84-11-048

Keszthely
Zalatour
Fő tér 1 ☎ 92-12-560

IBUSZ
Széchenyi utca 1-3 ☎ 92-12-951

Siófok
Siótour
Szabadság tér 6 ☎ 84-10-900

IBUSZ
Fő utca 174

Székesfehérvár
Albatours
Városház tér 6 ☎ 22-12-494

IBUSZ
Ady Endre utca 2 ☎ 22-11-510

Tapolca
Balatontourist
Kisfaludy utca 1 ☎ 87-11-179

Tihany
Balatontourist
Kossuth utca 20 ☎ 86-48-519

Veszprém
Balatontourist
Kossuth Lajos utca 3
☎ 80-13-750

Szabadság tér 21 ☎ 80-26-630

IBUSZ
Kossuth utca 6 ☎ 80-12-425

5

SOUTHERN HUNGARY

South of Budapest the Danube widens and the temperatures grow warmer. This is where Central Europe gradually, but perceptibly, becomes Mediterranean Europe. In Baranya, the southernmost part of the country, it can often get very hot in summer, while winter temperatures are rarely as uncomfortably cold as those of northern Hungary. While Budapest shivers in sub-zero winters, the spring flowers may already be out in the countryside here. Vineyards thrive on the slopes of the Mecsek Hills, an attractive range of low mountains which stretch in a broad arch to the north of the city of Pécs, the region's capital and prime destination for tourists. The Danube is broad and lethargic as it flows south, meandering through flat or rolling countryside dotted with farms surrounded by wheat fields, and past dusty towns where the daily afternoon siesta is taken as seriously as it is in Italy or the south of France. The Danube floods every spring, and the floodwaters have resulted in the formation of lengthy stretches of marshland and brackish lagoons which lie alongside its banks. Some of these have now been designated nature reserves, and are home to many hundreds of species of birds and other forms of wildlife.

The region has been fought over and settled by a variety of peoples. The Romans passed this way, as did the Turks, the early Celts and latterly wandering bands of Germans and Croatians. All have left evidence of their stay in the landscape or cultural life of the region. The last Hungarian town through which the Danube passes as it flows south into Croatia is Mohács, an unremarkable place were it not for the fact that near here, in 1526, one of the most decisive battles in Hungarian history was fought. The Turks routed the Hungarian forces and soon after gained control of Budapest. After the Turks finally left, at the end of the seventeenth century, the area was sparsely populated, and Croatians and Germans settled in the area. The Germans came from Swabia, an area of the Black Forest in south-western Germany around the upper stages of the Danube, and they simply reached this area by travelling down the river by boat. Because of the area's Turkish past, they gave the name 'Swabian Turkey' to the lands they settled, and although most Germans left the area after

World War II, there are still some German speakers around and some of the villages of the region have a distinctly German feel to them. Reflecting the diverse ethnic mix of the area, many villages in the very southern part of the region carry three names — in Hungarian, German and Croatian. Swabians also colonised other parts of Eastern Europe as the Turks left, including areas of Transylvania and what used to be Yugoslavia.

The most obvious place to head for in this region is Pécs, the largest town in southern Hungary where a modern, lively provincial city, nestling under the slopes of the Mecsek Hills, is built around a historical core that shows clear evidence of previous Turkish, Roman and medieval occupation. A substantial section of this chapter is given over to a description of the museums, art galleries and historical sites of this fascinating and diverse city. The first part of the chapter details the relatively few points of interest that lie between Budapest and Pécs. More interesting, particularly for nature lovers, are the excursions into Baranya that can be made from Pécs, which include the Mecsek Hills and towns in another range of hills, the Villányi-hegyseg, which lie along the Croatian border. Transport in this region is fairly easy; details of travelling to Pécs are given under the details for that city, and Pécs acts as a transport hub for the surrounding region. Travelling west-east, as opposed to north-south, is more difficult, on account of the obstacle posed by the Danube. The Danube covers a length of over 250km (155 miles) between Budapest and the Croatian border, but there are only two road bridges across the river along this entire stretch — at Baja and Dunaföldvár. Any road atlas will, however, show the vehicle and passenger ferries that exist at other locations.

Between Budapest And Pécs

Budapest To Szekszárd

Road 6, which heads south from Budapest towards Pécs, passes through some fairly uninspiring countryside, the monotony of which is not particularly relieved by any of the small towns on the way. Sixty kilometres (37 miles) downriver is the town of **Dunaújváros** (which means Danube New Town). Built in the 1950s (and originally named after Stalin), its beleaguered inhabitants live next to a huge steelworks which endlessly spews industrial smoke and effluents into the atmosphere. The industrial plants seem to stretch for miles along the main road through the town. Once considered a showpiece for a newly industrialised society, today Dunaújváros stands as a rather depressing monument to the follies of the Communist era. Like many of Hungary's old industries, the steel plant faces an uncertain future in a new economic era when businesses which lose money or are deemed inefficient are forced to close or rationalise their operations.

Another 40km (25 miles) along road 6, **Páks** is the site of Hungary's first, and so far only, nuclear power station which was designed by Soviet engineers and today supplies nearly 20 per cent of the country's electricity. There are currently discussions going on as to whether a second reactor should be built here, with many objecting to the expense of new development and fearing problems of radioactive pollution from whichever site is chosen to dump the nuclear waste. This aside, the only other thing of note is a Railway Museum situated in the old Páks railway station (dating from 1896) which contains a number of vintage steam trains. There is a well-known fish restaurant (*halászcárda*) situated on the main road which has a well deserved reputation for its *halászlé* (fish soup).

Just south of Páks there is a ferry over to the East Bank of the Danube and the small town of **Kalocsa**, where things brighten up considerably. Kalocsa was originally situated on the banks of the Danube but the river has since changed course and left the town standing a little embarrassingly in the middle of the plain with no particular reason for being there. King Stephen I founded the town in the eleventh century, declaring it to be an episcopal see and building a cathedral. Ravaged by Turkish forces and burned down in 1602, the town was completely rebuilt in the eighteenth century. Today Kalocsa derives its character as one of the main folklore centres of Hungary (folk art souvenirs are widely available throughout the town) and as the centre of 8,645 acres (3,500 hectares) of paprika growing country.

It is a 20 minute walk or short bus ride from the railway station to Szabadság tér, the main square. On the way you will see a sign just past the crossroads directing you to the Folk Art Museum on Tompa utca. Inside you will find pottery, paintings and embroidery for which Kalocsa is justly famed. Many samples are for sale and there is a small café attached.

Szabadság tér itself is dominated by the huge, ochre coloured cathedral in the back of which is situated a treasury house containing some magnificent gold and silver works including a superb bust of King Stephen I. Opposite the cathedral one finds the Archbishop's Palace which is also eighteenth century. The 120,000 volume library is visitable, and in pride of place is a Bible signed by Martin Luther.

Leave the square along István utca, to the left one will find the world's only Paprika Museum. Hungary actually grows 40 per cent of all the world's paprika and a fair proportion of it seems to be hanging in the museum. The atmosphere is consequently a little heavy and the captions are in Hungarian only. However, the exhibits are plain enough and all that is latest and best in paprika is available to buy. Further along István utca to the right is the more conventional Károly Viski Museum featuring traditional folk costumes, coins, photographs, bits of rock and some paintings by Peter Koroly. At number 76 there is a small museum dedicated to the sculptor Nicholas Schöffer whose work is quite jarringly modern for tradition-bound Kalocsa. A 'taster' of his work stands in front of the cathedral.

The twin-towered Baroque cathedral in the paprika and folklore town of Kalocsa

Szekszárd And The Forest of Gemenc

Thirty-four kilometres (21 miles) beyond Páks, the main road south to Pécs just skirts past **Szekszárd**, a pleasant, businesslike but ordinary town in the Sió Hills whose vineyards have produced wine since Roman days, and where a ceramics works produces black pottery which may tempt souvenir hunters who stop over here. Hunyadi utca is the main street, linking the railway and bus station in the south of the town, with the town's major crossroads at its northern end. On this road near the station is a large neo-Renaissance mansion housing the Béri Balogh Museum, with a good if predictable collection of peasant costumes, art work and other reminders of the lives of people who once lived in this region. At the other end of the town, Béla tér contains a statue which commemorates the plague of 1730. On one side of the square is the nineteenth-century County Hall, a white palace with the remains of an eleventh-century monastery and chapel in the courtyard. Beyond the square is Babits utca and the

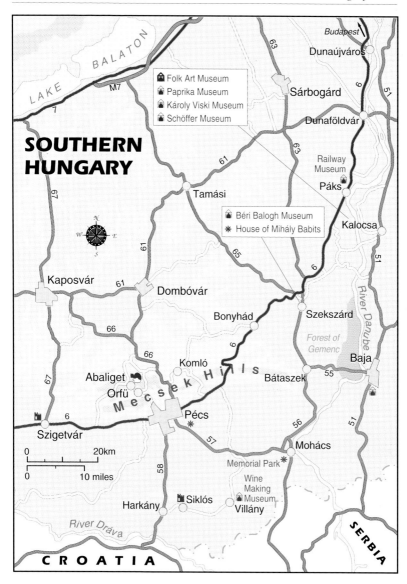

house of Mihály Babits. Babits was the editor of an interwar journal named *Nyugat* (*West*) which trod on the toes of establishment figures and featured the works of some of Hungary's most prominent authors. The collection is recommended only for specialists.

Before the Danube was tamed early in the twentieth century by a system of channels and canals which cut out many meanders the river made, it flooded regularly and the land on either side of its banks was an area of mud flats, reedy swamps and stagnant lagoons of trapped floodwaters. Now only a few of these areas remain, preserved havens for wildlife such as otters, deer, wild boar and birds such as falcon, hawks and eagles. The **Forest of Gemenc** is the most well-known of these areas, covering an area along the west side of the Danube between Gemenc and Baja, to the south-east of Szekszárd. Unfortunately, the place is not easy to visit. A miniature railway (with a couple of trains a day) runs through the forest from Bárányfok, on the road leading east from Szekszárd, to Pörböly, on road 55 west of Baja. At Gemenc there are boat trips which operate along the Danube and its numerous inlets in the forest. The best option is probably to arrange a tour with Tolna Tourist in Szekszárd, who organise excursions and, at the very least, should be able to provide some up-to-date information about how best to see the forest.

At **Baja**, on the East Bank of the Danube south-east of Szekszárd, and a long way off the Budapest-Pécs road, is one of the two bridges that cross the Hungarian stretch of the Danube, south of Budapest. The bridge here is road and railway combined, with rails built into the tarmac of the road section so it is closed when trains cross. Like Szekszárd, the town is pleasant and there is a small folklore festival in mid-July and a cultural festival in late August. Expansive Béke tér is the centre of things, enclosed on three sides by elegant buildings and on the fourth by an arm of the Danube. A bridge takes one across to Petőfi Island where there are boats and other water sports on offer, but the pace is generally fairly low-key. Festivals and other events take place on the island. Other than this, the only other points of interest are the local museum, named after a general Turr István and a Serbian Orthodox church, on Táncsics utca, which may be worth a look in if it is not locked, for its notable collection of icons.

☀ Pécs

Uranium mining towns are rarely popular with tourists, but Pécs (pronounced 'Paitch'), the largest town of southern Hungary, is the exception. Although the huge mine workings and high rise estates that surround Pécs always mean that reminders of the town's modern role — as an industrial community, a home to 150,000 people, and an important regional and educational centre — are never far away, the centre of the town is a world apart from other Hungarian cities of a similar size, with soaring palm trees, Moorish architecture, warm temperatures and elegant plazas lined with open-air cafés all lending a slight Mediterranean air to the place. Pécs is one of the most absorbing provincial cities in Hungary, with some good museums and galleries, and a variety of fine historical monuments, including the best examples of Islamic architecture in the country which, like the olive-skinned inhabitants, is a remnant of many centuries of Turkish occupation. The city is also a good base from which to visit many of the places described in this chapter, with good transport connections to towns to the west and east, as well as to Budapest, which is 198km (123 miles) away by fast road, or just over 3 hours' travelling time by express train from Déli station in the capital. Pécs is small enough to walk round on foot, although public transport may need to be used to travel from the centre to the railway or bus stations, and those without the use of a car will certainly need to use buses to get up to the TV tower above the city.

The Romans knew Pécs as *Sopianae*, and in the third century AD it was made the capital of the Roman province of *Pannonia Valeria*. There are a number of remains in the city dating from this time, most notably the early Christian mausoleum, below the cathedral. Stephen, the first king of the Hungarians, who is credited with bringing Christianity to the country, declared Pécs a bishopric in 1009, and during the Middle Ages the town became an important religious centre. In 1367, the first university in Hungary was founded here (making it the fifth oldest university in Europe). In 1543 the Turkish army gained control of the city, and after the indigenous population was expelled the town became inhabited by Greeks, Turks, Bosnians and Serbs, who built the Moorish and Islamic buildings that can still be seen in Pécs today. In 1686, when the Turks left, Pécs had been devastated by several decades of war, and the town recovered only slowly. The uranium mines were opened in 1954, since when the population has doubled. Now, the city is home to several well-regarded engineering and research institutions, which form the basis of its economy together with the important uranium mining and wine-making activities which are more immediately noticeable to tourists. Today Pécs gives the impression of being a bustling, prosperous place, as the busy western-style department store on Kossuth tér shows, while the presence of a large university gives the place a young, vibrant profile and enhances the strong and diverse cultural life of the city.

A Walk Round Central Pécs

The tour starts in Kossuth tér in the centre of town, which is just south of Széchenyi tér, the main square. Kossuth tér is dominated along one side by the Konzum Áruház department store, and at the east end of the square by the city's **Synagogue**. The Jewish community of Pécs now numbers about 400. A book of remembrance in the Synagogue lists the names of the 3,022 Jews who died during World War II, mainly at Auschwitz. The building itself is large and airy, a structure dating from the 1860s which is decorated with romantic frescoes and motifs.

Bem utca runs north from the square to Széchenyi tér, a broad, elegant, sloping plaza. At the bottom (southern) end of the square are two tourist offices and, outside the eighteenth-century Church of the Good Samaritan, a beautiful drinking water fountain, comprising four ceramic ox heads which were made at the Zsolnay porcelain factory in Pécs in 1912. In the centre of the square is the Holy Trinity Statue (1908), but the square's most dominating feature is the Catholic church at the top (north) end, the exterior of which clearly shows the building's former role as a mosque. The Turks used the stones of a medieval church that stood here to build

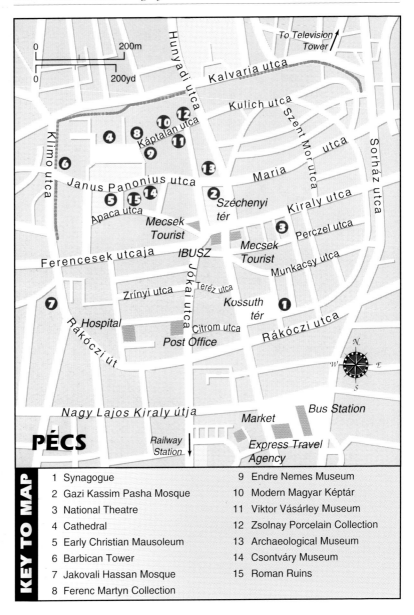

KEY TO MAP		
1	Synagogue	
2	Gazi Kassim Pasha Mosque	
3	National Theatre	
4	Cathedral	
5	Early Christian Mausoleum	
6	Barbican Tower	
7	Jakovali Hassan Mosque	
8	Ferenc Martyn Collection	
9	Endre Nemes Museum	
10	Modern Magyar Képtár	
11	Viktor Vásárley Museum	
12	Zsolnay Porcelain Collection	
13	Archaeological Museum	
14	Csontváry Museum	
15	Roman Ruins	

※ the **Gazi Kassim Pasha Mosque**, and inside it is possible to see the old Turkish windows and two prayer niches facing mecca. After the Turks left, the building once again became a church, and the minaret was pulled down in the eighteenth century. During this century many of the old Islamic features of the church were restored — with a crucifix hung over

A refreshing drink on a hot summer day quenches the thirst of a tourist in Pécs

the prayer niche, to appease any Christians who may fear that re-empha-
sising the building's former role might in some way be unethical. There
are two museums on the square, the Archaeological Museum (behind the
mosque) and a modern art gallery (opposite the statue). For more information on both, see page 153.

The main street of Pécs, Kossuth Lajos utca, runs east from the square,
joining it next to the ox-head fountain. A place to window-shop, wander
or observe the passing scene. The only real sight along here is the gleaming
National Theatre (Pécsi Nemzeti Színház) now open, and occasionally
showing revamped western shows which have been on in London or
elsewhere, after many years of restoration.

Janus Pannonius utca runs west from the mosque, past the Csontváry
Museum (see page 153) to the small park and square below the Roman-
esque-style **Cathedral** (Székesegyház). The oldest parts of the church date
from the eleventh century, but despite some Gothic and Renaissance
decoration and furnishings inside (mainly in the side chapels), which
come from previous churches which stood here, most of the building is
little more than 100 years old. On either side of the main altar there are
steps down to the five-naved, eleventh-century crypt, which provides
cool relief on a hot summer's day. In the fourth century AD the site of Dóm
tér, the square below the cathedral, was a large cemetery, and some steps
leading underground from just below the park take one down to the **Early
Christian Mausoleum** (Ókeresztény Mauzóleum). The site was discovered by accident in 1975, and is believed to be the burial place of a wealthy
inhabitant of the Roman city of Pécs who was interred here around the
year AD350. The site boasts some of the most significant archaeological
finds in Hungary. The wall-paintings, of Adam and Eve, and Daniel in the
Lion's Den, are fairly well preserved, as are the remains of a marble white
sarcophagus. As for the other graves of the once-extensive cemetery, they
are thought to have been gradually submerged by successive layers of
earth, and now lie deep below the square but some other tombs have been
excavated.

Along one side of the square is the Bishop's Palace. Behind this, a
circular **Barbican Tower** on Landler Jenő utca is a reminder of Pécs'
violent past, when thick city walls punctuated by bastions like this one
were maintained to defend the city against attackers. The tower was
heavily restored in the 1960s, with a park filling the moat. Other parts of
the city walls are also visible near here. A short distance south from here,
the **Jakovali Hassan Mosque** on Rákóczi utca, opposite the Pannonia
Hotel, is almost completely hidden by surrounding buildings. Built by the
Turks in the sixteenth century, the mosque then became a hospital chapel
before being reconverted back into a mosque in the 1950s. The excerpts
from the *Koran* and the other floral ornamentation on the inside of the
dome are original. The small interior is adorned with Turkish carpets and
a curved *minbar* (pulpit). Entrance to the mosque is through a small
museum next door (see page 153 for more information).

Museums And Galleries

Along Káptalan utca which runs east from the Cathedral

Ferenc Martyn Collection: temporary exhibitions, held in the house of one of the city's noted nineteenth-century artists.

Endre Nemes Museum: paintings by Endre Nemes (1909-1985) who was born near Pécs; other works of modern art.

Modern Magyar Képtár: a large gallery with a good collection of Hungarian art from the early part of the twentieth century. There is also an exhibition of the paintings of Béla Uitz (1887-1972), a Communist who lived for 50 years in the Soviet Union, whose work was largely influenced by his political beliefs.

Viktor Vásárhely Museum: paintings, sculpture and other sixties 'pop art' displayed in the house where the artist was born (in 1909). It is impossible to be indifferent to an artist like Vásárhely — his work will be absorbing to some, but will leave most cold.

Zsolnay Porcelain Collection: extensive collection of the decorative porcelain produced by the factory founded in Pécs in 1870. The museum is housed in one of the oldest houses in the city which was once the home of Gazi Kassim, who in the sixteenth century was the high priest of the mosque in the main square. In the same building are some abstract, sober works by the sculptor Amerigo Tot (1909-1984).

Other Museums And Galleries

Archaeological Museum: housed in a building behind the mosque in Széchenyi tér; focuses on the prehistory of the Pécs region, and on the history of the Roman city.

There is a **Gallery of Work** by local contemporary artists on Széchenyi tér.

Csontváry Museum: gallery of paintings by the artist Tivadar Csontváry Kosztka (1853-1919), who was virtually unknown in Hungary during his lifetime but after his death was widely noticed abroad; Picasso became a noted admirer. His huge, colourful canvases will surprise and delight many. The painter's favourite subjects are scenes from the Holy Land. Other canvases depict a unique view of nature and landscapes. Csontváry was largely self-taught and lived most of his life working in a pharmacy, dispensing medicines.

Jakovali Hassan Mosque: the small museum attached to the mosque displays items of Turkish armour, utensils, rugs and ceramics.

Other Points Of Interest In Pécs

Visible from all over Pécs is the 176m (577ft) high **television tower** (*tororny*), built on Misina Hill to the north of the city. A glance at a city map will show the number of the city bus that runs all the way up to it, via a small children's zoo (on Beloiannisz utca) and miniature railway halfway up the hill. To get there by car, follow Hunyadi János utca from the

The attractive centre of Pécs, one of the most interesting towns in Hungary

mosque on Szechenyi tér. At the top of the television tower is a restaurant and a very windy viewing gallery, each affording outstanding views over the city and the surrounding countryside. There are many marked walking trails in the hills around the tower, and just below the tower there is a short ski-tow and run. Another viewpoint over the city is the **Tettye Plateau**, where the ruins of a former monastery stand in a park.

On the first Sunday morning of every month, an important fair is held at Pécs, where livestock, crafts and all manner of things produced by people who live in villages near Pécs, are bought and sold. The location of the fair changes on each occasion, but tourist offices in Pécs should have information about where the next one will be held. As well as being an important centre for art lovers, Pécs has a strong and diverse cultural life. The city supports a symphony orchestra, and ballet, theatre and opera companies. Again, more information on current events should be available from tourist offices.

Exploring Southern Hungary: Excursions From Pécs

Pécs is undoubtedly the highlight of southern Hungary, but there are a number of places which can be visited as day-trips from the city. A number of villages in this part of Hungary have three names: one is Hungarian, the other German (dating from the time that Germans settled in the area in the Middle Ages) and the other Serbian or Croatian (reflecting the proximity of the border and previous infiltration of Serbs and Croats into this area).

The **Mecsek Hills** cover an area to the north of Pécs, actually sloping right down to the city centre at one point. Anyone wishing to walk in these hills should buy the tourist map *A Mecsek: Túristatérképe* from bookshops in Pécs). The main centres in the hills are Őrfü and Abaliget, both of which are a short distance away from Pécs (and linked to the city by frequent buses). **Őrfü** has two lakes (the further one is larger and busier), with opportunities for sunbathing, swimming and watersports; both lakes become very busy at weekends. **Abaliget**, close by, has a tiny lake, next to which is the entrance to some fairly ordinary caves. The best option is probably to head over the hills from either of these settlements, back to Pécs. A study of the map will show the number and variety of routes that are available.

Midway between Pécs and Barcs, a major frontier crossing on the border with Croatia, is **Szigetvár**, a town with a proud history. In 1566, the 2,400 soldiers in the castle here withstood for over a month an attack by 100,000 Turks. The siege ended when the Hungarian defenders broke out of the burning castle in a suicidal mission in which nearly all of them were killed, but which also cost the lives of a fifth of the Turkish army and that of its leader, the Sultan Suleyman II. The siege successfully delayed the seventh attempted assault on Vienna by the Turks, and the Magyar leader

Miklós Zrínyi was hailed as a national hero. The castle, now heavily restored and actually fairly ordinary, is at the end of Vár utca. In the centre of the grounds is a small exhibition about the events of 1566, and a small mosque that the victorious Turks erected to celebrate the life of Suleyman, their slain leader. Near the castle, in the square opposite the lion statue, is a Catholic church which, like many in this part of Hungary, still shows evidence of its conversion to a mosque by the Turks.

Twenty-three kilometres (14 miles) due south of Pécs along road 58 is **Harkány**, an enormous spa complex which, like the resorts in the Mecsek Hills, gets very busy with day-trippers from Pécs during fine weekends. There is only one reason to come here, and that is to lounge in the open-air thermal baths and pools, their waters rich in sulphur and other minerals and coming out of the ground at 62 °C (144 °F). Those after slightly more can arrange a wallow in a hot mud bath or a longer course of spa treatment at one of the hotels or medical establishments here, but, unlike some other spas, the architecture is nondescript and the place is not really that pleasant just to walk around. The healing qualities of the spa were initially discovered in the 1820s when a farm labourer, whose job required him to stand in a nearby swamp all day, was cured of rheumatism.

Six kilometres (4 miles) east of Harkány is **Siklós**, one of those hot, dusty towns where it permanently seems to be Sunday afternoon. The town's principal attraction is the castle, whose solid-looking walls and bastions are built on a slight mound above the centre. In it there is a dungeon full of various torture instruments, and various art and history exhibitions. A separate door from the main courtyard takes one into a nice chapel which boasts fragments of medieval wall-paintings and a rose-vaulted ceiling. There is also a hotel and wine-cellar within the castle walls. The castle dates from the first half of the fifteenth century. Most of what is seen now, however, is an impressive restoration of eighteenth-century rebuilding.

East from Pécs along road 57 is **Mohács**, another dusty town on a main road leading south into Croatia. Mohács is on the Danube and is one of Hungary's most important ports. There is no bridge here, but a ferry takes cars across to the East Bank (for the road to Baja see above and Szeged, Chapter 6). The significance of the town rests with it being synonymous with defeat. The loss of the Battle of Mohács in August 1526 marked the start of 143 years of Turkish occupation of Hungary. With a weak government, King Louis II of Hungary only organised an army against the Turkish threat after the Turks, under Suleyman I, had taken Belgrade and were marching north. A disorganised command resulted in a rout of the Hungarian forces by the Turks, and 25,000 Hungarians were killed including Louis and key members of the government, the church and the army, which meant that little effective opposition could be mounted against the invading force as it headed on northwards. By 1541 the Turks were in control of Buda and Hungary became part of the Ottoman Empire.

To commemorate the battle, the annual Busójárás Carnival is held in Mohács every year around the end of February or beginning of March, where townspeople parade through the streets dressed up in striking and frightening masks and costumes, which aim to welcome spring and scare off the Turks. The event is one of the most important and largest events of its kind in Hungary. Although now it is a tourist event to a certain extent, the townspeople take their annual festival seriously, and the roots of the festival are actually much earlier than the battle — hence the number of Serbs who also turn up, because this is in fact a much altered version of a Serbian carnival which dates from pagan days. Having said this, there is little else to see in Mohács itself during the rest of the year. A large church on Széchenyi tér in the centre of town was erected to mark the 400th anniversary of the battle, and nearby on Városház utca there is a museum which features some of the masks worn in the carnival. The site of the battle was to the south of Mohács. It is marked by a weird and sombre memorial park full of grotesque caricatures and carved wooden symbols depicting war and death. The park can be found along the road leading west towards Satorhely, from the Mohács-Udvar main road.

On the road between Siklos and Mohács is **Villány**, which has been the centre of an important wine-making area for over 2,000 years. There is a small Wine Making Museum in the town. On the hillside is a sculpture park where artists who attend the annual summer camp in Villány get to display their work.

Additional Information

Places to Visit
Abaliget
Caves
Entrance by lake in centre of village
Open: 10am-7pm, daily except Monday.
Limited opening times in winter, depending on how many people wish to see the caves at any one time.

Baja
Museum
Roosevelt tér
Open: Tuesday to Sunday 10am-6pm.

Kalocsa
Folk Art Museum
Tompa utca
Open: daily except Monday, 9am-5pm.

Paprika Museum
Szent István utca
Open: May to October, 10am-12noon, 1-5pm, daily except Monday.

Schöffer Museum
Szent István utca 76
Open: 10am-12noon, 2-5pm, daily except Monday.

Kardy Viski Museum
Szent István utca 25
Open: 9am-5pm, daily except Monday.

Mohács
Battlefield and Memorial Park
7km (4 miles) south of Mohács on road immediately east of Satorhely
Open: April to October, daily except Monday, 9am-5pm (opens at 8am June, July, August).

Museum in Mohács
Városház utca
Open: daily except Monday, 10am-6pm.

Páks
Railway Museum
Old Railway Station
Open: 10am-6pm, daily except Monday.

Pécs
Early Christian Mausoleum
Szent István tér
Open: daily except Monday, 10am-6pm.

Jakovali Hassan Mosque and Museum
Rákóczi utca
Open: 10am-1pm, 2-6pm, daily except
Wednesday.

Gazi Kassim Pasha Mosque
Top end of Széchenyi tér
Open: daily until 4pm in summer (until
12noon winter weekdays and 2pm
winter Sundays).

Synagogue
Kossuth tér
Open: May to October, 9am-1pm,
1.30-5pm, daily except Saturday.

Museums and Galleries
All museums and galleries on Káptalan
utca (as listed in text) are open 10am-
6pm, daily except Monday.

Archaeological Museum
Széchenyi tér
Open: 10am-4pm, daily except Monday.

Gallery of Work
Széchenyi tér
Open: 10am-6pm, Saturday; 12noon-
6pm, Monday, Wednesday, Thursday,
Friday; closed Tuesdays.

Csontváry Museum
Janus Pannonius utca
Open: 10am-6pm, daily except Monday.

Siklós
Castle
In centre of town
Open: mid-April to mid-October, daily
except Monday, 9am-8pm; mid-October
to mid-April, daily except Monday,
9am-4pm.

Szekszárd
Béri Balogh Museum
Mártírok tere
Open: daily except Monday, 10am-6pm.

House of Mihály Babits
Babits utca
Open: daily except Monday, 9am-6pm.

Szigetvár
Castle
At the end of Var utca
Grounds open: daily, mosque and

museum in centre of castle grounds,
open: April to October, 8am-6pm, daily
except Monday; November to March,
10am-3 pm, daily except Monday.

Villány
Wine Making Museum
Bem utca 8
Open: 9am-5pm, daily except Monday.

Tourist Information Centres

Dunaújváros
Koranyi Sandor utca 1
☎ 25-16-607

Harkány
Mecsek Tourist
Bajcsy-Zsilinszky utca
☎ 72-80-322

Mohács
Mecsek Tourist
Tolbuhin utca 2
☎ 711-10-961

Páks
IBUSZ
Táncsics utca 2

Pécs
IBUSZ
Széchenyi tér
☎ 72-12-176 or 72-12-163

Mecsek Tourist
Széchenyi tér 9
☎ 72-13-300

Szekszárd
IBUSZ
Széchenyi utca 19
☎ 74-11-947

Tolna Tourist
Széchenyi utca 38
☎ 74-12-144

Szigetvár
Mecsek Tourist
Zrínyi tér 2 (in Hotel Oroszlan)

6
THE GREAT PLAIN

The Great Plain, known in Hungarian as the Alföld or, more omi-
nously, the Puszta — which means 'Wasteland' — is Hungary's
wilderness country. Stretching east and south-east from Budapest, it
covers more than half the territory of Hungary, a vast expanse of flat,
desolate lowlands which continue beyond the country's borders into the
Ukraine, Romania and Serbia. The landscape of the Plain is a monotonous
patchwork of wheat fields, market gardens, orchards and rough grazing
land for sheep and cattle, interspersed with towns and villages which are
often as characterless as the countryside around them. In summer the
Plain often swelters under vast skies, giving rise to mirages forming above
roads and encouraging the locals to head indoors for a Mediterranean-
style siesta, sleeping away the dead heat of the afternoons. In winter a light
smattering of snow lends the area a haunting bleakness. The sheer emp-
tiness of the Plain is one of its most awesome aspects. During the twentieth
century, people have left the countryside in droves to work in the towns,
many of which are now fairly industrialised, with an emphasis on agricultural and food processing industries. They have left behind them depopu-
lated, neglected villages, and now isolated farmsteads, the traditional
tanya, are the most common signs of human habitation on the Plain. The
tanya is typically a collection of small buildings, where whitewashed
stone walls enclose courtyards full of untethered animals of all descriptions. Away from the towns, the *tanya* is often the only sign of life one sees
travelling through mile upon mile of unending nothingness.

The same process of depopulation also took place 400 years ago, when
peasants fled the land during the repeated advances of the Turkish army,
and sheltered in market towns such as Szeged and Debrecen, which began
to grow into important regional centres. After this time, the Turkish army
cut down many of the trees for timber, and large parts of the Puszta turned
into abandoned swamps and steppelands, inhabited only by wolves,
bandits, solitary herdsmen and wandering gypsies. It became a place
where few would venture voluntarily. One of the most infamous aspects
of Plains life was the regular flooding of the River Tisza, which flows

across the Plain in a series of wide loops and meanders. The Tisza rises in the Carpathians, in the Ukraine, and actually runs longer (within Hungary) than the Danube, of which it is a tributary (the confluence of the two rivers is just north of Belgrade). Whenever the Tisza flooded, huge lakes would be left in areas on both sides of the river's banks after the floodwaters had receded. These lakes would become saline and stagnant swamps and marshes, a haven for malarial-carrying mosquitoes and other unwelcome forms of wildlife, and would present farmers in the Plain with considerable problems. In 1879, the city of Szeged was destroyed by surging floodwaters of the River Tisza. It has since been rebuilt, and is now one of the largest cities on the Plain. Since this time, extensive flood control schemes have been implemented which have tamed the waters of the Tisza, so now the power of the river is harnessed to provide irrigation and hydro-electric power for the region. Increasingly, Hungarians who can no longer afford a holiday at Lake Balaton are taking breaks at the small resorts and water-sports centres that are appearing along its length.

With greater control of the River Tisza, the fortunes of the Plain began to change, and people gradually started coming back to the Puszta. During the nineteenth century it became frontier country, and like the American 'Wild West' it was soon populated by cattle ranchers, outlaws and rich prospectors who moved out of the cities in search of a new life. The origins of many of the traditions and folklore so often associated with Hungary are found on the Puszta. This was once the home of shepherds and the *csikós* (horsemen), daring and hardy cowboys who were glamourised by nineteenth-century poets and writers, and which are now presented by tourist brochures as vital symbols of Hungary's rich and colourful past. As usual, they tell only part of the story. It was left to writers such as Gyula Illyés, an English translation of whose book *People of the Puszta* might be found in second-hand bookshops in Budapest, to describe the real lives of most of the people who lived in the Plain. For the most part they were landless peasants who lived in abject poverty, often at the mercy of greedy landowners who established huge estates at the beginning of the twentieth century. In the 1950s, the Communist government tackled this poverty by establishing a system of collective farms along Stalinist lines. Everything was organised and owned by the State. But as the party line softened through the 1970s and 1980s, more private ownership of land and less State involvement allowed the Plains people to begin to supplement their State wages with private income. Progress has eroded poverty, but it is the scourge of traditionalists. The rise of modern, intensive farming now means that the legend of the *csiklós* now only lives on in the horse shows and elaborate festivals which are staged mainly for the benefit of foreign visitors. The crack of the traditional horseman's whip no longer breaks the deadening silence of the Plain. The sounds one is most likely to hear nowadays are those made by modern agricultural machinery, or by the steady stream of traffic which rumbles along the region's main highways which form some of the most important links between central and south-eastern Europe.

By turns eerie, dull, and forbidding, the Plain's sheer size and the distance between the comparatively few attractions it has to offer, means that it will not be high up on the itinerary of many travellers, which is a shame, for the surprises one occasionally encounters here can offer insights into Hungarian life that cannot be found in other, more visited parts of the country. Places of interest fall into two main areas: the south-western plain, to the west of the River Tisza, which includes the cities of Kecskemét and Szeged, and the Bugac National Park; and the Eastern Plain, around Debrecen, which is by far the largest city on the Plain. The latter area includes the Hortobágy National Park, where the wildlife and traditional society of the Plains can probably be witnessed to best effect. The areas north and east of Debrecen, near the borders of Romania and the Ukraine, are the poorest and least visited areas of Hungary, while in the south-east of the Plain, Gyula and Békéscsaba are so far off the beaten track that they are likely to be of interest only to adventurous people passing through this area on the way to Romania.

The South-Western Plain: From Budapest To Szeged

Road 5 (and a parallel, though only partially-built, motorway) run south-east from Budapest across the Plain to **Kecskemét**, 85km (53 miles) from the capital. Frequent bus and train services from Budapest take about 1½ hours to reach the town (most trains use Nyugati station in the capital, and continue on from Kecskemét to Szeged). Kecskemét is a large provincial city with a population of about 100,000, but the centre is reasonably compact, with the leafy main square, Szabadság tér, and the adjoining (and equally leafy) Kossuth tér, in the heart of things. A long, tree-lined avenue, Rákóczi utca, links Szabadság tér with the Katona József park in the north-eastern part of the town, on one side of which is the railway station (the bus station is nearby).

Kecskemét is one of the most pleasant towns on the Great Plain, with a couple of good hotels, some fine churches and a nice blend of architecture and greenery in the area surrounding the main square. The word *kecske* in Hungarian means 'goat', and the name of the town may go back to a thirteenth-century bishop who is said to have offered a goat to any convert to Christianity. Nowadays the town is famous for its fruit, rather than its animal products. It stands in the centre of Hungary's largest region of fruit orchards, which produce a variety of crops, the most famous of which are apricots. These are turned into *barackpálinka*, a very potent apricot brandy for which the town is famous. The town also has a strong cultural history, the composer Zoltán Kodály was born here (in 1882), and it is still a busy venue for theatre, opera and concert goers. The Zoltán Kodály Institute of Music Teaching in the town honours the composer, who with Bartók is

considered one of the founders of modern Hungarian music. Kodály
incorporated many Hungarian folk tunes into his compositions. He was
also a great teacher, and the 'Kodály Method' of music teaching — used
in the institute and in many other colleges all over the world — encour-
ages an active involvement in the process of learning music, and empha-
sises singing as the most important musical skill that students must learn.

Rákóczi utca joins Szabadság tér by two striking buildings. On one side
is the Technika Háza, a white building topped by an onion dome, whose
neat crenellations and mini-turrets form the heavily-restored but pleasing
façade of the town's old synagogue. It was built in the 1860s, although the
original dome fell off during an earthquake in 1911 resulting in the
construction of the striking Persian dome that now sits on top of the
Moorish octagonal tower. The synagogue was wrecked by the Nazis in
1944 and underwent extensive renovation in the late 1980s. The building
now serves as a congress hall and exhibition area — most temporary
exhibitions will be open to the public. On the other side of the road, the
Ornamental Palace (Cifrapalota) is adorned with multi-coloured ceramic
tiles, classic Hungarian art-nouveau, and the ideal building for hosting

The heavily embellished town hall at Kecskemét

An open-air market in Kecskemét

occasional art exhibitions. The other striking building on the square is the New College, housing a Protestant Museum, school, art collections, and a library.

Both Szabadság tér and the neighbouring Kossuth tér have pleasant gardens, with flower beds, ornamental trees and pathways. The most striking building on Kossuth tér is the town hall (Városháza), a deliberately ornate affair built in the 1890s (a time of rising Nationalism) which mixes folk designs and Gothic and Turkish motifs into what the architect, Ödön Lechner, considered to be a uniquely Hungarian style of architecture. Inside the building, the Ceremonial Hall is adorned with rich, patriotic murals. A carillion in the town hall chimes every hour, on the hour, playing tunes by Kodály, Mozart and others and entertaining people in the pleasant square in front of the building.

There are a number of churches in or near the square. The Baroque Old Church (Öregtemplom) is to the right of the town hall. It dates from the last quarter of the eighteenth century. On the other side of the square, opposite the eastern corner of the town hall is the town's oldest church. In medieval days it was used by Calvinists and Catholics, but since the seventeenth century it has been in the hands of the Franciscans. The Calvinist church nearby, dates from the 1790s.

Just in front of the town hall is the József Katona Memorial, in the form of a block of stone split in two. The Hungarian inscription reads 'One of Kecskemét's greatest sons broke his heart here'; it was on this spot that the dramatist József Katona (1791-1830) died of a heart attack. His most famous play was called *Bánk Bán* (1814) which was largely ignored during his lifetime but is now considered one of the most important works in Hungarian drama. Although the play is about a medieval conspiracy and rebellion, its strong Nationalist flavour has made it popular with Hungarian theatre companies for over 100 years. A little to the east of the town hall (to the left, as you face it) is the town's theatre, with an ornate neo-Baroque façade. The theatre is named after József Katona, and stands on a square which is also named after the playwright.

A short way beyond the town hall, on the corner of Gáspár András utca and Hosszú utca, is a worthwhile Toy Museum (Szórakaténusz Játékmúzeum). Exhibitions cover the history of toy manufacture and design. Visiting children are usually allowed to play with some of the toys on display. Very close by is an eighteenth-century town house which is now the location for an exhibition of twentieth-century Hungarian art (Naïv Művészek Múzeuma). In the other direction, the Bozsó Collection (Bozsó Gyűjtemény) can be found at Klapka utca 34 (this street leads off Rákóczi utca behind the Ornamental Palace). Bozsó was a local artist and his pictures and his extensive collection of local glassware, furniture, paintings and sculpture, all exhibited in his old house, are worth the trek up this dusty backstreet. There is also a History Museum in a building in the small park opposite the railway station, which is worth a quick look round while waiting for a train.

Between Kecskemét And Szeged

Road 5 and the main railway line follow each other south from Kecskemét towards Szeged (and the Serbian border), and there are some points of interest either on or a short way off this road, most of which are conveniently approached from Kecskemét, rather than Szeged.

Just a little way out of Kecskemét a small windmill stands by the roadside. It is a characteristic Great Plain windmill, and it dates from 1860 (although it has been moved twice). Further on, **Kiskunfélegyháza** boasts an ornate art-nouveau town hall, which forms a cheerful centrepiece to an unremarkable town. There is also a museum, at Vöröshadsereg 9. The building was a prison for over 150 years, and now part of the museum serves as a history of Hungarian prisons from the Middle Ages to the twentieth century. The displays relating to medieval torture are fairly gruesome. Some of the handicrafts and musical instruments made by prisoners are also on display.

However, most people in the region head for the **Kiskunság National Park** (Kiskunsági Nemzeti Park), which covers a large area of the plain to the south of Kecskemét. Deliberately, a variety of Great Plains landscapes are preserved here, including forest, rough pasture, marsh and dusty scrubland, and the area is a haven for many types of birds and animals, rare species as well as the traditional *puszta* fauna which include hardy breeds of sheep, horses and cattle. Specialist tours and information relating to the National Park are available from Bugac Tours in Kecskemét (Szabadság tér 1a), and it is advisable to contact them before setting off, if only to obtain the times of the horse shows and other spectacles that are arranged in the park — which are the main reasons for visiting it. The main entrance to the park is 3km (2 miles) south-west of the village of **Bugac**. In the village itself there are restaurants, rooms to let and a hotel. A narrow gauge railway (there are only two trains a day) links Bugac with Kecskemét (the station in Kecskemét is in the south-western part of the town, beside the road leading out to Kecel and Baja). Horse-drawn carriages regularly link Bugac station and village with the entrance to the park. At the entrance there is an information centre, a small Shepherd's Museum (Pásztormúzeum) with displays relating to the people and wild- life of the region, and a tourist bar and restaurant. Beyond it, along a dusty track, are the stables and some animal enclosures, where the horse shows take place and where some of the animals can be observed at close quarters. Apart from these, however, it is difficult to get close to *puszta* wildlife without going on a pre-arranged tour.

Half way between Kiskunfélegyháza and Szeged, a turning off the main road at Kistelek leads to **Ópusztaszer** and the Ópusztaszen Nemzeti Történeti Emlékpark, a memorial site which marks the spot where, in AD896, tribal chieftains showed their desire for a unified Hungarian State by allowing their blood to symbolically collect and blend in a wooden bowl. The event is often described as the meeting of Hungary's first diet (parliament), and celebrations are held here every 20 August (Hungary's

Horse-drawn transport in the Kiskunság National Park, near Kecskemét

National Day) to commemorate the event. The monument here was erected in 1896, the millennial year of the State the chieftains founded. *Cyclorama*, a huge canvas painted by Árpád Feszty, which depicts the ninth-century chieftain Árpád leading the Magyars into the Munkács Valley, and which was created for the 1896 celebrations, is on exhibition here. The excavated remains of a thirteenth-century church and monastery can also be seen on this site.

❋ Szeged

Szeged has a sophistication and liveliness that belies its position near the Serbian and Romanian borders. It is a pleasant and prosperous town with a consumer-friendly pedestrianised centre, an active cultural scene and an uncommonly (for provincial Hungary) vibrant night-life. This is due primarily to the presence of two universities here, the students of which played an instrumental role in the uprising of 1956. Further back in time, archaeological evidence suggests the area to have been inhabited as far back as the eighth century BC. In medieval times Szeged became a prosperous trading centre, principally for the unloading and distribution of Transylvanian salt. The town was razed to the ground by Mongol forces in 1241 and occupied by the Turks from 1543 to 1686. However, the most significant damage sustained by the town in modern times was in March

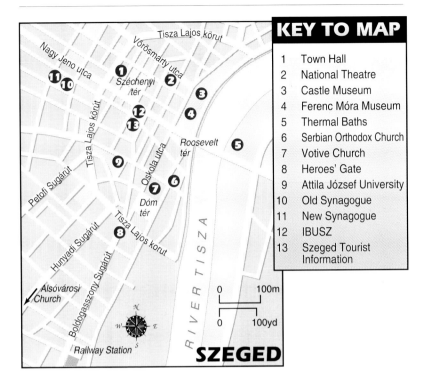

KEY TO MAP

1	Town Hall
2	National Theatre
3	Castle Museum
4	Ferenc Móra Museum
5	Thermal Baths
6	Serbian Orthodox Church
7	Votive Church
8	Heroes' Gate
9	Attila József University
10	Old Synagogue
11	New Synagogue
12	IBUSZ
13	Szeged Tourist Information

SZEGED

1879 when the River Tisza flooded the city and destroyed an estimated 6,000 buildings. This resulted in the centre of town being raised to a safer height and being completely redesigned. Today's city plan, with its broad avenues and grand sweeping boulevards, bears a marked similarity to that of Budapest. In recognition of the international aid received during reconstruction, stretches of the Grand Boulevard were named after cities that had made contributions. As with most of Hungary's urban centres, the post war period saw the construction of vast residential estates and the introduction of ugly industrial works. However, these are largely located in the Újszeged district of town over the river and away from the town's main attractions.

Begin your tour in the main town square, **Széchenyi tér**, which, with its trees, fountains, flower-beds and statues, is to all intents and purposes a mini-park. The neo-Baroque **town hall** stands at number 10. It dates originally from 1799 but was substantially rebuilt in 1883 after the Great Flood. Poet Mihály Babits (1885-1941) described it as 'like a lace-covered young woman dancing in the moonlight'. The two fountains in the square are entitled *The Blessing and The Angry* (Az Áldáhozó és a Romboló) and are allegories of the Tisza river (originally of Lake Balaton from where they were removed in 1934). Hungarians immortalised in the park include Ferenc Deák, Hungarian politician responsible for the 1867 Compromise, and Lajos Tisza, Minister of Labour and Transport responsible for the reconstruction of the city after the Great Flood.

Moving down Vörösmarty utca towards the Tisza one passes the **National Theatre (Nemzeti Színház)**, dating from 1883, before reaching the ruins of a thirteenth-century castle in the park by the river. After the Turkish withdrawal and up to the eighteenth century the castle was actually used as a prison but it was largely dismantled in 1882 during the reconstruction of the city. Presently it houses a small exhibition of local history and stonework. Also in the park is the **Ferenc Móra Museum** housed in a building known as the Palace of Education **(Közművel ődesi palota)**. Socrates and Homer welcome you through the entrance while inside is an enjoyable assortment of paintings, local history and archaeology. From here one could cross over the Tisza and take the waters at the thermal baths and swimming pool complex or join the sunbathing sensualists on the beach area at the riverside. If this does not appeal, take a walk down Oskola utca to Dóm tér which is dominated by the huge brown brick **Votive Church** (Fogadalmi templom), completed in 1930 and built with the intention of staving off any more natural disasters from the town. The façade contains representations of the twelve Apostles and the Virgin. The inside is richly decorated and boasts an enormous 10,180 pipe organ. In front of the church stands the Tower of Demetrius (Dömötörtorony) which stubbornly refused to be moved (even by dynamite) during the building of the church and so was left. The foundations date from the eleventh century. The octagonal tower was added in the thirteenth century.

Unfortunately, one's view of the church is rather spoiled by the 6,000 seat theatre situated in the square all year round and used for the Summer Theatre Festival. The festival began life in 1933, broke off during World War II and was revived in 1959. Various concerts, operas, plays and musicals are performed here during July and August. Details are available from the information office on Klauzál tér. On the north-eastern corner of Dóm tér is an eighteenth-century Serbian Orthodox church worth a peek inside for its Baroque iconostasis. The other sides of the square are flanked by university buildings and a theological academy. The busts of famous Hungarians adorn the perimeter of the square. Leave Dóm tér by its southern exit which leads into Aradi Vértanúk tere with its impressive equestrian statue of Ferenc Rákóczi, rebel leader during the 1703-11 War of Independence. Note also Heroes Gate (Hősök Kapuja), flanked by two imposing militaristic figures, built in 1936 in honour of the recapture of the country from Romanian hands in 1919.

From here walk northwards to Dugonics tér upon which is situated the **Attila József University** named after its most famous pupil which it expelled in 1924 for writing the poem *With A Pure Heart*. József was born of quite desperately poor working class parentage (his mother actually died of starvation) in the Budapest district of Ferencváros in 1905. After his dismissal from university he headed for Vienna and then Paris he came into contact with various radical left wing circles. On his return to

Budapest in 1930 he joined the Communist party (then an illegal organisation) but was expelled 3 years later by the emigré party leadership in Moscow upon his refusal to accept unchallengingly the orthodoxies of the party. His emotionally charged verse, deeply set in his own urban working class background, conveys a very powerful plea for radical social change. Disliked by his literary contemporaries and in conflict with his fiancée, József committed suicide underneath a train by Lake Balaton in 1937. A statue of József stands in front of the building.

From here it is a short walk north-west to the Jewish Quarter. The **Old Synagogue** on Hajinóczy utca dates from 1843 and has affixed to it a plaque showing the water level during the Great Flood. Just around the corner on Jósika utca is the enormous **New Synagogue** built in 1903 and boasting a huge 48m (157ft) high dome and beautiful stained glass windows depicting scenes from Jewish history and custom. History records the presence of a Jewish community in Szeged several hundred years before they were forced to either leave the town or consent to baptism during the Turkish occupation. Once the Turks had been removed from the town the Jews were allowed back and nearly 2,000 of them died during World War II.

Further out from the town centre on the lush Mátyás tér is the former Franciscan **Alsóvárosi Church**, built in 1498 and one of the most important Gothic monuments in Hungary. The Baroque tower and furnishings were added in the late eighteenth century and include a copy of the famous *Black Madonna of Czestochowa* (in Poland) said to be a portrait from life by St Luke (although it is actually not old enough). For anyone not keen on the walk, the church may be passed on a 45 minute city bus tour which departs hourly from outside Szeged Tourist on Klausál tér. Finally, 3km (2 miles) to the east of the centre of town, accessible by bus number 73, is **Tápé**, a local fishing community on the banks of the Tisza which has fought hard to maintain its customs and identity. There are several fine restaurants here and a private Ethnological Collection at number 4 Vártó utca. Also of interest is a church dating from the thirteenth century but substantially enlarged in 1939 with fourteenth-century frescoes on display in its Gothic sanctuary.

Roads from Szeged lead south, into Serbia, and east, into Romania. Thirty kilometres (19 miles) east of Szeged, the road to Arad passes through a dusty town called **Makó**, famous for the onions grown nearby and for some unremarkable thermal baths. Although Makó is a spa, there are no particular points of architectural interest here — save perhaps the neo-Classical town hall which dates from the 1830s, and a couple of churches but certainly nothing to make the town anything more than a place for a brief halt.

Szeged's most monumental landmark, the Votive Church

The South-Eastern Plain

Modest today in its attractions, **Békéscsaba** was, back in medieval times, ☀ an important settlement. The town suffered badly under the Turkish occupation and did not recover until the eighteenth century when it was revived by Slovak settlers. From the adjoining rail and bus stations it is a good 20 minute walk to the pedestrianised town centre so you may prefer to use bus 1, 2 or 7 instead. Most deserving of your attention once there is the Munkácsy Museum on Széchenyi utca near to the Körös canal. One room is devoted to the painter, an interesting selection of photographs, sketches and unfinished works cleverly set out to illustrate his working technique, the rest of the museum is devoted to a large display of posters

The façade of the Town Museum at Szeged

and a collection of stuffed animals. About 5 minutes walk from the museum at number 21 Garay utca is the Slovak Tájház with a display of traditional Slovák costumes. Further out, some 3km (2 miles) from the centre of the town, is an old corn mill, in operation until 1953, which has been turned into a museum. Local buses numbers 4 and 9 take you some distance towards it.

Fifteen kilometres (9 miles) south-east of Békéscsaba, along road 44 and very close to the Romanian border, is the settlement of **Gyula**, thought to have been named after the grandson of one of the seven original Magyar tribal chiefs. It is a relaxed small town with a permanent Sunday afternoon feel to it whose central point of interest is a stocky brick fortress which is situated in a small park near the town centre. The fortress originally dates from the end of the fourteenth century. It fell to the Turks in 1566 and was demolished after the War of Independence on orders from Vienna. It has however been restored and today its 3m (10ft) thick walls conceal a fully operational theatre in which plays are performed during the summer months. There is also a museum within the fortress and it is possible to climb the lookout tower. Beside the fortress is a sixteenth-century round tower, once used for storing gunpowder, now in use as a café. Opposite this is a small boating lake and a thermal pool complex which accounts for most of the visitors to the town. The waters are said to be good for rheumatism and arthritis but are only open during the summer. In the centre of the town, on Dürer utca, is a museum dedicated to the composer Ferenc Erkel, founder of the Hungarian National Opera and composer of the National Anthem, who was born in Gyula (at number 7 Apor Vilmos tér). The museum also contains a selection of paintings by Albrecht Dürer whose ancestors lived in Gyula. Finally, on Béké sugárút towards the railway station, is the György Kohán Museum featuring large and bold paintings of people and horses.

The Eastern Plain

Budapest To Debrecen

The distance by road from Budapest to Debrecen, unofficially the 'capital' of the Plain, is 226km (140 miles), along road 4 via Cegléd, Szolnok, Kisújszállás and Puspokladny. The main railway line between the two cities (most trains use Nyugati Station in the capital) follows the same route. There are usually about a dozen trains a day, most of which take 2½ to 3 hours. The following is a brief survey of some of the points of interest along the route taken by the road and railway line.

Seventy kilometres (43 miles) south-east of Budapest, road and railway line pass through **Cegléd** (most trains on the Budapest-Kecskemét-Szeged line also stop here). The town is an important railway junction, but has little else to recommend it although it is an important town, histori-

cally. A museum on Rákóczi utca commemorates the Peasants Uprising
of 1514, and also the uprising against the Habsburgs led by Lajos Kossuth,
one of Hungary's national heroes, in 1849. In 1877 over a hundred citizens
of Cegléd travelled to Turin, where Kossuth was living in exile, to ask him
to return to Cegléd as their member of parliament — which he did, to
immense popular acclaim. In 1894 many hundreds of Cegléd's citizens
walked from the town to Budapest to attend Kossuth's funeral. On
Szabadság tér is a huge Calvinist church, built in the 1830s and capable of
holding 2,000 people. Thirty-one kilometres (19 miles) further on, road
and railway cross the River Tisza at **Szolnok**, which has been an important bridging post since medieval times, when a castle (long since vanished) was established here. Once, timber and other goods from the
Carpathians were offloaded here, and Szolnok became the most important port and trade centre on the Tisza. Szolnok was destroyed in World
War II and today the town is grimly modern — certainly no place to arrive
on a gloomy Monday. Its few redeeming features are a Franciscan church
on Koltói utca, a regional and historical museum on the town's main
square, Kossuth Lajos tér, and, on the east bank of the Tisza, a hotel,
campsite and medical facilities associated with the town's thermal baths.

Nearer Debrecen, the road passes through **Karcag**, another important
railway junction and the centre of a large rice-producing area (there is a
huge rice-hulling mill in the town). Again, this town is not the most
enticing place to stop, although the Folk Art Museum on Horvath utca
may be worth a brief look. This area is well-known for its folk art,
particularly ceramics, and this and other museums in the town provide an
opportunity to see it. Twelve kilometres (7 miles) north of the town, along
the road to Tiszafüred, there is a thermal bath at **Berekfürdő**. There are
much nicer thermal baths, however, at **Hajdúszoboszló**, 22km (14 miles)
before the road and railway reach Debrecen (and therefore a popular
excursion from the city). Hajdúszoboszló is Hungary's largest spa and an
all-year resort. The 38°C (100°F) steaming brown waters have a salt con-
tent five times higher than the sea and are said to be good for arthritis and
muscular pain. They were discovered accidentally in 1925 during
drillings for oil and natural gas and within a year were being exploited for
commercial gain. The actual complex houses a large rowing lake, tennis
courts, swimming pools and even a cinema as well as the sixteen separate
indoor and outdoor thermal pools. In the immediate vicinity of the complex is a positive plethora of solariums, health clinics and hotels to cater
for the nearly one and a half million visitors the town absorbs every year.
Anyone wishing to escape all this may pay a visit to the Bocskai Museum
at number 12 Bocskai utca, named after a local Transylvanian prince who
led his people to victory over the Habsburgs in 1604. It contains various
military relics and an exhibition connected with the history of the baths.
Nearby, on Debreceni utca, is a present day Calvinist church (originally
founded in the fifteenth century) which has 20m (66ft) of a fifteenth-
century fortress wall hiding shyly behind it.

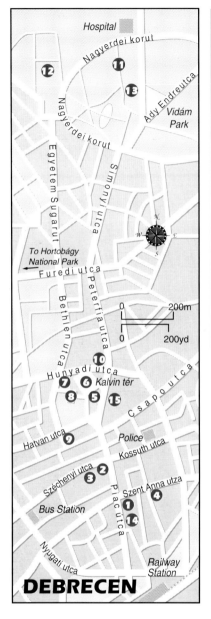

KEY TO MAP

1 Old County Hall

2 Small Church (Calvinist Kistemplom)

3 Diószegi House

4 St Anna Church

5 Great Church

6 Calvinist College

7 Cultural Centre

8 Déri Museum

9 Orthodox Synagogue

10 Medgyessy Museum

11 Nagyerdei Park

12 Kossuth Lajos University

13 Thermal Baths

14 Cooptourist

15 Hajdutourist

Debrecen ☼

With a population of some 217,000 the country's third largest city stands in the heart of protestant Hungary and as such states its case as a tourist destination simply and with dignity. Debrecen has a uniquely austere, no-nonsense atmosphere to it, the product of its long association with trade and the no-frills doctrines of the Calvinist religion. The city originally came into being through the fusion of three villages during the thirteenth century. After acquiring municipal status at the end of the fourteenth century it rapidly developed as an important market town and by the end of the fifteenth century it was playing host to eight annual trade fairs attracting Europe-wide interest. Visitors arriving by train are greeted by depictions of the famous old markets in the ticket hall. As a centre of trade and learning, Debrecen was particularly susceptible to the migrating ideas of the protestant, and specifically Calvinist, movement and in 1552 the local Catholic church was closed and it was decreed that only Calvinists could settle in the city. Three years later the Turks took hold of the city but, because it lay on the very border with the lands held by the Habsburgs and the independent princes, Debrecen managed to remain largely independent, though at a heavy cost in taxation. The independent spirit and civic pride engendered in this period managed to survive a heavy battering by Imperial troops during the War of Independence and in the early part of 1849 the rebel Kossuth government set up headquarters here after Budapest had been lost. In October 1944 Debrecen played host to the first post-liberation National Government.

Piac utca is the Debrecen's main street, running from the railway station (the bus station is a little to the west of the town centre along Nyugati utca) to the Calvinist Great Church after which it changes its name a couple of times before finally coming to rest at the entrance to the Nagyerdei Park. Tram number 1 runs the whole length and loops back again. Walking up Piac utca from the direction of the station the first attraction is the art-

The Calvinist Great Church at Debrecen, the largest town in eastern Hungary

nouveau **Old County Hall** (Régi megyeháza) at number 54. Constructed in 1912, the façade depicts armed *hajdús* while the stained glass windows in the main hall depict the seven Magyar tribal chiefs. The *hajdús* were the army of Istvan Bocskai. After victory in 1604 the prince provided them with land and they settled in communities prefixing *hajdú* to the name such as Hajdúszoboszló. Most were formerly bandits, runaway serfs and homeless peasants. Standing tall behind the Old County Hall down Szent Anna utca is **St Anna Church** which dates from the mid-eighteenth century. It is unusual insofar that it is a Catholic church and was financed by Cardinal Imre Csáky whose coat of arms may be seen above the portal.

Continuing up Piac utca, across the road stands the **Small Church** (Calvinist Kistemplom) sometimes referred to as the Csonka (mutilated) Templom on account of an onion shaped dome which was blown off during a violent storm in 1909. From here take a small detour left down Széchenyi utca. At number 6 is the **Diószegi House**, said to be the oldest house in Debrecen, dating from the end of the seventeenth century. Swedish King Charles XII stayed here on his way home from Turkey in 1714. Back along Piac utca, the building with the gilded art nouveau doorway at number 22 (across Széchenyi utca from the *kistemplom*) originally belonged to the First Savings Bank of Debrecen. On the other side of Piac utca, at number 20, is the neo-Classical town hall. Lajos Kossuth stayed in the left wing of this building during the first months of 1849.

Piac utca then widens into Kossuth tér which is dominated by the Calvinist **Great Church** (Nagytemplom). In keeping with the faith that inspired its creation the inside of the building is unadorned. It is an impressive structure nevertheless. It was here on 14 April 1849 that Lajos Kossuth announced the Declaration of Hungarian Independence to packed pews. Kossuth's worn armchair may be viewed next to the communion table. The church was built in neo-Classical style early in the nineteenth century and can hold up to 5,000 people. It also contains the largest bell in Hungary, forged from cannons used during the War of Independence. In the small park area in front of the church are statues of some of the leading figures in the 1848-9 uprising, including Kossuth.

Round the back of the Great Church, on Kálvin tér, is the **Calvinist College** (Református Kollégium) founded in 1538, though the original building was destroyed in the Great Fire of 1802 and the present structure dates from 1816. Today, the building houses a school, a theological college and a hostel as well as a library and two small museums open to the paying public. The college history museum is an engaging and evocative display of photographs and teaching implements together with a wholly reconstructed classroom. Opposite this is a colourful museum dedicated to ecclesiastical art. The library on the second floor boasts a collection of over half a million books, the oldest of which dates from the fifteenth century. Opposite the library is the oratory which in 1849, during the national uprising, housed the rebel parliament. It was the only large meeting hall with heating in the city. Brass plates on the benches show who sat where.

In December 1944 the provisional government met here as the Germans were being driven out of Hungary by the Soviets. A photograph on the back wall records the event.

To the west of the college, on Déri tér, is the **Déri Museum**, undoubtedly one of Hungary's finest. The four statues outside the main entrance by local sculptor Ferenc Medgyessy (1881-1958) won a grand prix at the 1937 Paris exhibition. They are representations of archaeology, art, science and ethnography. Inside the building are impressive Egyptian, Greek and Roman collections, an Oriental exhibition, a collection of medieval armour and coins, medals and paintings to spare. One of the many highlights is a room devoted to Hungary's most famous painter Mihály Munkácsy (1844-1900) which includes the huge *Ecce Homo*. Comfortable seats are provided for lengthy contemplation of this work which toured the world in the 1890s before being bought by wealthy Hungarian businessman Frigyes Déri who founded the museum. On viewing the painting in Dublin in 1898 James Joyce mused: 'It is a mistake to limit drama to the stage; a drama can be painted as well as sung or acted, and *Ecce Homo* is a drama'. Near to the Déri Museum, at number 1 Bethlen Gabor utca, is a **Postal Museum**. A little further out on Pásti utca is a neglected syna- gogue while at number 28 Péterfia utca, for anyone inspired by those figures outside the Déri Museum, there is a museum exhibiting the work of Ferenc Medgyessy.

The next cluster of visitable things is to be found in the **Nagyerdei Park** at the end of Simonyi utca in the northern suburbs. It is a pleasant place to walk in with a small zoo, an amusement park, a boating lake and a thermal baths complex complete with swimming pool and sunbathing area. Beyond the park lies Debrecen's largest building, the **Kossuth Lajos** **University**, and beyond that a botanical garden which is open during the summer only.

Near Debrecen: The Hortobágy National Park

Many people who visit Debrecen also visit the thermal baths at Hajdúszoboszló, but the most popular excursion for visitors to the city is to the **Hortobágy National Park**, where 640sq km (246sq miles) of unique *puszta* landscape is preserved. Road 33, which runs due west from Debrecen towards Tiszafüred, crosses the Hortobágy and goes through the village of Hortobágy itself, the centre of the park as far as visitors are concerned (trains and bus services run between Debrecen and Hortobágy as well; the railway station is right in the centre of the village). In the past, steam train services have operated in summer between Debrecen and Hortobágy. The village is 35km (22 miles) from the centre of Debrecen by road.

The Hortobágy is an eerie landscape of marsh, bog and rough pasture. In some places the soil is good enough for the land to be farmed, but elsewhere the land is left as wasteland — the true *puszta*. The area was once forested and densely populated, but invading Turkish hordes, and the flooding of the Tisza and other rivers, rendered the area poor for human habitation (although people began to return in the nineteenth century, when drainage canals were built across the area which allowed swamps and marshes to be reclaimed). The only hills are those once built for lookout purposes, and ancient burial mounds once constructed by the Cuman tribes who wandered across the Plains as nomadic pastoralists centuries ago. Millions of birds stop here on migration twice a year, in autumn and spring. Many bird varieties can be seen on the Hortobágy, including storks, heron, eagles, buzzards, mallards, osprey, terns, curlews and geese. They can be seen in many areas, but particularly at the Hortobágyi halastó lakes, west of Hortobágy village. Deer and boars live in the woody thickets, while otters and other mammals inhabit the reed beds and marshes surrounding the lakes and along the banks of the rivers. Distinctive *puszta* cattle (grey coloured, with horns) and Racka sheep (with corkscrew horns) can be seen in many areas, though they are no longer looked after by the rough-riding *csiklós* who, during the nineteenth

An ancient type of well, reconstructed on the Hortobágy puszta *near Debrecen*

century, would lead their herds across the area between wells, watering holes and pastureland. The area is very hot and dry in summer, and it is on this part of the Plain that mirages are most visible — mostly in the form of phantom lakes or ponds above dark, dry soil or, frequently, road surfaces. They are caused by the air at the ground surface becoming very hot, which causes light to be refracted and perspective and images to become distorted. Many nineteenth-century travellers were fooled by mirages here, which they often took to be shimmering, misty lakes.

Hortobágy village is a bit of a tourist honeypot, but there is at least an information centre here and other things to see and do. The main road crosses the River Hortobágy via the nine-arched bridge, a low stone bridge built in 1833 which features strongly in literature and paintings associated with the Hortobágy region. Beside it, the Nagycsárda is an inn and restaurant that caters for visitors to the village but which, in former times, was an important wayside halt and stables used by travellers and herdsmen. Behind the *csárda* is an art gallery featuring paintings of the *puszta* and the people and animals who live here. There are also two museums — a National Park Museum, which has exhibits relating to the human and natural life of the Hortobágy, and a Shepherd's Museum, with displays of costumes, carriages, and folk instruments once used by *puszta* herdsmen. There is also an open-air market, selling a variety of tasteful and tasteless souvenirs for visitors, and other facilities such as bicycle hire and even fairground attractions. Hortobágy village may be at the centre of the National Park but is not exactly the place to go to for peace and quiet.

This isolated farm is a typical scene of the Great Plain

✳   At **Máta**, a collection of stables 2km (1 mile) north of Hortobágy village, horse shows and other entertainments are often staged for visitors, where modern-day, state-employed *csiklós* in traditional costumes show off the skills that led to Hungary becoming known as a 'nation of horsemen'. Displays normally include controlled stampedes and bareback riding; things reach a head at the international horse show in Máta (first weekend of July) and the Hortobágy Bridge Fair (19 and 20 August). Horses also are bred and raised at Máta. Along the road west of Hortobágy is a small airfield, from where visitors can take 'safari' flights over the National Park in small propeller-driven aircraft. Arrangements can be made and more information obtained from one of the booths in Hortobágy. Several companies offer these flights.

North of Debrecen: Nyíregyháza and Nyirbator

Forty-five kilometres (28 miles) north of Debrecen along road 4 is the town of **Nyíregyháza**, the major attraction of which lies some 6km (4 miles) north of the town centre at Sostofurdo (meaning 'Salty Lake Bath') which plays host to a leisure complex containing thermal baths, swimming pools and a rowing lake. Across the road from the complex is a Village Museum, similar to those in Szentendre and Szombathely though this one also incorporates a riding school. Sostofurdo is surrounded by some 1,235 acres (500 hectares) of woods, ideal for rambling or picnicking in, and may be reached on local bus number 8 from outside the railway station in Nyiregyhaza. In the town of Nyiregyhaza itself the Andras Josa Museum at number 21 Benczur tér, named after a local archaeologist who was the first director of the museum, has rich archaeological and ethnological collections as well as rooms devoted to two famous sons of the town, painter Gyula Benczur (1844-1922) and writer Gyula Krudy (1878-1933). The centre of the town is dominated by three churches — Catholic, Lutheran and Uniate — which, together with an old synagogue on Sip utca, illustrate the religious diversity of the region.

Thirty-eight kilometres (24 miles) east of Nyiregyhaza is **Nyirbator**. While not much of a destination in its own right, anyone passing through should pay a visit to the town's unusual single nave Gothic Calvinist church. It was built between 1484 and 1488 on the orders of Transylvanian Viovode Istvan Bathori as a family burial church. Bathori's impressive Gothic tomb is on display inside and one of the original pews is on display in the National Museum in Budapest. The church was taken over by the Calvinists at the end of the sixteenth century. The 30m (98ft) high wooden belfry church dates from 1640. Until the late eighteenth century only Catholic churches were allowed to have stone belfries. The local Minorite (formerly Franciscan) church on Karolyi utca was also commissioned by Istvan Bathori in around 1480. It was plundered by the Turks in 1587 and restored in Baroque style in 1717. The richly decorated pulpit and altar were made in Presov, in Slovakia, around that time. Next to the Minorite church is an eighteenth-century former Minorite monastery which houses a museum dedicated to the Bathori dynasty.

North-Eastern Hungary: The Erdőhát

Squeezed up against the Ukrainian border, the Erdőhát is the only part of Hungary to be genuinely untouched by the trappings of the Hungarian tourist industry. Essentially the area consists of a succession of small villages, not especially picturesque — they are for the most part quite modern settlements and the scenery is too flat anyway — though containing certain points of reference (old mills, small medieval village churches and the like) upon which to hang your appreciation of the region. More to the point, the normal rules of sightseeing do not apply in the Erdőhát. The sight is the region itself. The colour and temper of local life that cannot be marked on any tourist map such as women sitting, swathed in black, on shaded roadside benches while their children play amongst the chickens splayed across the road. The people are the friendliest in Hungary. Dwellings range from the expensive and ultra-modern to the low farmhouses, crooked and colourful as a child's drawing, that extend themselves backwards to culminate in a small wooden barn and allotment. Listed below are some of the more obvious points of interest but the visitors to the region who take the most away with them will be those prepared to look for the 'sights' of the region themselves.

The main bases for exploring the region are Mátészalka, Fehérgyarmat and Vásárosnamény, each of little interest in their own right though **Mátészalka** possesses Catholic and Orthodox churches situated next to a thermal baths complex and a discarded synagogue on the road to the shopping centre. **Fehérgyarmat** has an attractive small wooden-spired church and **Vásárosnamény** contains a small museum dedicated to local embroidery. A little out of the way, **Vaja** (14km/9 miles north-west of Mátészalka) has a fifteenth-century Calvinist church (reconstructed in 1821) and a sixteenth-century fortified manor with museum that once belonged to Ádám Vaj, one of Rákóczi's supporters during the fight for independence against the Habsburgs.

Csenger, on the Romanian border, is one of the larger settlements and is connected by bus and train to Mátészalka and by bus to Fehérgyarmat. It boasts a lovely fourteenth-century red and black brick Calvinist church beautifully decorated with folk Baroque paintings. **Csengersima**, 8km (5 miles) north-east of Csenger, features a small Romanesque Calvinist church. The bus from Csengersima to Fehérgyarmat passes through **Jánkmajtis**, where there is a Catholic church originally built in Gothic style though substantially redesigned in the nineteenth century and a sixteenth-century Baroque manor house, but not through Gyugye which merits a stop on the basis of its tiny, beautifully decorated church. **Szatmárcseke** contains some unusual oaken grave markers and the mausoleum of the local-born poet Ferenc Kölcsey (1790-1838) who wrote the words of the Hungarian National Anthem. While over the River Tisza **Tarpa** (buses run from Fehérgyarmat and Vásárosnamény) boasts a large conical dry mill, entrance to which may be gained by reference to the address pinned to the door. **Csaroda** contains a rather self-consciously tall

Romanesque church dating from 1250 which was restored in 1971. Frescoes from the fourteenth century adorn the sanctuary, while the paintings on the ceiling of the nave are late eighteenth century. Further on, more small white wooden-spired churches may be found tucked cosily away in **Marokpapi**, **Vámosatya** (dating from the thirteenth century) and **Tákos**, where there is a folk Renaissance ceiling painting by Ferenc Asztalos dating from 1766.

Additional Information

Places To Visit

Békéscsaba
Corn Museum
3km (2 miles) north from centre of town
Open: 10am-6pm, except Monday and Saturday.

Munkácsy Museum
Széchenyi utca
Open: 10am-6pm, except Monday and Saturday.

Slovák Tájház
Garay utca 21
Open: 10am-12noon, 2-6pm, except Monday and Saturday.

Cegléd
Kossuth Museum
Rákóczi út
Open: 10am-6pm, except Monday and Saturday.

Debrecen
Calvinist College
Kálvin tér
Open: Tuesday to Saturday, 9am-5pm, Sunday, 9am-1pm.

Déri Museum
Déri tér
Open: April to October, 10am-6pm, November to March, 10am-4pm, except Monday and Saturday.

Great Church
Kossuth tér
Open: Monday to Friday 9am-12noon, 2-4pm, Saturday 9am-12noon, Sunday 11am-4pm.

Medgyessy Museum
Péterfia utca
Open: April to October, 10am-6pm, November to March, 10am-4pm, except Monday.

Postal Museum
Bethlen Gabor utca 1
Open: 2-4pm, Wednesday, Saturday and Sunday only.

Gyula
Erkel Museum
Dürer utca
Open: 9am-5pm, except Monday and Saturday.

Fortress
Open: 10am-5pm, except Monday and Saturday.

György Kohán Museum
Béké sugárút
Open: 9am-5pm, except Monday and Saturday.

Hajdúszoboszló
Bocskai Museum
Bocskai utca 12
Open: summer, 9am-1pm, 3-7pm, winter, 9am-1pm, 2-6pm, except Monday and Saturday.

Hortobágy National Park
Art Gallery
Open: April to September, 9am-5pm, October to March, 9.30am-4pm, except Monday and Saturday.

National Park Museum
Open: May to October, 9am-6pm daily.

Shepherd's Museum
Open: 9am-5pm, except Monday and Saturday.

Karcag
Folk Art Museum
Kálvin tér 4
Open: 10am-12noon, 2-6pm, except Monday and Saturday.

Kecskemét
Ornamental Palace
Szabadság tér
Open: 11am-6pm, except Monday and
Saturday.

Bozsó Collection
Klapka utca 34
Open: 10am-6pm, Friday to Sunday only.

History Museum
In the park opposite railway station
Open: 10am-6pm, except Monday and
Saturday.

Naïve Art Museum
Gáspár András utca 11
Open: 10am-6pm, except Monday and
Saturday.

New College
Szabadság tér
Open: 10am-6pm, except Monday and
Saturday.

Toy Museum
Gáspár András utca
Open: 10am-6pm, except Monday and
Saturday.

Kiskunfélegyháza
Kiskun Museum
Vöröshadsereg 9
Open: 10am-6pm, except Monday and
Saturday.

Kiskunság National Park
Open: 10am-5pm, daily May to October.

Pásztormúzeum
Open: 10am-5pm, daily May to October.

Nyírbátor
Báthori Museum
Károlyi utca
Open: 10am-6pm, except Monday and
Saturday.

Nyíregyháza
András Jósa Museum
Benczur tér 21
Open: 9.30am-5.30pm, except Monday
and Saturday.

Sóstófürdő Village Museum
Open: April to October, 9am-4pm
Tuesday to Friday, 9am-3pm Saturday
and Sunday.

Szeged
Castle Museum
In the park behind the Ferenc Móra
    Museum
Open: 10am - 6pm, except Monday and
Saturday.

Ferenc Móra Museum
Roosevelt tér
Open: 10am-6pm, except Monday and
Saturday.

New Synagogue
Gutenberg utca
Open: 9am-12noon, 2-5pm, except
Saturday.

Szolnok
History Museum
Kossuth Lajos tér 4
Open: 10am-6pm, except Monday and
Saturday.

Tápé
Ethnological Collection
Vártó utca 4
Open: 3-6pm, except Monday and
Saturday.

Vaja
Fortified Manor
Open: April to October, 9.30am-5.30pm,
November to March, 8am-4pm, except
Monday and Saturday.

Vásárosnamény
Embroidery Museum
Open: Monday to Thursday, 7.30am-
4.30pm, Friday, 7.30am-4pm.

Tourist Information Centres
Békéscsaba
Bekestourist
Andrassy utca 10
☎ 66-23-448

Express
Andrássy utca 29

Csongrád
Szeged Tourist
Felszabadulás útja 14
☎ 63-31-232

Debrecen
Cooptourist
Holló utca 4
☎ 10-770

Express
Piac utca 77
☎ 18-332

Hajdútourist
Kálvin tér 2/A
☎ 52-13-931

IBUSZ
Piac utca 11
☎ 15-555

Gyula
Békéstourist
Kossuth utca 16
☎ 66-62-261

Gyulatourist
Eszperantó tér 1
☎ 66-61-192

Hajdúböszörmény
Hajdútourist
Karap utca 2
☎ 55-11-416

Hajdúszoboszló
Hajdútourist
József Attila utca 2
☎ 52-62 214

Hódmezővásárhely
Szeged Tourist
Szőnyi utca 1
☎ 62-41-325

Kecskemét
Cooptourist
Kéttemplom köz

Express
Dobó körút 11

IBUSZ
Széchenyi tér
☎ 76-22-955

Pusztatourist
Kossuth tér
☎ 76-29-499

Mátészalka
Szatmar Tourist
Bajcsy-Zsilinszky utca 3
☎ 44-10-410

Nyírbátor
Nyírtourist
Szabadság tér
☎ 43-11-525

Nyíregyháza
Express
Arany utca 2

IBUSZ
Orszag Zaszlo tér 10
☎ 42-12-125

Nyirtourist
Dózsa György utca 3
☎ 42-11-544

Szeged
Express
Kigyó utca 3
☎ 11-303

IBUSZ
Klauzál tér
☎ 26-533

Szeged Tourist
Victor Hugo utca 1
☎ 62-11-711
and on Klauzál tér
☎ 21-800

Volantourist
Fekete Sas utca 28

Szolnok
Tiszatour
Verseghy park 8
☎ 56-11-829

7
THE NORTHERN UPLANDS

Hungary is surrounded by mountain ranges, the Alps to the west, the Carpathians to the north and east, but has no mountains of any great height within its territory. Nevertheless, the country's principal upland region, along its north-eastern border, is high enough and scenic enough to attract foreign tourists, even if the skiing facilities or walking opportunities do not come anywhere close to matching those in neighbouring Slovakia, Austria or Romania. The attractions in this region are fourfold: firstly there are the opportunities for walking — in the deeply forested Bükk or Mátra mountains, or in the wilder and more rugged limestone country in the very north-east of the country; secondly, in the form of historic towns, the most prominent of which is the wine-making city of Eger, which should feature on the itineraries of most visitors to Hungary; thirdly, the region holds many attractions for wine lovers, not only in Eger, but also in Tokaj, the small town where Hungary's most famous wine, Tokay, is produced for export all round the world; and lastly, some of Europe's most impressive limestone cave systems can be seen in this part of the country, by those willing to take the time and effort to reach them, for they are situated in an isolated region right up against the Slovak border. Despite the difficulties of travelling in this region — bus and train services are poor, distances are often comparatively long, and the roads are often not of the highest quality — this is an interesting area to visit, and away from the more obvious tourist spots such as Eger and Tokaj there is ample opportunity to experience what real provincial Hungary is like.

The Cserhát Region

Despite its proximity to Budapest, the Cserhát region which lies to the east of the Börzsöny Mountains (see Chapter 2) is little visited by Western travellers. The region lies between the towns of Balassagyarmat and Salgótarján, along the Slovak border. The Cserhát Mountains (if they deserve to be called that) are not particularly high, and the main reason for

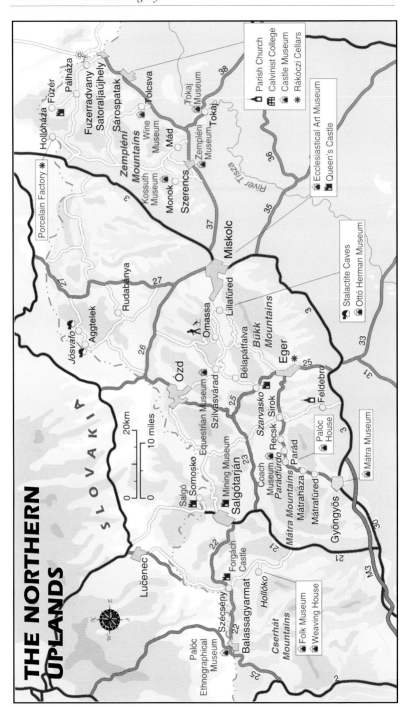

THE NORTHERN UPLANDS

Parish Church
Calvinist College
Castle Museum
Rákóczi Cellars

Ecclesiastical Art Museum
Queen's Castle

Stalactite Caves
Ottó Herman Museum

Porcelain Factory

Hollóháza
Füzér
Pálháza
Füzerradvany
Satoraljaujhely
Sárospatak
Tolcsva
Tokaj Museum
Zempléni Mountains
Wine Museum
Mád
Zempléni Museum
Tokaj
Kossuth Museum
Monok
Szerencs
River Tisza
Miskolc
Rudabánya
Lillafüred
Bükk Mountains
Aggtelek
Jósvafo
Omassa
Bélapátfalva
Eger
Ózd
Equestrian Museum
Szilvásvárad
Szarvasko
Sirok
Feldebro
Recsk
Paloc House
Parád
Mátra Museum
Mining Museum
Salgótarján
Coach Museum
Paradfürdo
Mátra Mountains
Parád
Salgó
Somosko
Mátraháza
Mátrafüred
Gyöngyös
M3
SLOVAKIA
Lučenec
Forgách Castle
Balassagyarmat
Hollókő
Szécsény
Cserhát Mountains
Folk Museum
Weaving House
Palóc Ethnographical Museum

20km
10 miles
0

38
36
35
37
27
21
26
25
33
31
3
30
21
22
23
24
25
2

N

coming here is to witness at first hand the culture of the Palóc peoples. They are an ethnic group who live in this isolated and economically backward region, who still sport traditional costumes and stage important folk festivals, making a real effort to keep their unique tradition and culture alive, especially as modernity, in the face of bleak mining and industrial settlements growing up in the eastern part of the region, seems to be encroaching on the area mercilessly. The Hungarian custom of *locsolkodas* — when the young men and boys of a village splash the local girls with water in return for an egg (all a thinly-veiled fertility ritual which takes place at Easter) — is kept alive here, in villages such as Hollókő, and it would be cynical to say that it was only done for the benefit of the passing tourist trade. Here, perhaps more than anywhere in Hungary, there is a genuine effort to preserve the ways of the past.

The traditional centre of the Palóc peoples is the town of **Balassagyarmat**, now a drab border town with little to recommend it except the Palóc Ethnographic Museum, with its excellent collections of the brightly-coloured costumes worn in the remote areas of this region. Having said this, however, most will want to press on into the rural areas to see the culture of the Palóc people at first hand.

The primary attraction in **Szécsény**, to the east of Balassagyarmat, is the Forgách Castle, an eighteenth-century mansion occupying the site of a former medieval fortress, which was destroyed by the Habsburgs during the War of Independence, after the Hungarian Diet had elected Ferenc Rákóczi as ruling prince in 1705 and declared the unification of an independent Hungary with Transylvania. The mansion now contains a museum, devoted to local history and hunting, and also to the Asiatic collections, mainly religious artefacts, of the explorer, Sándor Csoma Körösi. Down the road from here, a bastion from the original fortress exhibits various instruments of torture. On the main street, the Fire Watch Tower, dating largely from the nineteenth century, leans visibly from the vertical.

To the south-east Szécsény (the regular buses take 30 minutes) is **Hollókő**, which in 1988 became the first village in the world to be added to UNESCO's World Heritage List. Essentially, the whole of the lower part of the village is a living museum. Fifty-two homes are organised around a small fourteenth-century wooden towered church. The village has actually been the victim of a series of fires, but each time the houses have been rebuilt in traditional styles — the last time this occurred was in 1909. The inhabitants of the village are the Palóc peoples, who preserve their own dialect here and wear traditional folk costumes on public holidays. The costumes are displayed at the Folk Museum at Kossuth utca 82. The village is actually now geared very much towards the tourist industry, with house after house developed into souvenir shops, cafés and folk museums; there is even a post office and money-changing facility. All this does not however completely distract from the beauty of the village. Above the village are the ruins of a thirteenth-century castle, which one can climb up to. A full list of the museums here appears in the 'Additional Information' section at the end of this chapter.

Salgótarján essentially developed from the mid-nineteenth century as a coal mining town, but it was substantially rebuilt in the 1960s and the centre is modern, attractive and multi-purpose. It is also consequently completely lacking historical buildings due to two major floods which took place during the last quarter of the nineteenth century. In 1956 131 striking miners were shot dead by the ÁVO (Secret Police) in the aftermath of the Budapest uprising. The heavy dependence on inefficient heavy industry also means the town faces closure of local pits, and consequent high unemployment. The only real sight in the place is the Mining Museum on Ady utca, housed in the shafts of an old mine.

Accessible by local bus is the castle of **Salgó**, 8km (5 miles) to the north-east of the town, built in the thirteenth century on top of a 625m (2,050ft) high basalt hill. It has lain in ruins since the Turkish wars. There is, however, a tremendous view from the top into Slovakia and towards the castle of Somoskő. Though the town of Somoskő is in Hungary, the castle is just over the border in Slovakia so you will need a passport to visit it. It dates from the fourteenth century, and from one of its five towers one may survey the odd basalt formations nearby.

The Mátra Mountains

Although they are higher than the Bükk Range, the Mátra mountains do not offer as many opportunities as the other range, to the north-east. Nevertheless, their dense forests of beech and oak, and their secluded valleys and spa settlements mean that there is a fair amount to see and do here, even if the superior attractions of the Bükk mountains encourage one to push on eastwards without seeing everything. The proximity of the Mátra to Budapest means that they receive a lot of visitors, particularly at weekends. Many people in the capital own second homes in this area. The main town in the area is **Gyöngyös**, 60km (37 miles) from Budapest by motorway, and accessible by rail on a branch line from the main Budapest-Miskolc line. There are a few points of interest here, but most will want to pass through the town and head north into the hills. The main resorts are Mátraháza and Mátrafüred. Above the former resort is Mount Kékestető, the highest peak in Hungary (1,014m/3,326ft), where there are rudimentary facilities for winter sports. Hungarians make the most of these if they cannot afford the time or money to travel to the much higher mountains in Slovakia or Romania. There are, of course, many opportunities for walking in this area, and those interested in doing so should buy the large scale map of the region, *A Mátra Túristatérképe*, which shows all the places mentioned in this section in detail. The main road from Gyöngyös to Eger via Mátraháza, Parád and Sirok passes through the heart of the range, and most of the places mentioned in this section are on this road, along which there is a fairly good bus service.

Gyöngyös is at the centre of a wine-producing region, a pleasant but dull provincial town which appears to get what bustle and custom it does from visitors stopping off on their way up to the hills. Fő tér is the main square, lined with decaying but formerly handsome buildings dating from the nineteenth century, with St Bartholomew's Church standing at the northern end. The church was initially Gothic, and was substantially rebuilt with Baroque modifications in the eighteenth century. On Nemecz József tér, nearby, is a former Franciscan monastery and church, both built in the early eighteenth century. In the chancel is the coat of arms of the Barthori family, who built the church for the Franciscans. Those who wish to stay in Gyöngyös could make use of the hotel on the main square, or enquire at the tourist office there as to other possibilities. An old mansion at Kossuth utca 40 houses the Mátra Museum, a good collection of displays relating to the peasant and natural life of the Mátras, including a section on wine-making. This is a place to look round while waiting for the train on the Mátravasút, the narrow-gauge railway which runs up to the Mátra resorts, the southern terminus of which is next door to the museum.

From Gyöngyös there are two roads over to Eger, in the foothills of the Bükk mountains. The more scenic, but longer route goes through the settlements mentioned below. The faster route is along road number 3, via Kápolna. Seven kilometres (4 miles) north of Kápolna is the tiny village of **Feldebrő** with its parish church, which reputedly boasts the oldest church crypt in Hungary. The walls of the crypt are adorned with beautiful twelfth-century frescoes, depicting Christ, the Prophets and Biblical scenes, probably painted by a northern Italian artist. In the crypt is buried King Aba, who ruled Hungary from 1041 to 1044. The keys for the crypt may need to be borrowed from the *plébánia* (presbytery) behind the church.

The main road and the Mátrafüred branch of the Mátravasút run north from Gyöngyös to **Mátrafüred**, where the railway terminates. From now on those without their own transport will have to rely on the frequent bus service in this region. Mátrafüred is a resort town, with plenty of hotels and opportunities for things like swimming and tennis, but not much beyond this. The tourist information office is on the main road through the town, just up from the railway station. Plenty of paths start from here, but most will probably want to press on along the road which winds its way up to Mátraháza. Between the two resorts, just off the road, is a lake called Sás-tó, which offers opportunities for fishing and boating and around which there are more holiday homes, campsites and restaurants.

Mátraháza itself is another resort, this time more refined and relaxed, though with few possibilities for accommodation. Most of the buildings here are trade union hostels and hotels, with a number of sanatoria and medical facilities secluded behind the rows of trees along the road. A number of paths start at the small car park just by the junction for the road that runs up to Kékestető. It is a walk of 1 hour 15 minutes along the path marked with yellow squares over the hills to Lajosháza, a tiny hamlet which is the terminus of the western branch of the Mátravasút — there are trains from here back to Gyöngyös. A longer walk, taking just under 3 hours, takes one along the path marked with green squares, then with blue markers, to the resort of Galyateto to the north-west. Here, the Grand Hotel has a swimming pool and there is a spectacular view over the mountains from the look-out tower on Péter hegyese, a short walk away.

A road (and a blue-marked trail) runs up the hill from Mátraháza to **Kékestető**, the highest peak in Hungary. The fact that there is a road up to the top, along which buses travel frequently (there are even some direct buses from Budapest to the summit) shows that this is not a particularly steep nor impressive mountain. But people come up here for the limited opportunities for winter sports (there are two ski runs and tows), and to go up the enormously high television transmitter, which has a restaurant and viewing galleries half way up affording outstanding views over the entire range and beyond. In theory it is possible to see the High Tatras in Northern Slovakia from here.

The Northern Mátras

From the summit of Kékestető it is a pleasant walk of just under 3 hours through eerily silent forests to Parádfürdő (the last bit of the walk is along a minor road). The neighbouring villages of Parád and Parádfurdő are also the next settlements along the road from Mátraháza. At **Parád** is the Palóc House (Palóc ház), full of peasant costumes and other artefacts which show the former lifestyles of the local Palóc peoples. There is also an exhibition of wood-carvings in the village. At **Parádfürdő** is the Coach Museum (Kocsimúzeum) situated in a building beside the main road, displaying a magnificent collection of wonderfully restored old coaches once used by the Hungarian nobility. There are some horses stabled nearby, which occasionally pull the coaches in shows. The English word coach derives from the fact that the coach was invented in the village of Kocs in western Hungary, which is pronounced (in Hungarian) *coach*. Parádfürdő itself is a small, genteel spa, with many elegant nineteenth-century buildings surrounded by parkland. The sulphurous waters that bubble up from the ground here are thought to cure digestive problems and other ailments.

A little way beyond Parádfürdő is the village of **Recsk**, in whose quarries thousands of political prisoners, sent here by the Stalinist regime of Hungary in the 1940s and 1950s, were forced to work in conditions of virtual slavery. The concentration camp was closed in 1953, but it was not until 1991 that a memorial to those who suffered here was erected, outside the quarry a little way from the village. Beyond Recsk is **Sirok**. Above the village, to the north, and accessible on a blue-marked track that runs steeply up from the main part of the village, is the ruined castle Siroki várrom. The castle dates from the thirteenth century and from the summit there are beautiful views over both the Mátra and the Bükk. Twenty kilometres (12 miles) beyond Sirok the road enters Eger.

The Bükk Mountains

The Bükk range, which stretches between the cities of Eger and Miskolc, which are both worthy of a visit themselves, is probably the most popular and interesting range of mountains in Hungary, even if the peaks here are not quite as high as those in the Mátra mountains, to the west. The Bükk mountains are heavily forested, like most ranges in Hungary, and their accessibility means that some areas can become quite crowded at busy times. The extensive network of colour-coded forest trails and paths, which can be seen on the map *A Bükk: Túristatérképe*, can take visitors away from the busier areas and into the heart of the Bükk, with its numerous streams, waterfalls, caves and gorges. The National Park area of the range covers 98,800 acres (40,000 hectares). Here, the wildlife of the region — including deer, many rare species of birds such as rock thrushes, Imperial eagles and woodpeckers, badgers, and a number of different types of woodland orchids — find their habitat within the dense covering of trees, and are protected by strict government conservation laws. Although protected, parts of the Bükk have been, or are still, exploited by man, and there are numerous limestone quarries, logging areas and iron ore mines, the products of which are used in the iron and other metal plants in Miskolc and the industrial cities to the north. The Bükk is a limestone area, which results in steep slopes and precipitous gorges and cliffs in some areas, and the numerous caves that are dotted around the hills once provided shelter to early man. Beech (*Bükk* in Hungarian) is the main covering, a species of tree which thrives well on limestone soils. The highest peak is Istálló-skő (958m/3,142ft), which can be reached from the resort of Szilvásvárad, to the north of Eger. Another popular resort, in the east of the range, is Lillafüred, to the west of Miskolc. The roads linking Eger and Miskolc, which cross the central part of the range, give motorists good views over these mountains, but the only way to see them properly is on foot.

   The cities of Eger and Miskolc are jumping-off points for the western and eastern parts of the Bükk range, respectively. Both cities are described in this section, together with details of how to approach the Bükk from either direction.

Eger

With its 175 listed historical monuments, wine-making traditions and proximity to the Bükk mountains, Eger is one of the most popular destinations within Hungary. There is archaeological evidence of a settlement here dating from the Stone Age. The first generation of Hungarian settlers also came here and at the beginning of the eleventh century King Stephen made it an episcopal see. The town was largely destroyed by the Mongol forces in 1241 but was revived by the influx of a large number of settlers from Western Europe and during the latter part of the fifteenth century became a major centre of Renaissance culture.

Historically speaking, Eger is most famed for the events of October 1552 when a force of 2,000 under the command of István Dobó managed to withstand a siege upon the town's castle by a Turkish force numbering over 10,000. The Turks' eventual retreat after a month caused great celebration throughout Europe. The events of 1552 are described in the popular Hungarian novel *Stars of Eger* (1901) by Géza Gárdonyi which pays particular attention to the role played by the town's women who hurled rocks, boiling fat and lots worse down upon the infidel from the castle walls. The Turks however had the last laugh in 1596 when the city defended by a garrison of foreign mercenaries surrendered in under a week. Much to their surprise, most of the defending soldiers were slaughtered upon the opening of the castle gates.

Eger remained in Turkish hands until 1687, and the minaret in the town centre is the most northerly monument of the Turkish occupation of south-eastern Europe. By the time of the withdrawal there were barely 3,500 people living in the town and this included some 600 Muslims who stayed behind and converted to Christianity. In 1702 the castle walls were pulled down on the orders of Emperor Leopold I who feared their use by independence fighters. Indeed, during the 1703-11 War of Independence the town became a rebel stronghold and Eger's Bishop Telekessy was the only Catholic prelate to declare himself against the Habsburgs. In common with many Hungarian towns the present day Baroque centre dates from the reconstruction of the mid-eighteenth century and this is what lends the town much of its considerable charm.

The railway station is some 15 minutes walk away from the centre though there is a frequent bus running to the centre along the main road, Deák Ferenc utca. The bus station is in the centre of town behind the huge, neo-Classical **Cathedral**. There has been a church on this site ever since King Stephen established an episcopal see here in the eleventh century. The present day structure was built between 1831 and 1836 and was designed by József Hild who also designed the basilica at Esztergom. At the bottom of the steps leading up to the Cathedral are statues of two Hungarian kings; to the right King Stephen and to the left St Ladislas. The beginning of the second flight of steps is watched over by statues of St Peter and St Paul. Above the tympanum on the church are allegorical statues of Faith, Hope and Charity flanked by the winged angels of Divine Truth and Love. All the statues are the work of Italian-born Marco Casagrande (1806-80). Interior decorations are largely the work of J.L. Kracker (1717-79), a Viennese artist who came to Hungary in 1764 and died in Eger. Nearby on Széchenyi utca is the Baroque Archbishop's Palace.

Directly opposite the Cathedral is the **Lyceum** which dates from 1785. Originally a Catholic training college, it is now a teacher training college but some sections are open to the public. The library on the first floor features a superb ceiling fresco of a session from the Counter-Reformatory Council of Trent (1545-63) painted by J. L Kracker and his son-in-law

József Zach in 1778. The foreshortening is not quite right but it is still an impressive piece. Many of the portraits are of real people and the four corners represent the decisions of the council. An information sheet in English tells you all the details about the ceiling and the library which contains Hungary's only Mozart autograph and boasts 76,000 volumes. Upstairs is a small astronomical museum and, at the very top of the tower in the east wing, the Camera Obscura. Visitors are admitted in groups into a darkened room by a curator who operates the mirrors that provide a unique view of the city. A 'must' for all voyeurs. The curator sells post-cards of himself at the end of the showing!

From the Lyceum, walk down Kossuth utca. The **Franciscan Church** on the right dates from the mid-eighteenth century and was built from the remains of a mosque which once stood here. Opposite at number 9 the **County Hall** is worth a look for its beautifully ornate wrought-iron gates which are decorated with various coats of arms, motifs and allegorical figures. They date from 1761 and are the work of Henrik Fazola (1730-99). From here turn left into Eger's main square, **Dobó István tér**. On the south side of the square is an eighteenth-century Baroque **Minorite Church**. The Latin inscription above the entrance reads 'Nothing is enough for God'. The exterior was restored in the 1960s though unfortunately the interior was not, nevertheless the altarpiece by the now familiar J. L Kracker is worth attention. On the square itself stand two sets of statues commemo-rating the events of 1552. To the east stands István Dobó flanked by a knight and a woman and to the west is the 'Monument to the Gallant Border Warriors'. A short walk north of the square, on Knézich utca, is an early seventeenth-century fourteen-sided **Minaret** which may be as-cended. The mosque of which it was a part was demolished in 1841. From here walk to the Castle entrance, passing some seventeenth-century Turk-ish baths on Dózsa György tér on the way.

Walk up from Dózsa György tér to the lower gate of the **Castle**, which dates from the 1580s when the original thirteenth-century structure was strengthened against further Turkish attack. On the right is a large bronze relief celebrating the events of 1552. Follow the path up (pausing to take in the great view of the town below) to the **Museum Complex**, the entrance to which is through the gateway. One ticket pays for all the various bits inside. To the left as you enter, on the upper floor, is a Picture Gallery boasting a Tintoretto and numerous works by Mihály Munkácsy. Directly opposite the entrance is the Gothic Bishop's Palace, the ground floor of which houses the small Hall of Heroes containing the red marble tomb of István Dobó. On either side of the tomb are statues representing the defenders of the castle. In the stone cases are some of the bones of the victims of the siege discovered during excavations. Upstairs is a museum dedicated to the history of the castle.

To the east of the museum complex are the ruins of the **Cathedral of St John the Evangelist** which date originally from the eleventh century. Rebuilt after Mongol molestation, the building fell into disuse after being

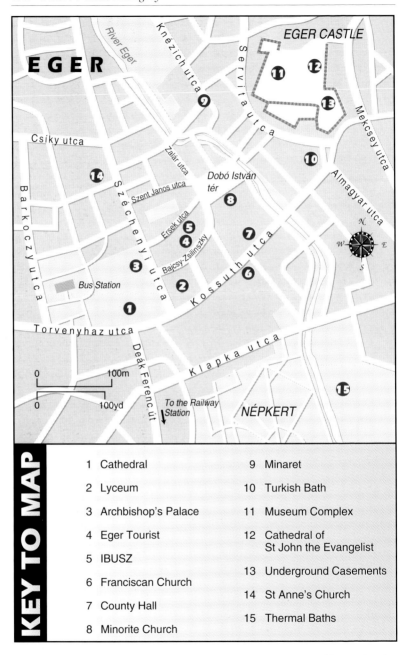

KEY TO MAP

1 Cathedral	9 Minaret
2 Lyceum	10 Turkish Bath
3 Archbishop's Palace	11 Museum Complex
4 Eger Tourist	12 Cathedral of St John the Evangelist
5 IBUSZ	
6 Franciscan Church	13 Underground Casements
7 County Hall	14 St Anne's Church
8 Minorite Church	15 Thermal Baths

largely destroyed by fire in 1506 and was used as an arsenal by both sides during the Turkish occupation. Final demolition came, as ever, courtesy of the Habsburgs at the beginning of the eighteenth century. Next to the ruins is the entrance to the **Underground Casements**, visitable only on a guided tour which lasts half an hour. It is a fascinating place but unfortu-

With its many historic monuments and thermal waters Eger is one of Hungary's most compelling highland towns

A day out in Eger

nately quite poorly presented. There is a seemingly endless introductory spiel from the tour guide and only 50m (164ft) of actual subterrania is explored. Upon emergence one may pay tribute to the remains of author Géza Gárdonyi (1863-1922) who wrote *Stars of Eger*. Be warned though, as the words on the stone betray: 'Only his body lies here'. In Gárdonyi's former home, at number 28 Gárdonyi utca, is a small museum dedicated to the author.

There are a few more places of interest a little further away from the town centre. At the end of Széchenyi utca stands the Baroque **St Anne's Church** built in 1733 from the stones of a mosque which stood here. On a hill overlooking the town is a Copf Serbian Orthodox Church dating from the late eighteenth century. Last, but not least, one cannot visit Eger and escape unaware of its reputation as a wine producing town. One could pay a visit to the small **Wine Museum** at 1 Városfal utca 1 or alternatively simply sample the produce in one of the various wine taverns around the centre. Anyone feeling more adventurous might like to venture out to the wine cellars in the Szépasszony Valley, west of the town. Essentially local vineyards produce four types of wine; Egri Bikavér (Bull's Blood, the city's most famous wine), Muskotály (Muscatel), Lcányka (a medium dry white) and Medoc Noir (a rich, dark red). During the September harvest there are numerous wine-related events going on throughout the town including a parade of floats.

North From Eger Into The Bükk

Heading north from Eger, road and railway pass through the village of **Szarvaskő**, where there is a ruined thirteenth-century castle, and then through **Bélapátfalva**, where there is a very well preserved Romanesque church which somehow managed to survive the devastation of this area by the Turks. The church was founded in 1232 by a group of Cistercian monks who settled here from France. The church is signposted from the main road (though is a fair walk from the railway station).

Szilvásvárad is the next settlement along this road and is 26km (16 miles) north of Eger. It is the main starting point for walkers who approach the Bükk range from the western end. Although it is easy to see this area on an excursion from Eger, there are a number of hotels and other possibilities for accommodation in the resort. There is a tourist office on the main road which should be able to help with accommodation. Szilvásvárad lies at the foot of forested hills and was once owned by the Pallavinici family, an aristocratic landowning family who supported the Fascists during World War II and whose land was taken away from them by the government in 1948. The town then became a workers' holiday resort, with many trades unions owning holiday homes to which their members would head for their annual summer break (this was the traditional way of organising holidays in all Communist countries). The horse-breeding tradition of the Pallavinici family lives on, however, in the stud farm that exists here where Lippizaner horses are bred. Lippizaner horses are usually white or grey, and small but thickly built. Some of them can be seen in stables next to the Equestrian Museum at Park utca 8, where there are also displays relating to the use and breeding of these particular horses. There is also a horse-riding track in the village, where Hungary's annual coach-driving competition (the Bükk Championships) is normally held, at the end of August.

From Szilvásvárad there are paths and a narrow gauge railway (origi- nally built for logging) up the beautiful **Szalajka Valley** (cars cannot get the whole way up the valley; there is a car park where the road termi- nates). Half-way up the valley there is a Forestry Museum, which shows how woodmen and charcoal burners lived and worked. They were once the only inhabitants of these hills. The railway ends in a clearing in the forest near a small lake, overlooked on three sides by high and thickly forested hills.

Possibilities for walks in this region are numerous. From the railway station in the clearing it is possible to walk up to the Istállóskői Cave (*barlang*) along the paths marked with green triangles. The path is popu- lar, and snakes up through the forest to a huge limestone cave in the forest. Just below the cave, another path leads off from the main path (though still marked with green triangles) and heads down, past some towering lime- stone cliffs and then steeply up to the summit of Istállós-kő (959m/ 3,146ft). This walk will take a good couple of hours and is more of a scramble than a walk at times. The summit can be approached much more easily from a path which leads off the Szilvásvárad-Miskolc road (marked with yellow triangles). Paths in this part of the mountains are numerous and dense, but are sometimes not that easy to follow. A careful study of the map will show the many other possibilities there are for walks. One idea may be to walk across the central part of the range (by a number of different routes) from Szilvásvárad or the upper part of the Szalajka Valley over to Ómassa and the Garadna Valley, from where there are narrow gauge trains (and buses) down to Lillafüred and then Miskolc.

For those who approach **Miskolc** from the south, coming by road or rail from Budapest, the first impression of the city is a distinctly uninviting one, of scores of similarly drab residential blocks scattered up the hill- sides, surrounding an industrial core which is criss-crossed by numerous radial roadways and busy interchanges. This is Hungary's second largest city, and is not the place to arrive on a wet Monday. It is a grimy place, with important steel and arms factories on its outskirts, and although there are one or two things to see and do here most visitors regard Miskolc as merely the gateway to the eastern part of the Bükk range rather than a city which is likely to attract tourists.

The city is 179km (111 miles) from Budapest by road, with motorway for part of the way, and other parts of the journey covered by fast dual carriageway. From Eger, there are two ways to reach Miskolc — the slower way, across the mountains (via Répáshuta), which brings one to Lillafüred or the faster route, via Mezőkövezd, which involves travelling

a greater distance but on flatter, faster roads. There are regular buses between Eger and Miskolc; travelling between the two cities by train normally involves changing at Füzesabony. There are numerous trains from Budapest to Miskolc (most use Keleti station in the capital). The fastest, Hungary's new Inter-City trains, are first class only and take 1 hour 45 minutes. Other services take up to half an hour longer. The main railway station in Miskolc is Tiszai, a short tram ride away from the centre. Conveniently, there is only one tram line in the city, running from the main railway station, right through the centre along the main shopping street, and then right out to the western outskirts of the city, terminating at Diósgyőr vár. The main bus terminal is at Búza tér, close to the centre of town. There is a second railway station, Gömöri, which is also fairly close to the centre of town. There are a number of hotels in the city, both in the centre and at Miskolc-Tapolca, but most will want to head out into the hills to find somewhere to stay. There are also two campsites around Miskolc-Tapolca. Those who are planning to look round Miskolc should invest in a street plan of the place, since many of the things worth seeing are on the city's outskirts and would be impossible to find otherwise. There are bookshops and tourist offices supplying maps along the main shopping street.

Széchenyi utca (which becomes Bajcsy-Zsilinsky utca further east) is the main shopping street through the city, and is pedestrianised for much of the way. Some of the buildings have Baroque façades, others are of the concrete-functional variety. The place is usually lively and bustling, however, even if one has to dodge speeding trams every couple of minutes. Kossuth utca runs north from the Pannónia Hotel and IBUSZ office on the corner of Kossuth utca and Széchenyi utca, into Paloczy utca and the square Deák tér. At number 7 on the square, trees almost obscure the Greek Orthodox Church, founded in the late eighteenth century by the descendants of the Greeks who had fled from the advancing Turks. The church has a superb 16m (52ft) high iconostas which is inset with the 'Black Mary of Kazan', presented to the church by Tsarina Catherine the Great of Russia. The Mount Athos Cross, also in the church, is decorated with precious stones and was brought here by the first Greek Settlers in 1590. Next to the pathway up to the church is an Ecclesiastical Art Museum, which displays Orthodox religious treasures from all over Hungary. Paloczy utca runs east from the square to Hősök tere, with a Minorite Church and Monastery dating from the 1730s on the northern side of the square, and the city's Synagogue on the south side. Before World War II over 11,000 Jews lived in the city. Now the Jewish population numbers about 250, the size and beauty of the still-functioning synagogue a poignant reminder of the city's once large population of Jews.

Avas Hill rises to the south of Széchenyi utca; a television transmitter stands at its summit. At the bottom of the hill is a Gothic Calvinist church,

Looking over the rooftops to the main medieval market square, Dobó István tér

dating from the 1560s, with a wooden roof and a separate wooden belfry
which stands next to it. The overgrown churchyard has been in use for
over nine centuries. On the other side of the road is the Ottó Herman
Museum, with a good collection of folk costumes and pottery. Between
the church and the TV tower, a dense network of paths and tracks takes
one up the hill, past tiny villas which all contain wine cellars, some of
which are over five centuries old, and run deep into the hillside. There is,
predictably, a good view over the city from the TV tower. On good days
it is possible to see as far as the Carpathian Mountains in Slovakia.

Miskolc-Tapolca is a southern suburb of Miskolc, and can be reached
by one of the city's buses. This is a popular spa resort, where there are
many hotels and holiday homes, and people crowd round the numerous
langós stalls while loudspeakers deliver pop music to the hordes of bathers. Not a place to go for a quiet afternoon's bathing or relaxing, but given
the drabness of the rest of Miskolc it is easy to see why so many people
head this way at weekends. There is a boating lake, a large open-air
swimming pool, and at the far end of the resort are the *barlang fürdő* (cave
baths), where bathers can relax in a number of natural warm-water caves
and grottoes, including one which boasts a 'thrashing shower' which
gives bathers a natural massage. The water in all the baths and medical
establishments comes from a depth of 900m (2,952ft), is mildly radioactive
and has a temperature of about 30°C (86°F). There are medical baths all
around the resort, where people are supposedly cured of mental or
nervous disorders.

In the far western part of the city, at the end of the tram line, is Diósgyőr
vár, the Queen's Castle. It was built in the fourteenth century by the
Angevin King Louis the Great, initially as a defensive fortress in the style
of southern Italian castles, but soon came to be used as a royal residence
for Hungarian queens — hence its name. Situated at the foot of the Bükk
mountains it was also, predictably, used by Hungarian kings and princes
as a base for hunting. Crudely restored in the 1960s, the castle looks quite
impressive close up and there are good views from the four solid-looking
square towers, back towards Miskolc, and, in the other direction, over the
Bükk mountains. The castle's courtyard is a venue for open-air concerts
in summer, some of which are held as part of the Miskolc Summer Festival
of plays, concerts and other performing arts. Details of this, and the
folklore festival held at the beginning of July (reputedly one of the best in
Hungary), can be obtained from tourist offices in the town.

West From Miskolc Into The Bükk

The road that runs west through Miskolc, past Diósgyőr Vár, then runs out
and into the Bükk mountains. The pretty resort of **Lillafüred**, a world
away from the industrial grime of Miskolc, yet on the city's bus network,
is the first settlement the road passes through on leaving Miskolc. There
are two ways to get there other than driving. Firstly, there are buses there
from Majális Park, on the western edge of Miskolc (take a bus from the

centre or main railway station to Majális Park which also stop on the main road near the castle); or, there is a narrow gauge railway which runs from Miskolc up to Lillafüred (and then on into the Garadna Valley, another branch runs along the Csanyik Valley, to the north). The terminal in Miskolc is on the main road which runs west from the centre to the castle and Lillafüred. The tram stops close to it.

Lillafüred is a small, secluded village, hidden in a steeply wooded valley and situated next to a small lake, called Lake Hámori, where boats can be hired. People skate on it in winter, when it freezes over. A distinctive 1920s hotel, The Palace, is on the other side of the road to the lake. There are three stalactite caves in the village. Above the road to Miskolc is the Szeleta Barlang, where important archaeological remains from the Ice Age have been discovered, while in a deep grotto in the valley immediately below the hotel is the entrance to the Anna Cave, where there are a number of limestone chambers to explore. Above the railway station, along the road to Eger, is the István Cave, probably the most interesting of the three, with many pools and stalagmite and stalactite chambers. Beyond this is the Ottó Herman Museum. Ottó Herman, who died in 1944, was a noted ethnographer and naturalist who lived in this house for much of his life, collecting butterflies, beetles and other wildlife specimens from the surrounding forest. Stuffed and mounted examples of the many insects, birds and other small mammals that he caught can be seen in the museum.

The next village on the road and railway beyond Lillafüred (take the road that runs along the lakeside in Lillafüred) is **Újmassa**, where an old nineteenth-century foundry has been preserved. It was first used by a locksmith from Eger, who exploited the local reserves of iron ore. Beyond Újmassa there is access to more walking country. The narrow gauge railway continues up to Garadna, while the road (and buses from Majális Park in Miskolc) continues a little way beyond this to **Ómassa**, a real mountain village where the inhabitants store wood for the winter in sheds by their houses, and where the tiny wooden-built dwellings are spread out up the hillside. Ómassa is the starting point for many walks. An examination of a map will show all the possibilities, but some suggestions are as follows: west of Ómassa is Bánkút, a small ski resort where there are a number of ski lifts and tows. Above the resort there is a lookout tower on the summit of Mount Bálvány (956m/3,140ft). It is possible to walk over the central part of the Bükk from Bánkút, to the peak Istállós-kő, the railway in the Szalajka Valley, or to Szilvásvárad (see section above for all these places). Well to the south of Bánkút is the mountain plateau Nagy-mező, where wild horses graze in summer. It is also possible to walk from Ómassa over the ridge to the railway station at Farkasgodor-Orvenyko, which is the terminus of a branch of the narrow gauge railway from Miskolc. Times of the trains should be checked in advance at Miskolc if this walk is to be attempted.

A lakeside hotel in Lillafüred, one of the prettiest resorts in the Bükk Mountains

The Aggtelek Region

The Baradla limestone cave sytem in the Aggtelek region is one of the longest in the world and is a major draw for visitors, despite its being so far away from anywhere. The three entrances to the caves are to be found at the villages of **Aggtelek** and **Jósvafo**, and on the road linking them (the Béke cave system is a separate cave system, close to Jósvafo). The two villages are situated to the north of Miskolc, in bleak and remote country-side right on the Slovak border. The cave system runs under the Slovak border and there is another entrance on the Slovak side, at Domica. However, the border crossing at Aggtelek can only be used by Hungarians and Slovaks, so it is not possible to cross over to look at these caves. However, tours taken from Aggtelek sometimes cross under the border and take visitors into Slovak territory. There are no rail connections here, but there are direct buses to the two villages from Eger, Miskolc and the industrial towns of Ózd, Kazincbarcika and Putnok, which lie to the south. There are even direct bus services from Budapest, although this is a very arduous journey to make. There are hotels in both locations, adjacent to the cave entrances. Aggtelek is the more popular site, with a jumble of car parks, refreshment stalls and hotel buildings seemingly in the middle of nowhere. The two villages themselves have little of interest to visitors bar the entrances to the caves, although Jósvafo is prettily situated, and it has an old church with wooden gravestones and memorials in the cemetery.

Parts of the Baradla cave system were known to Stone Age man. Important archaeological finds have been made here. The Béke cave system has only been discovered recently in 1952. The temperature in the caves is a constant 10° or 11°C (50 or 52°F). Take warm clothing, and bear in mind that it can be wet underfoot and overhead. The caverns and passages in these cave systems have been formed by water running along cracks and joints in the limestone, and widening them by dissolving the rock. The dissolved minerals (mainly calcium·carbonate) are then deposited when the water drips off the ceilings of caverns, creating stalactites, and, when the drops splash onto the floor of the caverns, more calcium carbonate is deposited, forming a stalagmite. Occasionally stalagmites and stalactites can grow together, forming columns. Many of the caverns and tunnels are dry, the water that formed them long since having taken a different route through the limestone.

The Baradla Cave System

All three entrances to the Baradla system afford access to an incredible subterranean world of lakes, grottoes, narrow passages, caverns and stalagmites and stalactites in a dazzling array of shapes and formations. The caves stretch under the ground for 22km (14 miles), 5km (3 miles) of which is under Slovak territory and at each entrance there are various tours on offer, some of which are up to 6 hours duration. These are recommended for cave buffs only — 6 hours is a long time to be underground in wet and musty passages. At the Aggtelek entrance there is an exhibition relating to the caves, and various reptiles are displayed in cages that are far too small for them. There are also species of cave wildlife, bats and small rodents, that are rarely glimpsed by visitors to the caves. Short tours (usually about an hour in length) of the cave systems are available at both the Aggtelek and Jósvafő entrances. Longer tours are also available from these entrances, but the main entrance for the longer tours is at the Vörös-tó entrance on the road half way between the two villages. The Aggtelek entrance is probably best for shorter tours and seems to be used by more people than the Jósfavő entrance. In the cave system one can see the 'Hall of Giants', one of the largest single caverns in Europe, 120m (394ft) in length and up to 40m (131ft) high, and the world's largest stalagmite, over 25m (82ft) high and 8m (26ft) in diameter at its base. There is usually an opportunity to travel in boats along an underground river, although this depends on water levels in the river. Concerts are sometimes given in the caverns here, in the evenings. Look out for the posters advertising them at the Aggtelek or Jósvafő entrances.

The Béke Cave System

There is only one entrance to this separate, but lengthy, cave system, much of which remains unexplored. Its existence has only been known since 1952. In 1973, explorers discovered a lengthy network of passages and caverns when they penetrated a 30m (98ft) high underground waterfall. The entrance is beside the road just as one enters Jósvafő from Aggtelek, shortly before the Jósvafő entrance to the Baradla caves. These are difficult caves to explore and a tour is fairly demanding. They are wet and cold, so take warm waterproof clothing. Helmets are issued at the entrance. The caves contain an underground sanatorium, as the air in them is thought to be beneficial to asthmatics.

Excursions Above Ground

The countryside around Aggtelek and Jósvafő is wild and hilly, and displays typical features of karst landscapes — bare rocky outcrops, gorges and precipitous cliffs, and waterfalls and sinkholes. Do not walk too close to the border, which is still heavily policed. Those who walk in this or any other border regions would be wise to take their passports with them. The map *Aggtelek, Jósvafő és Kornyekenek Túristatérképe* should be used to plan walks and excursions in this region.

Two walking tracks link Aggtelek and Jósvafő. The trail marked with blue markers, which goes over the tops of the hills, takes 1 hour 35 minutes to walk. It divides at the Aggtelek end, one trail marked with blue triangles, the other marked as a blue/yellow trail; both trails rejoin at the Aggtelek caves. The other trail, marked with green markers, takes 1 hour 55 minutes and is along a remote valley. Both trails start and finish next to the entrances to the caves in both villages. From Jósvafő village there are paths which head north and north-east into the remote countryside around the border, much of which is inaccessible by road. There are many pretty farming villages in this region, which can be explored on foot or by car. At **Rudabánya**, to the south-east of Aggtelek, there is an iron-ore mine and refinery. The mineral has been mined here since the time of Louis the Great, and in 1967 the jawbone and teeth of a 10 million-year-old monkey was found here. It is thought to be a distant ancestor of man, and has been named *Rudapithecus hungaricus*. The jawbone is on display at the entrance to the mine. There is also a Gothic church in the village, with a wooden ceiling painted in the seventeenth century.

The Zempléni Mountains

The Zempléni mountains stretch north-eastwards from the town of Szerencs, over into Slovakia. Apart from the wine-producing town of Tokaj, these remote, deserted mountains, home to wolves, wildcats and eagles, amongst many other species of wildlife, see few tourists, making the trek northwards from Tokaj to the medieval castle at Sárospatak, or the distant villages beyond it, all the more rewarding for those more adventurous travellers prepared to make the journey up here.

The Southern Zempléni

Two towns lie on the southern limb of the Zempléni, Szerencs, which is really just a gateway town to the mountains, and Tokaj, a town well worth visiting in its own right.

There is very little to recommend in **Szerencs**, a dull place on the road and railway line that run east from Miskolc. The chocolate factory here, now owned by the Swiss consortium Nestlé, produces most of the chocolate in Hungary. At the far end of the town to the railway station, surrounded by a small park, is an old castle and manor house which now houses the Zempléni Museum, including one of the largest collections of postcards in the world, numbering 700,000, donated to the museum by a doctor in the town. The entrance to the castle is from Rákóczi utca. The castle was built in the middle of the sixteenth century and was once owned by the Rákóczi family, who fought for Hungarian independence against the Habsburgs. In the Gothic Calvinist church, which is surrounded by a medieval fortress wall, a Rákóczi prince and his wife are buried. The town is a focus for transport routes into the surrounding region, with buses fanning out from here to many villages in the Zempléni, and trains heading north into the western part of the Zempléni, east to Tokaj (and then to the northern part of the Great Plain), and north-east to Sárospatak. The town's railway and bus stations are next door to one another.

Half an hour by train — or 19km (12 miles) along the road — from Szerencs is **Tokaj**, a small town which lies at the centre of one of the most important wine-producing areas in Hungary. Tokaj is the most famous small town in Hungary. Lying at the confluence of the Tisza and Bodrog rivers, its winding, narrow streets overlooked by the vineyards that produce Hungary's most exclusive wine, Tokaj is, however, something rather less than the sum of its parts. Inevitably it is the wine that attracts most of the visitors to the town, but there are a few points of architectural note. If arriving by train turn left from the station and then left again under the bridge along Bajcsy-Zsilinszky utca. At number 15 is the former Rákóczi-Dessewffy House (now used as a college). At number 44 Rákóczi utca stands the Town Hall built in 1790 in the style of Louis XVI. In the centre of the old town, at number 7 Bethlen Gábor utca is the Tokaj Museum dedicated to the history of Tokaj wine while a little further along the street, at number 17, the Greek Orthodox church plays host to an exhibition of contemporary paintings. Meanwhile, across the river, there are some ruins of a fourteenth-century castle. There are a huge number of small, private cellars, particularly on the hillside above the main street. The most famous pilgrimage is to the Rákóczi cellar at number 15 Kossuth tér where 20,000 hectolitres of wine are stored in twenty-four chandelier-lit passageways totalling some 1½km (1 mile) in length. The cellar was used as an important meeting place during the 1703-11 War of Independence.

Many pretty villages in the southern part of the Zempléni are accessible from both Tokaj and Szerencs. At **Tolcsva** an old manor house now contains a wine museum. **Mád** boasts an eighteenth-century synagogue, with the old Rabbi's House and Religious School nearby, and Old Jewish cemetery in the northern parts of the village. At **Monok** is the eighteenth-century manor house where Lajos Kossuth, one of Hungary's greatest politicians, was born. It is now a museum. In the 1848 revolution against the Habsburgs, he was elected president of an independent Hungary that never was. After the defeat of the Hungarians in 1849, he escaped from the country and lived in Britain and America, dispensing radical politics and espousing Hungarian Nationalism, before dying in exile in Turin in 1894.

Road number 37 and a railway line head north-east from Szerencs to **Sárospatak**, a small town with a fine castle and other monuments, and a town that was once, thanks to its Calvinist college, one of the intellectual centres of Hungary — a position which the town is now actively trying to regain. In the ninth century, this area was the first to be settled by the Magyar settlers who came here from central Asia.

There has been a castle here since the thirteenth century. In the sixteenth century, the Perényi family that owned the castle gradually rebuilt the medieval fortress in Renaissance style, changing its role from a defensive castle into a residential palace. The Rákóczi family that owned it during the seventeenth century enlarged the palace further. As a result the two parts of the castle now co-exist rather awkwardly in an eclectic but handsome jumble of architectural styles. After World War II the castle was restored and converted into a large museum, with displays covering the history of the castle, the Rákóczi family, and the War of Independence. There is also an art gallery, and some of the old castle rooms can be seen, including the old Banqueting Hall. Guided tours also take in the medieval parts of the castle, known as the Red Tower, including the dungeons, and the Knights Hall where parliamentary sessions were held during the 1703 War of Independence.

The Parish Church on Kádár Kata utca, which leads to the castle entrance, is one of the largest Gothic buildings in eastern Hungary. There is a huge Baroque high altar inside, which was brought here from the Carmelite Church in Buda Castle after their order was banned in 1784. Organ recitals sometimes take place here. At the north end of Rákóczi utca is the Calvinist College, founded in 1531, and where the great humanist teacher and educationalist Cormenius once taught. In the sixteenth century a printing press set up in the college was used to print his textbooks. The Counter Reformation forced the college to be moved for a time, to Košice in eastern Slovakia. It moved back here in 1703. Many eminent Hungarians have studied here, including the politician Lajos Kossuth and the writer Zsigmond Móricz, and the college is now one of the most famous in the country. The college has long-standing ties with England. English has been a special subject here for many years, and language courses are held here every summer. The buildings are now early nineteenth century and inside there is a Calvinist Museum, and also a Great Library. Tours of the building are available.

Finally, there are some interesting modernist buildings in the town, designed by the architect Imre Mákovecz and built in the 1970s. The best

The ruined castle perched above the village of Füzér

known is the House of Culture on Eötvös utca, between the castle and the station, the façade of which represents a giant insect. This is where many concerts are held during the town's small summer festival in July / August. The apartment block further along the street, on the corner with Rákóczi utca, is similarly distinctive.

The North-Eastern Zempléni

Ten kilometres (6 miles) beyond Sárospatak road and railway pass through **Sátoraljaújhely** before passing into Slovakia. This is another town which is more useful as a transport centre rather than being interesting itself. There is a white wooden church outside the station, and the main square, Ady tér, is pleasant (Baroque Town Hall at number 5), though nothing more. The whole place gives the impression of being a rural backwater, which is what it is, for it is from here that the highest and most interesting parts of the Zempléni mountains can be reached. Those that are not progressing any further beyond here could hike up Mount Magas 509m (1,670ft), above the town. There is an 18m (59ft) high look out tower on the summit, from where the High Tatras can often be seen. There is also a ski run. There was bitter fighting here between the Hungarians and the Nazis in 1944.

The road which runs north-west from the town towards Bozsva and Gonc skirts the northern edge of the Zempléni and allows access to the highest parts. Leaving Sátoraljaújhely, the first place the road passes through is **Széphalom**, where in a park beside the road there is the mausoleum of Ferenc Kazinczy, a language teacher who championed the use of the Hungarian language during the nineteenth century, when it was under threat from the German-speaking Habsburgs. The mausoleum is in the style of a Greek Orthodox home and is built over the spot once occupied by his house. Further on at **Füzérradvány**, a tiny village off the main road, the old Castle Garden has been converted into an arboretum of oaks and pines, which now provide a haven for wildlife such as snakes. At **Pálháza** there is a Calvinist church with a wooden bell tower dating from the eighteenth century. A narrow-gauge forest railway (*erdei vasut*) runs from here to **Rostálló**, in the mountains, the starting point for many hikes. **Hollóháza**, reached by a turning off the main road, is the most northerly village in Hungary, and is famous for its porcelain factory which dates from 1831. There is a museum and a shop here, selling brightly coloured products of the factory.

The biggest draw for travellers around here, however, is the ruined castle situated on a steep bluff above the tiny, picturesque community of **Füzér**. It was built in the 1260s and for a time held the Hungarian crown jewels. The castle was blown up after the defeat of the Hungarians in the War of Independence in the early eighteenth century. There is a magnificent view from the ruins, over the Zempléni range. By the picturesque church in the village, a track marker post gives times and track details for many destinations in the mountains. This is a good starting point for hikes in Zempléni, for anyone equipped with a map and good supplies of food and water (there are very few settlements in these hills).

Additional Information

Places to Visit

Aggtelek
Stalactite Caves
All caves open: 8am-5pm (3pm October to April).

Balassagyarmat
Palóc Ethnographical Museum
Open: 9am-5pm, except Monday and Saturday.

Eger
Castle Museum Complex
Open: 9am-5pm, daily. Only the Hall of Heroes and the underground fortifications are open on Monday.

Géza Gárdonyi Memorial Room
Gárdonyi utca 28
Open: 9am-5pm, except Monday.

Lyceum
Széchenyi utca
Library open 9.30-12noon, Tuesday to Sunday, astronomical museum open 8.30am-1.30pm, Tuesday to Friday and 9.30am-12noon, Saturday and Sunday (closed in winter).

Minaret
Knézich utca
Open: 9am-5pm, daily.

Wine Museum
Városfal utca 1
Open: Tuesday to Saturday 12noon-10pm.

Füzérradvány
Arboretum
Open: 9am-5pm daily.

Gyöngyös
Mátra Museum
Kossuth utca 40
Open: 9am-5pm, except Monday and Saturday.

Hollóháza
Porcelain Factory
Open: May to September, 9am-5pm, October to April, 10am-4pm, except Monday and Saturday. Closed December to February.

Hollókő
Folk Museum
Kossuth utca 82
Open: April to September, 10am-4pm Wednesday to Sunday, October to March, 10am-2pm Thursday, 12noon-2pm Friday, 10am-4pm Saturday and Sunday.

Palóc Folk Furniture & Art Museum
Kossuth utca 99
Open: April to October, 10am-6pm, except Monday and Saturday.

Weaving House
Kossuth utca 94
Open: April to October 9am-5pm, except Monday, Wednesday and Saturday.

Lillafüred
Ottó Herman Museum
Open: 10am-6pm, except Monday and Saturday.

Stalactite Caves
Open: April to October, 9am-5pm, November to March, 9am-4pm daily.

Miskolc
Ecclesiastical Art Museum
Deák tér 7
Open: April to October, 10am-6pm, November to March, 10am-4pm, except Monday and Saturday.

Ottó Herman Museum
Felszabadítók út 28
Open: 10am-6pm, except Monday and Saturday.

Queen's Castle
Open: April to October, 9am-6pm, except Monday and Saturday.

Monok
Kossuth Museum
Open: 10am-1pm, 3pm-6pm, except Monday and Saturday.

Parád
Palóc House
Open: 9am-5pm, except Monday and Saturday.

Parádfürdő
Coach Museum
Open: April to October, 9am-5pm daily,
November to March, 9am-4pm, except
Monday and Saturday.

Salgótarján
Mining Museum
Ady utca
Open: 9am-5pm, except Monday and
Saturday.

Sárospatak
Calvinist College
Rákóczi utca
Open: 9am-5pm, Monday to Friday,
9am-1pm, Sundays and holidays.

Castle Museum
Open: March to October, 10am-6pm,
November to February, 10am-5pm,
except Monday and Saturday.

Parish Church
Kádár Kata utca
Open: 10am-2pm, except Monday and
Saturday.

Rákóczi Cellars
Behind Borostyan Hotel
Open: 7am-7.30pm, except Saturday
and Sunday.

Szalajka Valley
Forestry Museum
Open: April to November, 9am-4pm,
except Monday and Saturday.

Szécsény
Forgách Castle
Open: summer 10am-6pm, winter 9am-
4pm, except Monday and Saturday.

Széphalom
Mausoleum of Ferenc Kazinczy
Open: 10am-6pm, except Monday and
Saturday.

Szerencs
Zempleni Museum
Open: 10am-12noon, except Saturday
and Sunday.

Szilvásvárad
Equestrian Museum
Park utca 8
Open: 9am-5pm, except Monday and
Saturday.

Tokaj
Tokaj Museum
Bethlen Gábor utca 7
Open: summer 9am-5pm, winter 9am-
3pm, except Monday and Saturday.

Tolcsva
Wine Museum
Open: 10am-12noon Tuesday and
Friday to Saturday, 2-4pm Thursday.

Újmassa
Foundry
Open: 9am-5pm, except Monday and
Saturday.

Tourist Information Centres

Eger
Eger Tourist
Bajcsy-Zsilinszky utca 9
☎ 11-724

Gyöngyös
Mátratourist
Fő tér ☎ 37-11-565

Hollókő
Kossuth utca 68

Mátrafüred
Mátratourist
Vörösmarty utca 4.

Miskolc
Borsod Tourist
Széchenyi utca 35 ☎ 46-50-666

IBUSZ
Kossuth utca 2 ☎ 46-37-731

Salgótárjan
Nógrád Tourist
Erzsébet tér 3 ☎ 32-10-660

Sárospatak
Borsod Tourist
Kossuth utca 50 ☎ 41-11-073

IBUSZ
Rákóczi út 3

Sátoraljaújhely
Express
Kossuth tér

Szilvásvárad
Eger Tourist
Egri ut 22 ☎ 36-20-155

8
What To Do In Hungary

Hungary offers far more opportunities to the visitor beyond conventional sightseeing — everything from watersports to horseriding, star gazing to displays of folk dancing, visits to the theatre and cinema to watching horse riding, and Grand Prix motor racing or football matches. Budapest is the centre for many of these activities, especially as regards the theatre, cinema and concert scene, with the Balaton an important region for sporting and outdoor activities. But many locations in Hungary offer these activities to varying degrees. The cultural scene in many provincial towns and cities is very varied, especially in summer when many places hold art or folklore festivals. This chapter details what is on offer in Hungary in all these areas and, more importantly, where to find information about the ever-changing sporting and cultural scenes. Where relevant, specific information relating to Budapest is given; other places are mentioned in more general terms.

General Information

There are a number of booklets and leaflets detailing the sporting, cultural and entertainment scene in Hungary, published monthly or yearly and available from tourist offices and hotel reception desks all over the country. Some will cover Budapest and the provinces, others will relate specifically to Budapest (and may only be available there). One publication to look out for is *Programme in Hungary*, a free booklet published monthly in English and German and which seems to be widely available. It has information on concerts, opera, ballet, theatre, casinos, exhibitions, sporting events, arranged sightseeing tours, folklore performances and details about spa treatment and thermal baths, all presented in two sections, one for Budapest and one for the provinces. It is full of hundreds of useful addresses, opening times and other details — a 'Bible' for anyone staying in Hungary for any length of time who wants to see what the country has to offer beyond what has been described in the preceding chapters of this book.

Another booklet, *Budapest Panorama*, gives the low-down on Budapest's entertainment and sporting scene. Again, it lists details about the full range of entertainment on offer, including classical, rock and jazz concerts and recitals, opera, ballet, cinema, temporary exhibitions, details about both spectator and participatory sport, addresses and comments about restaurants, clubs and casinos in the capital, and also important practical information such as the addresses of embassies, hospitals, car rental facilities, airline and tourist offices, Western Banks, and how to make telephone calls or send a parcel or telex abroad; a useful update of what is contained in the Fact File section of this book. Again, it is published monthly, costs nothing, is freely available and should be consulted by anyone wanting to make the most of their stay in the capital. Finally, there are a number of English-language newspapers published in Budapest. They contain news and views about Hungary — interesting for anyone who wants to know more about contemporary Hungarian politics or society — and also a listings section for the week ahead. *Budapest Week* is a newspaper published on Friday, available at news stands all over the central part of the capital, which provides similar information, on a weekly basis, to the booklets already mentioned. Look for other newspapers or magazines which carry similar information. In Hungary's free-market economy, the number of titles available is likely to mushroom.

Finally, another source of information in Budapest is the touch-screen computer in the IBUSZ office at Petőfi tér 3, open 24 hours a day. On this, you can call up information on anything from restaurants to opera, nightclubs to where the lost property offices are in the capital, taxi firms to the addresses of doctors or hospitals. The machine then prints out the information for you. An invaluable service.

Music

Hungary has a long classical and folk music tradition, and has produced many world-famous composers, conductors and performers, whose contributions to Hungarian culture are outlined in the introduction to this book. The classical music scene is flourishing everywhere; the pop music scene is less developed, with few Hungarian bands known outside the country — but adventurous visitors might want to turn up at a rock concert they see advertised on fly-posters put up around city centres, and see what there is on offer. Western bands sometimes play in Budapest and other cities. These events will be more heavily advertised. In Budapest, major Hungarian (and sometimes foreign) rock bands perform at the Petőfi csarnok, a huge youth centre in the Városliget (City Park). In theory they should be able to supply details in English ☎ 142 4327. Those interested could also check out the Rock Café in Dohány utca 20, Budapest VII; other venues are listed in magazines such as *Budapest Panorama*. Occasionally the Népstadion, the huge sports arena in the east of Budapest, stages

Western bands. The British group *Queen* played there in 1985. Nearby is the Budapest Sportscsarnok, a similar venue (though much smaller).

Jazz is popular in Hungary but jazz fans may find it more difficult to seek out the concerts and events. The 'concerts' sections of listings magazines may show some jazz concerts, but there is rarely a separate section marked 'Jazz'. Most jazz performances take place in jazz clubs and bars, in billiard halls and nightclubs. Currently the most famous group is the *Benkó Dixieland Band*. Ask around in tourist offices in Budapest to find out when and where they are playing, although they often tour abroad. In Budapest the best place to look for events are in the English language newspapers or on posters stuck up around town. Some jazz venues in the capital are the Annex Jazz Club in the Hotel Erzsébet, Károly utca 11-15, Budapest V; the Merlin Theatre (see under 'Theatres and Cinemas'); the Jazz café in Balassi utca 27, Budapest V; and the Vendeghaz Café-Restaurant Jazz Club at Hidfo utca 16, Budapest III.

The classical music scene is more varied and concerts are usually of the highest quality. In the summer, in particular, foreign orchestras give concerts in Budapest and other cities. At this time of year there are often concerts staged in towns which see a lot of visitors — for example, Szentendre, Eger, Keszthely, Esztergom or Sopron. Country houses such as Fertőd (Chapter 3) often stage concerts. A more unusual setting for a chamber concert is deep underground in limestone caverns such as those at Aggtelek, in north-eastern Hungary. Churches and cathedrals, such as the abbeys at Tihany beside Lake Balaton, or Pannonhalma (Chapter 3), are venues for organ recitals. Martonvásár, south-west of Budapest (Chapter 4) is where Beethoven lived for a time, and concerts of his music are now staged in the open air, on an island in the lake in the grounds of the house, on summer evenings. The music scene in the provinces tends to be busiest during the summer or during festivals (see Feature Box on pages 216 & 217 for a comprehensive list of regional festivals). The concert scene in Budapest is busy and varied all year round. Venues in the capital include the Matthias Church, on Buda Hill, and St Stephen's Basilica, in Pest. Concert halls include the two at the Franz Liszt Academy of Music at Liszt Ferenc tér 8, Budapest VI, or the Vigadó, a huge, beautiful concert hall near the Danube at Vigadó tér 1, Budapest V. Many tourist offices (eg Tourinform) carry information about concerts, and there are leaflets (unfortunately some only in Hungarian) with very detailed listings of concerts that are on offer. There is a central ticket and information office for all Budapest's concerts at Philharmonia, Vörösmarty tér 1, Budapest V, right in the centre of town, which also supplies information about concerts at Martonvásár (Chapter 4), including pre-arranged travel there and back. The opening times are 10am-6pm Monday to Friday, 10am-2pm Saturday. The office is closed on Sunday and shuts every day for lunch from 1.30-2pm.

Folk music is the way to experience uniquely Hungarian music and is performed all over the country. Visitors may experience anything from a group of musicians playing in a hotel restaurant, to attending concerts given at any one of the country's huge provincial folk music festivals. These festivals will normally include displays of folk art and other traditions. Again, check the listings magazines for what is on offer. Many provincial towns stage concerts and shows during the summer. The Táncház, an institution developed in the 1970s, is where folk music and dancing is performed, and the audience is always encouraged to get involved. Some folk ensembles play music from specific regions such as Serbia, Croatia or Transylvania. In Budapest there are many venues and ensembles. Some are held in the open air in summer. The Budapest Folklore Centre, with music, dance, folk art and more besides, is at Fehérvári utca 47, Budapest XI. Listings magazines and tourist offices should be able to give the full rundown. Concert halls such as the Vidagó are sometimes the venue for folk concerts. Some hotels and restaurants have special folklore evenings but you will normally have to pay to eat or stay there to take part. In Budapest the folklore concerts can sometimes be distinctly touristy. A more genuine encounter with Hungarian folk music might be had in the provinces.

Nightlife And Eating Out In Budapest

Any listings magazine or newspaper will carry addresses and details of restaurants, clubs, discos, casinos and bars in the capital. The restaurants and bars right in the centre of town and around the castle tend both to be pricey and geared towards tourists. The restaurants section of the *Budapest Panorama* booklet lists restaurants according to their class and price, and also carries lists of restaurants with folklore programmes and those which specialise in Hungarian cuisine, or in the cuisine of other countries. Choices on offer in Budapest include Mexican, Japanese, Serbian, Chinese, French, Thai, Italian, Argentinian, Czech, Korean, Greek and others. There are also addresses of kosher and vegetarian restaurants. Reservations in most restaurants are advisable in the evenings. Those who really want to dress up and splash out will enjoy Gundel, the most famous restaurant in Budapest, on Állakerti körút 2, in the City Park. In Budapest, many restaurants will be able to provide menus in English. Many Western fast food chains are beginning to sprout in Budapest and in provincial cities as well. Home-from-home options, the interiors of which look exactly the same as the same chain's restaurants on the other side of the world, include Pizza Hut, McDonald's, and Burger King. Their addresses are well advertised. There are many Hungarian fast-food outlets operating too, and many stalls set up in the street sell hot snacks, drinks or ice cream during the day.

The numerous *kávéház* (coffee houses) in Budapest were once the focus for the city's cultured and intellectual citizens. Up until World War I, they were the haunt of writers, artists and politicians, who formed a sophisticated elite in Budapest society and who gathered at their favourite *kávéház* to work and talk as much as anything, regarding the coffee house as both a social club and work place. Now it is mainly tourists who populate the coffee houses and *cukrászda* (patisseries) in the capital, since only they can afford the high prices. The *kávéház* and *cukrászda* are virtually indistinguishable. Both serve coffees, other drinks and delicious ices, pastries, cakes and desserts. Many are still full of character. They can be found all over Budapest. Some of the ones to look out for are as follows: the Gerbeaud is in Vörösmarty tér, right in the centre of Pest, a popular tourist haunt with delicious cakes on offer, where you can sit outside in the square and watch the city go by; the New York, Teréz körút 9-11, Budapest VII, has sumptuous art-nouveau decor, and there is a restaurant attached; and the elegant Astoria Kávéház, in the Astoria Hotel at Kossuth utca 19, which was reputedly the haunt of spies in cold war days.

Details and addresses of clubs, casinos and bars can likewise be found in *Budapest Panorama* or the English-language newspapers. Most in the centre of Pest tend to be expensive and cater for an international clientele. A number of boats on the Danube have been converted into clubs, casinos or restaurants, and these chug up and down the river until late into the night, their floating guests watching live dancing or folklore shows, or gambling away in the casinos on board. Many of the largest international hotels have pricey discos, clubs, restaurants and gambling halls.

Opera, Ballet And Musicals

Hungarians take their opera and ballet seriously as they do their classical music concerts. Formerly high state subsidies, which are increasingly under threat as all art forms begin to adapt to a more market-led economy, mean that the opera and ballet scene is varied and of high quality. Many Hungarian opera and ballet companies perform abroad, and foreign companies perform in Budapest and other cities. Tickets are often hard to get, but are far cheaper than for similar shows in Western cities. A visit to the opera can be a real experience. Opera is normally performed on a lavish scale, with performers being given ovations after particularly momentous operatic numbers. The main venue for opera in the country is the State Opera House at Andrássy utca 22, Budapest VI. The interior boasts huge chandeliers and other similarly grandiose items of decoration. Former directors of the State Opera Company include Gustav Mahler and Otto Klemperer. Needless to say, people dress up to come here. The Box Office is on Dalszínház utca, round the corner from the entrance. Opening times are Tuesday to Saturday 10am-1.45 pm, and 2.30-7pm, Sundays 10am-1pm, 4-7pm, ☎ 153-0170. Tickets can also be bought at some hotel desks and travel agents. There are guided tours of the Opera House before some performances. The repertoire includes works by Hungarian composers such as Bartók, and also works by Verdi, Mozart, Puccini etc. New productions are premiered in the spring and autumn.

Festivals And Annual Events In Hungary

January
Farsang, the New Year ball season, all over Hungary.

February
Busójárás Carnival in Mohács, one of the liveliest carnivals in provincial Hungary.

Filmszemle, Budapest film festival.

March
15 March: the 1848 revolution is remembered, especially in Budapest where everyone is seized by a sudden rush of patriotism. Flags are waved, crowds gather at various spots in the capital to commemorate the revolution.

Budapest Spring Festival: '10 days, 100 places, 1,000 events'. Concerts, ballet, exhibitions, opera, folklore, theatre, with many international performers taking part. Some events are held outside the capital. One of the most important events in Budapest's year. Similar spring festivals are also in Sopron, Kecskemét and Szentendre.

Easter
In some provincial places (for example Hollóko, Chapter 7) the custom of *locsolkodas*, an old fertility ritual, is revived. Boys and men splash cologne or water on girls and receive a painted egg in return. Churches are always packed and there are many services held.

1 May
Open-air celebrations in many places, although the old Communist

The Opperetta Theatre at Nagymező utca 17, Budapest VI, stages light operetta or Western musicals. *La Cage aux Folles* and *Chess* have been staged here, while other theatres in the capital have staged *Les Misérables* and *Cats*. Seek out details at hotels or tourist offices, as these shows are likely to appeal to visitors. Hungary's most famous musical, a smash-hit in the 1980s, is *István a király* (Stephen the King), which is about the attempts of King Stephen to Christianise the Magyars in the eleventh century. It may still be playing in a theatre in Budapest. The Erkel Theatre, Köztársaság tér 30, Budapest VIII, is a modern theatre and the largest in Hungary, which stages opera, musicals and ballets, specialising in performances by modern dance companies and visiting foreign companies such as the Bolshoi. Another interesting venue is the open-air theatre on Margaret Island, which stages anything from opera to rock concerts on practices of grand displays and marches on this date have been abandoned. Beer tents are set up in Budapest's parks, and the date is still recognised as a 'workers' holiday'.

June
Festivals at Sopron and other towns. Concerts at Zsámbék, the ruined church to the north-west of Budapest. Equestrian events at Szántód-puszta; Slovak folklore festival at Bujak; Pécs Summer Festival with open-air concerts and theatre performances.

July
Hortobágy and Kiskunság equestrian events; Debrecen Jazz Festival; Szombathely International Bartók Festival; Szeged Summer Festival.

August
Esztergom International Guitar Festival, every odd year (1993, 1995 etc); Hortobágy Bridge Fair, usually 19-20 August (equestrian events); Tata festival, includes open-air concerts, plays, opera; Debrecen flower carnival, usually last week in August.

20 August is St Stephen's Day, and the National Day of Hungary. Events and celebrations all round the country. In Budapest, over a million people line the banks of the Danube and watch the spectacular fireworks display above Gellért Hill, which starts at 9pm.

September
Autumn Arts Weeks in Budapest from late September into October with concerts, plays, opera, theatre, exhibitions.

Savaria Arts Festival in Szombathely (continues into October).

summer evenings. Performances of large scale operas such as *Aida* have occasionally taken place in the Népstadion sports stadium. Listings magazines will carry details of venues and performances, as will tourist offices or the Philharmonia office (see under 'Classical Music') in Budapest. The ballet company of the State Opera House performs in the theatres mentioned in this section, and at other venues. There is a central box office in Budapest which deals with most opera, ballet, musical and theatre performances, and also arrangements for some rock or classical concerts; it is at Andrássy utca 18, ☎ 111 2000.

The opera and ballet scene is far more subdued outside Budapest. Most large cities have a theatre which may stage operas or play host to dance companies from time to time. Look out for notices or try to seek information from local tourist offices.

Shopping

In Communist days, visitors from the Soviet Union and other Eastern Bloc countries would come to Budapest to stare, goggle-eyed, at the quality and variety of goods that were on offer in the shops. Hungary's comparative wealth, and the growing importance of a more consumer-led, capitalist style economy which began to emerge in the 1970s and 1980s, ensured that the capital's main shopping street, Váci utca, became the most Western-looking corner of anywhere in Eastern Europe, a place where window shoppers could feast their eyes on luxury goods that were sold in smart-looking shops that were unknown back home. To the Western visitor, Váci utca is less of an eye-opener, but throughout Hungary there are many quality goods and souvenirs to buy, and the prices are extremely reasonable. Western consumer goods, such as electrical equipment, cameras, , quality clothing and jewellery, are best looked for in Budapest. Other goods, such as ceramics, books, records, antiques, wines, or goods and souvenirs made from wood, leather or silver are available in many other towns and cities, although there will be far less choice on offer. Some practical details on shopping are given in the Fact File section. This section simply describes what to look for in the shops in Budapest and other cities.

In Budapest, Váci utca, which runs south from Vörösmarty tér in central Pest, is the main place to look for fashionable goods, books and jewellery. Tourist souvenirs are sold all over the city, but especially in the streets in the castle district. Entertainment-listing booklets such as *Budapest Panorama* usually carry sections on shopping, listing specialist shops which sell fashion goods, antiques, records, books, sports equipment etc. A visit to a big department store can be interesting. In Budapest there is a big department store, called the Skála Metró, across the road from Nyugati station (there is an entrance from Nyugati metro station). The ground floor contains a food hall as good as anything you will find in the country. This is the place to look for Hungarian wines or spirits to take home. The upper floors sell clothes, electrical goods, books, records, tapes and furnishings. It is also fun to visit food markets in the capital, where stalls are piled high with paprika, fruit and vegetables, bread, cheese and fish which can sometimes be seen swimming around in glass tanks, and bought from there. An indoor market is a *vásárcsarnok*. The two largest indoor markets in the capital are on Vámház körút, close to Szabadság-híd bridge and at Rosenberg hazaspar 13. Both are atmospheric places, alive with bustling shoppers and garrulous stall owners. They are both open until about 6pm on weekdays, until 2pm on Saturdays and are closed on Sundays. Outdoor markets are known as *piac*. There are good open-air markets on Lövőház utca, close to Moszkva tér, and on Garay tér, just beyond Keleti station. They tend to be open during the same hours. Finally, mention must be made of the Esceri flea-market, where all manner of junk, antiques, and second-hand goods are sold from ramshackle stalls in a dusty, windswept location in south-east Budapest. Everything

A colourful fruit and vegetable market near Moszkva tér, Budapest

After a cutural tour of Budapest visit Váci utca, a pedestrian mall with charming window displays

What To Buy In Hungary And Where To Buy It

Antiques

Some antiques cannot be taken out of the country. Expensive antiques are probably best bought at hard-currency shops (see Fact File section). Any goods bought in these shops are automatically suitable for export. In Budapest there is often a craft fair at the Petőfi Csarnok in the Városliget on Saturday and Sunday mornings. There are antique shops in the capital on Váci utca. Pricey antiques likely to appeal to tourists are availble in shops on Castle Hill or look for addresses of shops in listings magazines.

Books

A number of bookshops along Váci utca in Budapest sell books about Hungary in foreign languages, or stock the works of Hungarian authors translated into English. Many Hungarian publishers produce coffee table books on Hungary with text in English. The biggest foreign-language publisher in Hungary is Corvina. Most provincial towns have a bookshop, where maps, guides or other books in English are occasionally sold. In Budapest there are second hand bookshops at Gerloczi utca 7, and Múzeum Körút 13-15.

Ceramics

Herend, Pécs and Kalocsa are all pottery-producing towns. Buy their wares there, or in shops in Budapest. Again, Váci utca is the best place to start looking. Porcelain figurines are popular, as are vases and other items of glassware.

Clothes

There are expensive and fashionable clothes and shoe shops along Váci utca, Budapest. Clothing sold in department stores is often of reasonable quality. Again, listings magazines carry addresses of clothes shops.

Dolls And Puppets

These have long been popular in Hungary. Many are sold in antique shops. Marionettes can be bought in tourist centres such as Szentendre, often dressed up in regional costumes.

Food And Drink

Paprika (in sachets), salami (the best brands are *téli*, *Csabai* and *Gyulai szalámi*) or Hungarian wines and spirits can be bought in supermarkets and exported though be wary of any import regulations that the country you take these products back to might have. For more ideas, see the 'Food and Drink' section in the Introduction to this book.

Records And Tapes

These are inexpensive and are available everywhere. Recordings of Hungarian classical and folk music artists are usually reasonably priced and are of high quality. Compact discs are only found in a few outlets. There is a good music shop in Budapest on Martinelli tér, open until 9pm 7 days a week, selling Hungarian and Western recordings. Many records imported from the West are sold more cheaply than they are in Britain or America. Hunting around can yield some real bargains.

seems to be on offer, from Habsburg bric-a-brac to dodgy-looking electrical goods, spares for bikes and cars, old books and records, even unwanted bits of military paraphernalia from the departing Russian army. An absorbing place to look around, but beware of the pickpockets. The market is open 6 days a week and can be found at Nagykörösi utca 156, near that road's junction with Hoffher Albert utca, in Budapest's XIX district.

Spas And Thermal Baths

There is a long tradition of drinking and bathing in spring waters that bubble up from the ground in numerous locations in Hungary. The Romans knew about some of the springs, and established spas at various locations in the country, the waters of some of which are still used to cure patients of various ailments, as they take an intensive course of bathing and drinking the waters of the particular spa that they have been advised to attend. Most spa towns are relaxing and interesting places to visit, with carefully laid-out parks, areas of woodland and elegant, if gently decaying, nineteenth-century buildings.

Hungarian Spas

Balatonfüred: on the shores of Lake Balaton, an elegant spa which has received a good number of internationally famous politicians, artists, writers etc into its sanatoria. World-famous heart hospital.

Balf: near Sopron and the Austrian border; popular with foreigners. Muscular, skin and digestive disorders are treated.

Bükfürdő: another resort in the far west of Hungary. Developed only in the last few decades into an expensive, modern resort, specifically geared towards wealthy foreigners.

Harkány: in the warm south of the country, a very popular spa with outdoor pools and many medical facilities. Crowded on warm weekends in summer.

Hévíz: near the western shores of Lake Balaton. Radioactive mud may not sound like something which pulls in the crowds, but most here come to bathe in Europe's largest thermal lake. Another popular and busy spa, the waters of which are supposed to treat muscular disorders. The nearby pleasures of Lake Balaton mean that this is another spa with a varied international clientele.

These are Hungary's principal spas. Others exist, mentioned in the text of this book in the relevant chapters. In most spas it is possible to bathe and taste the waters. Courses of medical treatment are best booked before leaving for Hungary, through IBUSZ or another travel agent.

Steam Baths In Budapest

The Romans developed a spa at *Aquincum* in the northern part of Budapest, which fell into disuse after they left. But one of the benefits of over

150 years of Turkish occupation of the capital has been the establishment
of a number of Turkish baths in the city, which are popular with both
tourists and Hungarians. Now, 70 million litres of water gush from the
city's springs every day, at temperatures of up to 70 °C (158 °F), and they
feed over a dozen thermal bath complexes. It is possible to hire towels,
bathing costumes etc at most of these establishments, and an afternoon
spent relaxing in the warm waters of one of the city's Turkish baths, after
a morning's gruelling sightseeing, is a good way to arrange one's time in
the capital. Some baths have both swimming pools, and thermal baths in
which people wallow, rather than swim. There are always separate warm
baths and medical facilities for men and women; some bath complexes
have swimming pools, which can be used by both sexes. At all establishments it is possible to have a variety of medical treatments, including
massages and spells in the sauna and steamrooms, for which one has to
pay for over and above the cost of the ticket which gives access to the hot
baths or swimming pool. A number of bath houses, especially the Gellért
baths, are architectural delights in themselves and could easily count as
'sights' of Budapest.

Császár Bath, and **Lukács Bath**, Frankel Leó utca, Budapest II
Both part of the National Institute for Rheumatology and Physiotherapy.
Under reconstruction and possibly closed for long periods. Nineteenth-
century building housing spa facilities whose waters were known 1,000
years ago, and which were developed by the Turks. However, the water
is sulphurous.
Baths: open 6.30am, close 6pm weekdays, 1pm Saturdays, 2pm Sundays.
Swimming pool: opens 6am, closes 7pm Monday to Saturday, 4pm Sundays.

Gellért Baths, Kelenhegyi utca 2-4 (in same building as Gellért Hotel)
Built in 1913, this is very popular with tourists. High prices and over-
sumptuous decor, tend to discourage all but the wealthiest Hungarians.
Popular with Budapest's wealthy society in the 1930s, and still retains a
certain air of exclusivity. Very warm baths to wallow in, plus indoor and
outdoor pools, the latter with a wave machine and sunbathing area. Full
range of saunas, massages etc available. Possibly the best baths in the
capital. The staff here speak English and this is a good place to learn about
the whole system of thermal baths before visiting other complexes.

Baths: opening times as for Császár Baths.
Swimming pool: opens 6am to 6pm daily.

Király Baths, Fő utca 84, Budapest II
Another elegant nineteenth-century spa building. Its name translates as
the King's Baths. A small complex, limited facilities for swimming but a
fine place in which to wallow away an afternoon.

Open: Monday to Saturday 6.30am-6pm, closed Sunday.
Men only, Monday, Wednesday, Friday; Women only, Tuesday, Thursday, Saturday.

Rác Baths, Hadnagy utca 8-10, Budapest I
Another bath house dating from Turkish times.
Open: as for Király Baths.

Rudas Baths, Döbrentei tér 9, Budapest I
Built by the Turks in the sixteenth century. The octagonal pool they designed still remains. Nice interior decor. Swimming pools and drinking cures for digestive complaints. Reputedly popular with the capital's gay community.

Baths: open as for Császár Baths.
Swimming pool: opens 6am, closes 5pm Monday to Saturday, 12noon Sundays.
Entire complex for men only.

The ornate thermal baths in the Gellért Hotel, Budapest

Széchenyi Baths, in the Városliget (City Park), adjacent to Széchenyi Fürdő metro
Another very large bathing complex. There is a statue outside to the geologist who discovered the springs and founded the baths in the nineteenth century. Frequently crowded.

Baths: open as for Császár Baths.
Swimming pool: opens daily, 6am-6pm.

Thermál Hotel, northern tip of Margaret Island
Luxurious modern bathing complex, popular with foreigners who stay in the hotel next door to the baths and attend a full course of treatment. Exclusive and expensive air about the place, and a little out of the way. Restaurant and nightclub, and full medical facilities on offer.

Baths and pool: open daily, 7am-7pm (first Tuesday of every month: closes 3pm).

Sports

Spectator

Details of these are usually given in listings magazines and Budapest's newspapers. In the provinces there are football matches, sailing races (mainly on Lake Balaton), equestrian events including racing and horse shows, bowling, volleyball, cycling, motorbike speedway and many other competitive sport events. In Budapest there are rowing races on the Danube (August), and cycling, basketball, football, tennis, hockey, ice hockey, swimming and shooting events. Larger events in the capital include international football matches, held at the Népstadion stadium in Pest, which has a capacity of 76,000. Next door is the indoor arena, the Budapest Sportscsarnok, a venue for events such as ice hockey, tennis or basketball. Both can be found on Kerepesi utca in the eastern part of Pest, and are served by Népstadion Metro station. Budapest's two main soccer teams are Ferencvárosi, based at Üllői utca 129, Budapest IX, and Honvédkispest, at Új temető utca 1-3, Budapest XIX. Matches are played in the afternoons at weekends, and occasionally in the evenings midweek. Swimming and waterpolo competitions are held at the Komjádi bela Pool on Frankel Leo utca in Buda.

Loversenyter, at Albertirsai utca 10, Budapest X (metro: Pillangó utca) is the venue for flat horse racing, which usually takes place on Saturday, Sunday, Wednesday or Thursday afternoons. There are trotting races at the Ügetőpálya track at Kerepesi utca 11, Budapest VIII, usually on the same days. Individual races are advertised in listings magazines. The Budapest Grand Prix motor race, first held in 1986, is held at the Formula 1 track at Mogyoród, 20km (12 miles) north-east of Budapest. Tickets can be bought in advance from tourist offices in the capital. The event normally takes place in early August and is held over 3 days. HÉV trains from Örs vezér tere run to Szilasliget, half a mile from the Hungaroring Grand Prix ground. The Budapest marathon is run in late April or early May, from the Népstadion to Római-fürdő.

Participatory Sport And Outdoor Activities

The best place to head for sports such as tennis and volleyball, and swimming and water sports, is any of the resorts around Lake Balaton, which are specially geared up for this sort of thing. These sports are normally organised through hotels, who will often be able to rent out equipment. Skiing is not particularly big news in Hungary. There are ski-lifts and runs in the Mátras and Bükk mountains, amongst others. Many locations all over Hungary offer horse-riding, especially sites in the Great Plain such as Hortobágy (Chapter 6) — enquire at local tourist offices. Specialist horse-riding holidays can be arranged from outside Hungary by IBUSZ or other firms. In Budapest there is a specialist agency dealing with riding holidays: Pegazus Tours, at Károlyi Mihály utca 5.

Many Westerners come to Hungary to hunt. The game in the country's hill regions includes fox, stag, roebuck, deer and pheasant. Those who want to hunt should make arrangements before they come to Hungary. IBUSZ offices in Britain and America should be able to arrange hunting package holidays. A useful address in Hungary is Huntours at Retek utca 34, Budapest II. Those who want to go angling in the country must obtain a permit, from the Hungarian Anglers Association (Magyar Országos Horgász Szövétseg) at Október 6 utca 20, Budapest V. Around Lake Balaton, fishing permits can be obtained from tourist offices.

Sporting Grounds And Facilities In Budapest

Billiards — Billiard saloon, Krisztina körút 15, Budapest XII
  and Gold Club, Kertész utca 17, Budapest VII
Bowling — Hotel Novotel, Alkotás utca 63-67, Budapest XII
Horse riding — Metro tennis Camping, Csomori utca 158, Budapest
XVI and Petneházy Country Club, Feketefej utca 2-4, Budapest II
Mini-golf — Hotel Flandria, Szegedi utca 27, Budapest XIII
Skittles — Hotel Tusculanum, Záhony utca 10, Budapest III
Squash — City Squash Club, Marczibányi tér 13, Budapest II
Swimming — pool on Margaret Island and in Thermal Hotel Helia
Tennis — SAS Club hotel, Törökbálintl utca 51-3, Budapest XII
  and Flamenco Tennis, Bartók Béla utca 63, Budapest XI
  and Thermal Hotel Helia, Karpát utca 62-4, Budapest XIII

There are skiing grounds in the Buda Hills at Normafa and Jánoshegy in winter. Many people skate on the frozen-over lake in the City Park in Budapest in winter.

Theatre And Cinema

The theatrical tradition in Hungary is strong, and most provincial towns have a theatre with a regular theatrical company. Whether foreign visitors want to sit through anything in Hungarian, however, is another matter. Most listing magazines have sections which provide details of theatrical performances in English, whether by Hungarian companies or by visiting theatre groups from English-speaking countries. These rarely take place outside Budapest and are most likely to take place in summer. In Budapest an important venue is the Merlin Theatre at Gerloczy utca 4, Budapest V. Another venue for English-language plays is the courtyard of the Budapest Hilton near Buda Castle. The Katona Theatre at Petőfi Sándor utca 6 is the most important Hungarian-language theatre in Budapest. The company based here has toured abroad to critical acclaim. Theatre which transcends the language barrier includes mime (see listings magazines for details) or puppet theatres (*bábszinház*) which put on shows for children in the afternoons (shows in the evenings tend to be political or social satirical shows intended for adults). In Budapest there are puppet theatres at Népköztársaság utca 69, and at Jokai tér 10.

Films shown in Hungarian cinemas tend either to be in Hungarian anyway, or are dubbed into the language. Listings magazines tend to ignore films, but Budapest's weekly English-language newspapers carry a list of films exhibited in the capital's cinemas that are shown with English dialogue intact (ie with Hungarian subtitles for Hungarian speakers). You will rarely find films shown in their original language outside Budapest's few art-house cinemas that specialise in showing foreign films. The letters 'Mb' beside a film title means that it is dubbed into Hungarian. Times of showings are often given in a very confusing manner: ½ 8 means 7.30, for instance ('half to eight o'clock'). There is a film festival held in Budapest every year in February, attended by foreign distributors and critics.

The Planetarium in the Népliget Park in Budapest (close to Népliget Metro Station) also doubles as a laser theatre in the evening, when hourlong shows of extremely loud rock music, accompanied by an amazing laser show on the inside dome of the building, are put on. The programme varies but includes music by Genesis, Queen, Jean Michelle Jarre and Pink Floyd. A different laser show accompanies the music by each band. There are usually two or three showings every evening. The programmes of the laser theatre are well advertised around town and in listings magazines. Tickets can be bought at the Planetarium or the main theatre box office at Andrássy utca 18 in central Budapest. Magic Lantern shows combining film, acting and mime are staged at the Nulladik Színház at Csengery utca 68, Budapest VI.

HUNGARY FACT FILE

Accidents And Emergencies

For procedures involving road accidents and breakdowns, see under 'Driving in Hungary'.

The following telephone numbers apply all over the country:
Police 07
Fire 05
Ambulance 04 (hospital - *kórház*)

Violent crime in Hungary is quite rare but the number of thefts has increased quite dramatically in the post-Communist era and as such it is wise for visitors to take special care of personal possessions. Make sure car doors and hotel rooms are locked (especially at night) and do not leave jewellery, money or cameras lying around but make use of the hotel's safe. The Budapest Central Police Station can be found at 16 Deák Ferenc utca (by Deák tér metro station, ☎ 1123-456). It is open 24 hours a day and, if in Budapest, should be telephoned in preference to the 07 number as it is more likely there will be someone there who speaks English. The police (*rendőrség*) wear blue and grey uniforms and are quite markedly polite to tourists (though they will often ask to see papers if travelling in border regions).

Accommodation

The great increase in the availability of private rooms in the last couple of years has meant that finding somewhere to stay in Hungary, even in high season, is rarely a serious concern though there is still a severe shortage of lower grade hotel rooms during the summer so anyone planning to arrive late in a town or simply seeking peace of mind is advised to make a reservation. It is possible to do this from abroad either through travel agents (Danube Travel in London provides this service for a fee) or by contacting hotels directly yourself — information offices abroad can provide lists of hotels. If already inside Hungary, bookings can be made in the Budapest head offices for the provincial branches of the three nationwide hotel chains; Hungar Hotels (Petőfi utca 16 ☎ 118-3393), Pannonia (Rákóczi út 9 ☎ 114-1886) and Danubius (Martinelli tér 8 ☎ 117-3652). Information offices in Budapest can provide a booklet called *Camping and Hotels* which covers

227

the whole country. If arriving in a town without accommodation it is best to head first for the local tourist information office. All tourist offices in Hungary also act as accommodation offices and most should be able to find accommodation for you in hotels, pensions or private houses, or give information about campsites. The addresses of these offices are given in the 'Additional Information' section at the end of each chapter.

Most hotels (*szálloda*) belong to the Hungar Hotels, Pannonia or Danubius chains and are graded by a star system. Five star establishments meet all the world standards for five star luxury — each room will be equipped with a bath, telephone, radio, television and small refridgerator — though they are only to be found in Budapest and around Lake Balaton. Four star hotels are marginally more modest while three star ones do not always provide private baths or television sets. Two star hotel rooms are unlikely to have a bath or shower while one star establishments will be quite spartan and may not provide breakfast, though will generally be clean and very cheap by Western standards. Prices vary according to star rating, season (prices can drop by over a quarter in winter) and locality (for Budapest and Balaton expect to pay an average 20 per cent extra). One hangover from the Communist era is that some hotels might still have different price bands for foreign and domestic tourists though this practise is dying out. A reservation is highly advisable for anyone travelling alone as single rooms are not in abundance.

Pensions (*panzió*) are appearing in ever greater numbers at the most popular tourist destinations. They come in two grades and will offer catering facilities. Generally they will undercut the prices of local hotels with similar ratings though there are no hard and fast rules as to their relative expense. Motels may sometimes be found on the outskirts of the major towns along the main highways. Often they will form part of a larger tourist complex that might include a camping site, swimming pools, thermal baths etc. Once again price and quality are constant variables.

Often the cheapest option for a room in the centre of town will be a private room (*szoba*). Local tourist offices will have information about these and can book you in directly or you may alternatively simply knock on the door — watch out for the '*szoba kiadó*' or '*zimmer frei*' signs that proliferate around Balaton and the Danube Bend. Again single beds are harder to come by and rates may be higher if you stay fewer than three nights. Breakfast can often be provided for an additional sum. It is an increasingly popular way for Hungarians to earn a little extra money and it does provide an opportunity to see the inside of a Hungarian home though the people who rent these out are rarely able to converse in a foreign language (some will have a smattering of German; very few will speak any English) and pretty much keep themselves to themselves. Host and premises will have been vetted by the agency (if rented through one) and will consequently be of a quite acceptable standard (there are no such guarantees when accepting an offer from a tout) and there may be a television or radio in the room and the possibility of cooking and washing facilities. One last word of warning: most Hungarians seem to own dogs, often of the large and ferocious variety, but the owners will always assure visitors that their slavering pets are quite harmless.

Towards the cheaper end of the market details of local tourist hostels (*túrista szálló*) may be obtained from regional tourist offices. They are basically the equivalent of the Western youth hostels (which only currently exist in Budapest) and though they will often be the cheapest place to stay facilities will be minimal and the majority of beds situated in very cramped dormitories. Vacant colleges (*kollégium*) open their doors to paying guests over the summer holiday (roughly from the beginning of July to mid-August) and also at weekends throughout the year. Details again will be available at the local tourist office. Usually the spartan rooms will simply contain two beds, two desks and a sink but they are very cheap and often quite well located. The locations of these facilities will often change every year. There is a national network of youth tourist offices (Express) which are the best place to find out about this sort of accommodation.

There are over 200 camping sites (*kemping*) in Hungary. They are especially plentiful (and crowded) around Lake Balaton (where they are also the most expensive) and there are seven sites in Budapest, the majority scattered around the Buda Hills. They are graded from one to four star but all have running water, shower facilities, toilets and a 24 hour reception service. The more elaborate boast restaurants and shops. Most open from May to September only though a few stay open all year and offer reductions during the low season. Members of the International Camping and Caravanning Club are entitled to discounts. Information offices can supply leaflets as to the exact whereabouts and opening times of each site. Campsites may also offer bungalows (*üdülőház*) which usually house two to four and range from those with hot running water, kitchens and a sitting room to the most basic of wooden huts. Camping rough is illegal.

Budapest: With an estimated 5 million visitors each year and only 60,000 beds the situation in the capital is not ideal but even at peak times it will be possible to find a room within your price range. The city has an excellent cheap internal transport system so even if you are some way from the centre all will not be lost (the transport system comes to a halt around 11pm but taxis are quite affordable). In the high season many of the cheaper hotels and pensions will be booked up so if you arrive without a place to stay the best option will probably be a private room. These may be booked through tourist agencies (Budapest Tourist, Cooptourist, IBUSZ, Express, Volántourist), which have offices at all the major points of entry to the capital by air, train, bus and boat. There are many private and official accommodation agencies at Ferihegy Airport, and at the three main stations. Hotels may also be booked through IBUSZ which acts as agent for the Pannonia and Hungar Hotels chains. Offices generally open 8am-6pm daily though there is a 24 hour accommodation service available at the IBUSZ office situated at Petőfi tér 3 (☎ 1185-707) (nearest metro: Deák tér, and also close to the Danube landing stages).

Those who are looking for the cheapest options in Budapest should simply get off the train at one of the three main stations and take which ever offer of hostel accommodation made by touts there seems the most reasonable. Representatives from many private hostels in the capital hang around the stations looking for likely guests, and are in particular abundance when the major international train services roll in. Often they will provide a minibus service out to their particular hostel which will vary in terms of quality, cost and distance from the city centre. The latter may not really be a serious concern, as the public transport system is so good (although some of the suburbs are a little grim). The main Express youth travel office is at Baross tér, by Keleti Station.

Accommodation may be booked in advance at the following locations:

GB
Danube Travel
6 Conduit Street
London W1R 9TG
☎ 071 493 0263
Agents for IBUSZ.

Hungarian Air Tours
3 Heddon Street
London W1R 7LE
☎ 071 437 1622
Agents for Pannonia
   Hotels.

USA
IBUSZ Travel Bureau
630 Fifth Avenue
Rockefeller Center
Suite 24-55
New York, NY 10111
☎ 582 7412

Hungar Hotels-Pentatours
Norwalk
Connecticut 06856
PO Box 305
☎ 655 6700

Hungarian Hotels Sales Office
1888 Century Park East
Suite 827
Century City
Los Angeles, CA 90067
☎ 448 4321

Climate

June, July and August tend to be the warmest months when temperatures regularly reach into the mid 30°C (86°F). The heat is only really a problem in Budapest, where high humidity, large crowds and pollution may conspire to produce discomfort. In winter by contrast it is not uncommon for temperatures in the capital to fail to rise above freezing. All buildings and public transport are centrally heated but many parts of Hungary have little to offer the visitor during the winter months and so the mild springs and autumns (where average temperatures nudge the 20°C/68°F mark) are much the most pleasant times to visit the country. There is little variation in temperatures across the country. Generally, in summer, it gets warmer and drier the further south or east one travels. Be warned that the weather can change rapidly in a short space of time, especially in the summer when the high humidity levels often cause short rainstorms in the late afternoon or evening.

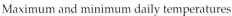

Maximum and minimum daily temperatures

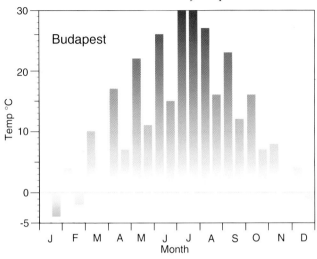

Average monthly rainfall

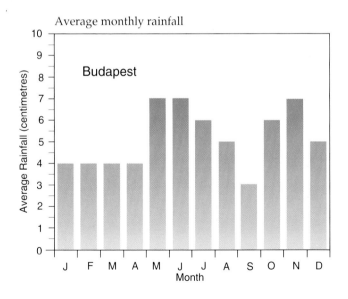

Communications

Post

Hungary's postal system is generally considered to be reliable. Local post offices (*posta*) are normally open 8am-6pm Mondays to Fridays and 8am-2pm on Saturdays, main post offices operate 7am-8pm Mondays to Saturdays. To avoid queuing in post offices one may purchase stamps (*bélyeg*) and postcards (*levelzőlap*) at hotels and tobacconists. Postboxes are painted red and decorated with a hunting horn. Mail to Great Britain usually takes just under a week — remember to send it airmail (*légiposta*). When sending a letter poste restante remember to write the surname of the recipient first (to be on the safe side when picking up such mail ask for it to be looked for under both first and last names) and then simply address it 'Poste Restante, Posta...' and then the name of the town. It will be held at that particular town's main post office. Mail can take up to 2 weeks to arrive from Western Europe. When collecting one should take a passport though you will not always be asked to produce it. Post offices also handle telephone, telegraph and telex services; telegrams (*távirat*) may be sent by dialling 02.

In Budapest, the main post office is at Petőfi utca 13, Budapest V, open 8am-6pm weekdays, until 2pm Saturdays, closed on Sundays. This is probably the best place from which to pick up poste restante mail (the desk is in the hall immediately to the left as you go in the building).

There are post offices open 24 hours a day at Térez Körút 51, Budapest VI, and at Baross tér 11C, Budapest VIII (near Nyugati and Keleti stations, respectively; Déli station also has a post office).

Telephones

Hungary's telephone system is somewhat less reliable and requires a good deal of patience. Local calls may be made from public telephones and are very cheap. Booths for local calls will be coloured either yellow or grey and once inside lift the receiver, put your money in and then wait for a dialling tone. For long distance or international calls use a red booth (illustrated instructions for use are pinned up inside. NB these phones are *very* unreliable). International dialling codes from Hungary are: UK 0044 (then miss out the first zero from the area/town code), USA and Canada 001, Australia 0061. For long distance calls within Hungary dial 06 before the area code. It will generally be a lot less complicated (but more expensive) to telephone abroad (and internally) using a post office or hotel. Simply write down the number required and hand it to the receptionist or post office clerk and then pay after the call. The country code when dialling Hungary from abroad is 36 and the code for Budapest is 1. In Budapest and around Lake Balaton there are now appearing phonecard machines — phonecards for which may be purchased from most post offices. There is an English language directory enquiry service operating in Budapest 7am-8pm (with a limited service on Sundays and holidays) on 1172-200.

In Budapest, the best place from which to make international calls (and also from which to send a telex or a fax) is the Telephone Bureau at Petőfi utca 17-19, Budapest V (weekdays 7am-9pm, Saturdays 7am-8pm, Sundays 8am-1pm). They also stock telephone directories from many countries.

Currency And Credit Cards

The Hungarian unit of currency is the *forint* (Ft or HUF) which comes in 20, 50, 100, 500, 1000 and 5000Ft notes and 1, 2, 5, 10 and 20Ft coins. There are 100 *fillér* to 1 *forint*; these *fillér* coins are practically worthless but still in circulation. There is no longer any compulsory money exchange and no longer any difficulty in finding places to change money. Banks, hotels, bureaux de change, information offices and even some larger campsites and department stores all provide this service. Banks and tourist offices still offer much the better deals. Generally they open 9am-5pm weekdays and 9am-2pm Saturdays, and virtually all will cash traveller's cheques or Eurocheques. Remember to take your passport. Do not be tempted to change money on the streets; any potential advantage will be small, it is still illegal and it is extremely likely that you will be ripped off. It is virtually impossible to change money anywhere on a Sunday. In Budapest, though, there are some exchange offices open long hours, and the one in the IBUSZ at Petőfi tér 3 is open 24 hours a day.

The safest way to carry money is by traveller's cheques though once outside Budapest, even along the Danube bend and around Balaton, it may be a little harder to change them and so it is advisable to bring along an amount of German or Austrian currency to smooth over any difficulties. Major credit cards (including Amex, Visa, Carte Blanche, Eurocard and American Express) may be used to hire cars, buy plane tickets and for payment in larger hotels, restaurants and many shops in central Budapest but, once again, outside the capital their usefulness decreases. Eurocheques may be cashed to the value of 15,000Ft in banks and information offices. One may transfer money from abroad by telex via the Hungarian National Bank in Budapest (Szabadság tér 6). This takes anything up to a week from the UK. There is an American Express office in Budapest at Déak Ferenc utca 10, Budapest V.

It is advisable not to overestimate your expenditure by too much as only 50 per cent of any remaining *forints* may be re-exchanged at the border up to a maximum of $100. Any amount in excess of this should be handed to the customs office who will issue an official receipt containing details of how to have the amount transferred to your home address in hard currency. To be able to re-exchange *forints* it is necessary to produce the receipts from the original transaction.

In common with other East European countries, many expensive transactions (eg car hire, bills in the more expensive hotels) may be made in Western currency (by credit card or Eurocheque). Some private souvenir stalls may ask for payment in Western currency (particularly Deutchmarks) and a 5DM tip is always more gratefully appreciated than a tip in the local currency.

Customs Regulations

Customs formalities at the Hungarian border are minimal and delays only occur at road crossings when entering from Austria or Romania. At the airport and international boat landing stage there are green and red customs channels; use the former if you have nothing to declare. Visitors can bring in 250 cigarettes (or 250g of tobacco), 2 litres of wine and 1 litre of spirits. All personal items, such as cameras, cassette players, TV sets and bicycles can be brought in duty free though special permits are required for CB radios and for sporting guns and ammunition. Customs regulations actually change quite frequently so it may be worth contacting the Hungarian Consulate for up-to-date information. Pets may be brought into the country only with a valid health certificate issued at least 8 days before arrival. There is a compulsory veterinary check at the border. On leaving Hungary the only surprise customs problem concerns food. One is only allowed to take out of the country enough food (up to the value of 100Ft) to last the outward journey. Medicines, tools, works of art and some antiques may require special export permits. Full details can be supplied by travel agencies or by the Customs Office in Budapest at Szent István tér 11/b. Goods purchased in hard-currency shops may be taken out duty free — the receipt acts as an export permit. It is forbidden to arrive with or take out more than 100Ft but there is no restriction on the amount of foreign currency that may cross the border either way.

Most goods in Hungary include a 25 per cent VAT charge which may be claimed back in hard currency at the border. For this one must spend the equivalent of at least 25,000Ft in hard currency in the one shop and ask for a VAT certificate. One must also prove with exchange receipts that one has changed the equivalent amount or more in hard currency.

Driving In Hungary

National motoring organisations (eg the AA in the UK) will have information on motoring in Hungary and should be consulted by those intending to drive in the country before they leave home. In Hungary, information on motoring can be obtained from the Magyar Autóklub, Rómer Flóris utca 4a ☎ 115-2040.

Driving Conditions

There are four categories of roads in Hungary. Motorways (*autopálya*) are prefixed with an 'M' and run from Budapest to Győr (M1) and Lake Balaton (M7). Two unfinished routes run towards Miskolc (M3) and Kecskemét (M5) and an orbital motorway around the capital (M0) is also under construction. Highways (numbered 1 to 8) radiate out of Budapest to be joined by secondary roads identified by two or three digits, the first digit of which denotes the highway that it joins. Finally there are a large number of unnumbered back country roads which do cars few favours. Most through roads are of good quality though the condition of roads in the towns can be quite variable. The biggest problem that one is likely to face, however, is the driving habits of the locals who combine a talent for improvisation with some plain bad-mannered aggression to produce a quite worrisome cocktail that fellow drivers (and pedestrians!) should be extremely wary of. The other major cause for adjustment is the relative slowness of the general flow of traffic in Hungary — most of the cars on the road being clapped out Trabants and Wartburgs. All in all drivers should take time to absorb the culture of the road and certainly any decision to drive in Budapest should not be taken lightly. In Budapest, drivers should be wary of trams which move very fast through the city and may suddenly appear from odd directions. Rather than face the problems of frequent traffic jams, scarce parking space, confusing one-way systems and the potential novelty of a tram network it is highly recommended that visitors instead make use of the city's cheap and extensive public transport system.

Documents Needed
To be able to drive in Hungary one needs an international driving permit (which is easily obtainable from national motoring organisations for a small fee) and third party insurance. While it is not strictly necessary to be in possession of a Green Card it is a wise precaution to have one. If necessary insurance can be purchased at the border but this only covers damage to third parties in Hungary. If using your own car it is probably best to check with your present insurance company to see if you are covered. Cars must be fitted with a nationality plate or sticker and rubber mudguards. Motorists are also required by law to carry a red warning triangle (for display in the event of an accident), a set of replacement bulbs and a first aid kit. It is not permitted to lend a foreign-registered car to anyone.

Motoring Rules And Regulations
Drive on the right and overtake on the left. It is not uncommon for Hungarian drivers to try to pass you on the inside so be vigilant — the accident rate in Hungary is one of Europe's highest. All drivers and front seat passengers must use seat belts and children under 6 may not travel in the front. Drinking and driving is absolutely prohibited and the law in this area is very strictly applied. The speed limits are 120kph (74mph) on the motorways, 100kph (62mph) on the highways, 80kph (50mph) on other roads and 60kph (37mph) in built-up areas. The police are very strict about speed limits and offenders will be fined on the spot. It is prohibited to overtake near pedestrian crossings, to repeatedly switch from lane to lane on highways or to blow the horn in built-up areas (except to prevent an accident). At road crossings the vehicle coming from the right has the right of way unless otherwise indicated and pedestrians take precedence over cars turning onto the road. Trams always have right of way. Outside of towns be very wary of livestock, horse-drawn wagons, bicycles and railway level crossings, most of which are clearly signalled by blinking lights but unprotected by barriers and should be approached slowly. On highways and secondary roads it is prohibited to reverse, stop at islands or make U-turns. At night and in poor visibility headlights should be dipped. Motorcyclists and their passengers must wear helmets. Parking in Budapest is a nightmare. Much of the inner city is closed to traffic not displaying a special permit (issued to residents and service operators) and any car left in a prohibited zone will be towed away. One's best bet is to try one of the multi-storey car parks along Martinelli tér and Aranykéz utca. In provincial towns the problem is much less acute. Many will have automatic parking-ticket machines or alternatively you may be approached by a parking attendant.

Fuel

Filling stations (*benzinkút*) are dotted along the motorways and main highways at intervals of 10 to 30km (6 to 19 miles) and on minor roads at intervals of about 50km (31 miles). They usually open 6am-10pm though there is a 24 hour service operated by Shell and some AFOR (the state petrol company) stations on the main roads and around the capital. Fuel comes in three octane ratings — 86 (normal), 92 (super) and 98 (extra). Lead-free fuel (*olomentes benzin*) is available at some fifty stations nationwide, a map showing their location is available at the border or from the Hungarian Automobile Club at Rómer Flóris utca 4a in Budapest. Queues at filling stations are common so it is best to fill up. Most pumps are not self-service and a small tip will be in order. Diesel can only be purchased for coupons available at IBUSZ offices, border crossings and hotels.

Breakdowns And Accidents

In the event of a breakdown contact the Hungarian Automobile Club (Magyar Autó Klub) who run a 24 hour breakdown service ☎ Budapest 1691-831, 1693-714. There are emergency telephones every 2km (1 mile) along the motorways. The service is free for members of affiliated motoring organisations if the repairs take no longer than one hour. In the UK the AA is affiliated. Obtaining spare parts for Western-made cars is a major problem both in terms of price and availability though the situation is becoming much brighter in the capital. The Hungarian Automobile Club at Rómer Flóris utca 4a ☎ 1152-040 will be able to point you in the direction of a suitable private garage. Accidents should be reported to the Hungaria Biztositó insurance department in Budapest at Gvadányi út 69 (☎ 2526 333) within 24 hours. If someone is injured the police should also be notified (☎ 07). In the case of either an accident or breakdown remember to put out the red warning triangle 50 yards behind your car.

Volanspec Car breakdown and servicing co is at Ifjugarda utca 117, 1151-Budapest (☎ 160-0200).

Car Hire

The minimum age requirement to be able to hire a car is 21 and the driver should be in possession of a valid licence at least one year old. All bills must be paid in hard currency, traveller's cheques or by credit card. Several international car-rental firms (eg Hertz, Avis, Europcar, Inter Rent) have arrangements with Hungarian agencies and cars may be ordered in advance from these companies before entering Hungary or from hotel reception desks and travel agencies within Hungary. In Budapest these agencies are IBUSZ (Martinelli tér 8, ☎ 118-4158), Cooptourist (Ferenc körút 43, ☎ 113-1466) and FŐTAXI (☎ 122-1471). Outside the capital IBUSZ, Volántourist and Cooptourist offer the same service. Cars available range from Ladas to Toyotas, price obviously varies according to model. A minimum deposit in hard currency will always be required as well as an insurance payment per day.

Avis is at Martinelli tér 8, Budapest V (☎ 361 118 4158, fax 361 118 4859, telex 225545).

Hertz is at Ferihegy Airport terminal 1 (8am-10pm daily ☎ 157 86180);

terminal 2 (same times ☎ 157-8606), and in central Budapest at Kertesz utca 24-28, Budapest VII (daily 7am-7pm ☎ 111-6116).

Road Signs
Road signs follow the standard international pictographs, though some information is displayed in Hungarian. The most common ones to look out for are Útépítés (roadworks), Kerülőút (diversion), Zsákutca (no through road) and Kőomlás (falling rocks). A flashing amber traffic light means that you should proceed with caution. At junctions the yellow diamond gives priority. This is ended when a black cross is put through the diamond.

Embassies

GB
Harmincad utca 6
Budapest V
☎ 1182-888

USA
Szabadság tér 12
Budapest V
☎ 1126-450

Canada
Budakeszi út 32
Budapest XII
☎ 1767-686

Hungarian Embassies and Consulates abroad:

GB
35b Eaton Place
London SW1
☎ 071 235 2664

USA
3910 Shoemaker Street NW
Washington DC 20008
☎ 202 362 6730

223 East 52nd Street
New York
☎ 212 752 0661

Canada
7 Delaware Avenue
Ottawa K2P OZ2
☎ 613 232 1711

Entry Formalities

Citizens of the United States, Canada and EC countries (except Portugal) do not need visas to enter Hungary and may stay up to 90 days in the country as long as they have a full valid passport. Australians, New Zealanders and other nationalities, however, still do require visas and these may be obtained at Hungarian consulates abroad or at road crossings at the border or on arrival at Budapest airport. Visas may not be obtained at rail crossings or at the passenger dock in Budapest. For those who need them, visas come in two varieties; tourist visas are valid for 30 days stay with the option of multiple entries, while transit visas allow a 48 hour stay (though you cannot enter and leave the country by the same border section). Visas are not required by children included in their parents' passport and travelling with them. Applications for visas may be made in person or by post to the Hungarian consulate. Applications in person rarely take more than 24 hours, you will need to take your passport, two photographs and the requisite fee with you. If you want to apply by post you must first obtain an application form by sending an SAE to the consulate. Tourist visas may be extended twice, thus in practise it is possible to stay for 90 days, by making an application at the police station nearest to your place of residence in Hungary at least 48 hours before the visa expires. The process takes no more than 15 minutes. You may be asked to produce evidence to show that you will be able to support yourself financially for the additional period.

After 30 days stay all visitors are required to register their address with the police. People in hotels, hostels, campsites, guesthouses and pensions are automatically registered so this only really need concern those staying in private accommodation with friends or relatives. Should you need to do this get an alien's registration form (*lakcímbejelentő lap küföldiek részére*) from the local post office, have it signed by your host and take it to the local police station. Lost passports should be reported to the police and your consulate. If found they will be sent to the aliens' registration office at Andrássy út 93 in Budapest.

In Budapest, passport photographs can be obtained from the photomat machine in the Corvin department store at Blaha Lujza tér. Lost passports are sent initially to KEOKH at Andrássy út 93 in Budapest.

Essential Things To Take

Most medical and food supplies that visitors will need can be obtained in the country, but it is wise to bring all regularly needed items and basic medical or first aid items from home, especially if spending a lot of time away from the capital. Those who are planning to do some walking should bring proper shoes and other equipment (including if possible a good map) from their home country. Tap water (*csapvíz*) is safe to drink everywhere in Hungary unless otherwise labelled (*nem ivóvíz*). The electric current in Hungary is 220 volts. Plugs used are the standard continental type (round, two-pinned) so British and North American appliances will need a standard continental adaptor which will allow the use of 13 amp square-pin plugs. Shavers can be used in either standard shaving sockets or the ordinary wall sockets. Hungarian television works on the Secam system so televisions and videos brought from Britain will either have to be dual-system or adjusted.

There is no problem obtaining most international brands of colour print film (Kodak, Fuji, Agfa etc). However, Western brands of colour transparency film can be hard to find, and the East European or Russian brands that are most common in Hungary are poor quality and often cannot be processed back in the West. Film processing is available in most towns. In Budapest and the other main urban centres there are labs that can process films in a couple of hours. Ofotért, Főfotó and Fotex shops sell photographic items and equipment and offer a developing and printing service. Long-life batteries are readily available but black and white film is more difficult to come by. The airport security machines at Ferihegy will not harm your films.

Facilities for the Disabled

Unfortunately Hungary offers very poor facilities for people with disabilities. Ramps do sometimes exist at public places where there are steps but in general facilities for access to public buildings is poor for wheelchair users.

Illness and Health Care

No inoculations are required for Hungary. Foreigners may receive first aid treatment and transport to hospital free of charge. All other treatment will be charged. EC citizens may also receive free emergency health care and emergency dental treatment but will be charged for drugs and non-emergency care and it is certainly wise to take out some kind of travel insurance that will cover loss of money and possessions as well as medical treatment. For an ambulance ☎ 04. The standard of hospitals (*kórház*) varies enormously, there is a 24 hour casualty department in Budapest at Hold utca 19 behind the US Embassy. Emergency dental work is provided by the dental surgery clinic at the Institute of Stomatology at Mária utca 52 in Budapest ✈☎ 1330-189).

Hotels and tourist offices can direct you to medical centres and local doctors' offices. Your Embassy in Budapest will have lists of English-speaking doctors and dentists — most will be in private practice but will be relatively cheap in comparison with the West. Pharmacies (*gyógyszertár* or *patika*) normally open 9am-6pm Monday to Friday and 9am-12noon Saturday. A sign in the window will give the address and telephone number of the nearest 24 hour pharmacy (ügyeleti szolgálat), of which there are several in Budapest (eg at Teréz körút 95 ☎ 111-4439). Basic medicines available include Kalmopirin (an aspirin-type pain reliever), Quarelin (for headaches) and Demalgon (for toothaches). Condoms (*óvszer*) and insect repellents (eg *Vietnámi balzsam*) are stocked in pharmacies but not generally toiletries, cosmetics or photographic items.

Language

Hungarian belongs to the Finno-Ugric group of languages which includes Finnish, Estonian and some languages spoken in the very northern regions of the former Soviet Union. As a result there are very few words with which most visitors are going to feel any familiarity. English is widely spoken in hotels and information offices in Budapest but much less frequently outside the capital where German is very much the language of tourism. German is very widely spoken in Transdanubia and around Lake Balaton and it may well be worth your time to brush up on a few key words and phrases. A Hungarian phrase book and English-Hungarian dictionary are wise investments and for anyone who does fancy a go there is a positive side to things; the Roman script is at least familiar, the country is devoid of any regional dialects and Hungarians do tend to speak their language very clearly.

The Hungarian language can look, and sound, very daunting; prepositions (eg to, with, in) are simply added to the end of nouns rather than placed before them to produce words of a formidable length, difficult to pronounce because of the abundance of accents and 'double letters' (cs, gy, ly, ny etc). All letters are spoken and plurals are indicated by the endings 'ek', 'ok' or 'ak'. Adjectives precede the noun and negatives are produced by putting 'nem' before the verb. 'The' in Hungarian is either 'a' (before a consonant) or 'az' (before a vowel). The indefinite article (egy) is often omitted. Words are thankfully devoid of grammatical gender. The bewildering number of diacritic markings above letters mean that often words are pronounced in a completely different way to what one would expect were they written in English. Furthermore, many vowels are sounded quite differently - eg, 'a' is pronounced like the 'o' in God. So the town of Balassagyarmat in northern Hungary is in fact pronounced something like 'Bolosho-dyurmot'; numerous other examples exist.

A few useful Hungarian phrases:
Yes/no — *igen/nem*
Hello/goodbye — *jó napot/viszóntlátásra*
Please/thank you — *kérem/kösönöm*
Excuse me — *bocsánat*
Where/when/how — *hol/mikor/hogy*
Good/bad — *jó/rossz*
Large/small — *nagy/kicsi*
Left/right — *bal/jobb*
Early/late — *korán/késoőn*
How much is it? — *Mennyibe kerül?*
I don't understand — *Nem ertem*
English/American — *Angol/Amerikai*
Hotel — *szálloda*
Church — *templom*
Entrance/exit — *bejárat/kijárat*
Toilet — *mosdó*

Days of the week:
Monday — *hétfő*
Tuesday — *kedd*
Wednesday — *szerda*
Thursday — *csütörtök*
Friday — *péntek*
Saturday — *szombat*
Sunday — *vasárnap*

Maps

Tourist offices in each city and town have available city-plans for sale. Alternatively bookshops and news-stands should also sell them. In Budapest there are a large number of maps available ranging from free advertising sheets to imported atlases. The best city map is probably the *Budapest Atlasz*, available from bookstores all over the city and containing maps of the whole of the city, and also information and addresses of places of interest, museums, hotels, restaurants, camp sites, nightclubs, cinemas, theatres, information offices, hospitals, and transport offices. At a country-wide scale the definitive road atlas of Hungary (*Magyar Autó Atlasz*), published by Cartographia of Budapest, also contains sketch maps of most Hungarian towns. Hiking maps should be purchased wherever possible (even at home) as they are sometimes not available. They contain keys in several languages, including English. The bookshops along Váci utca in Budapest are a good place to look for maps of various parts of the country.

Measurements

The metric system is used in Hungary. The only slight variant from standard European practice is that products in food markets are generally labelled and sold in dekagrams (10 dekagrams = 100 grams). Conversions are:

1kg (1,000grams) = 2.2lb
1 litre = 1¾ pints
4½ litres = 1 gallon
8km = 5 miles

Media

Foreign newspapers, especially international newspapers (eg the *International Herald Tribune*, or the *International Guardian*) can be bought all over Budapest, occasionally turn up around the Balaton, but are very difficult to find anywhere else. German and Austrian newspapers and magazines can be bought all over the country. In Budapest there are a number of English-language papers produced specifically for English speaking residents or visitors, which contain news (with a Hungarian slant) and also much up-to-date information and addresses for visitors, with reviews of films, night-clubs, restaurants etc. These remain oriented towards the capital, however, and are rarely seen outside Budapest. Sky, MTV and CNN can be watched by guests in many hotels and are occasionally beamed into restaurants and bars. Hungarian Channel 1 also shows subtitled, uncut BBC news after 11pm on weekdays. The best source of internationally-oriented news and features is the BBC world service, which can easily be picked up in Hungary between 24.80 and 49.59 MHz; use lower frequencies at night, higher ones during the day. For more information on reception consult the information office at Bush House in London before leaving for Hungary.

Opening Hours

The opening hours of the main places of interest to tourists are given in the Additional Information section after each chapter. Almost all museums shut on Mondays and a good number of the smaller ones on Saturdays too. Generally they open 10am-6pm though there may be early (and occasionally complete) closure during the winter. Often entry to museums will be free on one day of the week, usually either Wednesday or Saturday. Entrance is usually not permitted during the last half hour of opening time.

Access to churches is less predictable. Large churches which are major monuments are usually open throughout the day, though they may prohibit sightseeing during services. Otherwise, outside service times, access may be restricted to the porch or, in small towns and villages, the church will be kept locked in which case entry may only be gained by rousing the verger. His address should be pinned to the door, if not look for a house with a *'plébánia csengője'* sign by the doorbell — a small tip would be in order in such circumstances. Most of Hungary's remaining mosques have now been converted into museums.

Most shops and tourist attractions close on national holidays: 1 January, 4 April, 15 March, 1 May, 20 August, 25 and 26 December.

Outdoor Activities

Cycling
Though Hungary is an ideally flat country for it, cycling is not common and it is even illegal not just on motorways but on most major trunk roads. Bicycles can, however, be taken on the train and it is possible to hire them at some stations — in Budapest at Déli and Keleti railway stations (☎ 1228-049 for further information). Help with routes may be obtained from the Hungarian Cycling Federation in Budapest at Szabó János utca 3 (☎ 1836-965). IBUSZ also organise cycling tours lasting up to a week around Budapest and Lake Balaton. In Lake Balaton and other areas, it is often possible to hire bicycles but the machines on offer are often in very poor condition. Anyone who wants to do some serious touring by bicycle in the country should bring their own bike or try hiring a better model in Austria and cycling it in from there.

Horse-Riding
Hungarians have traditionally been great horse riders and there are strong traditions of equestrianism in many parts of the country, particularly around the Great Plain. Horse-riding package-tours depart from many points around the country though particularly around Lake Balaton, on the Great Plain and in the Northern Uplands. A brochure *Riding in Hungary* is available from information offices (IBUSZ, Cooptourist etc). In Budapest at Ferenciek tér 5 there is a specialist agency called Pegazus Tours which also organises such trips. Tours last about a week to ten days; alternatively it is possible to arrange treks lasting just an afternoon. It may be best to enquire at Hungarian Tourist offices abroad, and arrange a riding holiday with them, before coming to Hungary.

Walking
Walking is most fruitful in the highland region stretching from the northern shore of Lake Balaton, across the Danube Bend to the far north-eastern corner of the country. Trails are marked with coloured symbols (painted onto trees and rocks). These correspond with routes marked on maps with the symbols K (*kek* - blue), R (*piros* - red), S (*saga* - yellow) and F (*zöld* - green). In some areas, track marker posts, situated at path junctions or in villages or hill resorts, give times (in hours) for walks. In other places these signs are non-existent. Walks are not as clearly signed or marked as they are in neighbouring countries like Slovakia and Austria where the scenery is more spectacular, if the walks a little steeper.

Other Pursuits

Sailing and windsurfing equipment may be hired in resorts around Lake Balaton and Lake Velence. Mini-golf is also popular around Lake Balaton but for the real thing you will have to venture to the Kisoroszi course 38km (24 miles) north of Budapest. For angling in the lakes or rivers you will require a permit from the Hungarian National Fishing Association at Október 6 utca 20 in Budapest or from the travel agency Siótour in Siófok, on the southern shore of Lake Balaton. Most thermal bath complexes have swimming pools and many of the larger hotels will have their own private ones. Finally, several Hungarian tour operators offer hunting holidays. Wild boar and foxes are hunted all year round, stag, roebuck, deer, pheasant and waterfowl seasonally. Further information can be obtained from MAVAD at Úri utca 39 and VADEX at Krisztina körút (both in Budapest).

Public Conveniences

Public toilets are to be found in train and metro stations and in parks and squares — a nominal payment will be expected in the saucer by the entrance. The hygiene generally leaves much to be desired and museums, hotels, restaurants and fast food chains provide much better alternatives. They will be indicated either *'mosdó'* or 'WC', *férfi* = men, *nöi* = women.

Public Transport

Public transport in Hungary is remarkably cheap by Western standards and anyone travelling to, from or within Budapest will be mightily impressed by the speed and efficiency of bus, train, tram and metro services. Unfortunately anyone travelling away from the spoke-like transport system emanating from the capital will invariably have to contend with late, dirty and infrequent services that finish early.

Within Cities

The size of most provincial Hungarian towns renders public transport moribund as all the major points of interest will be within walking distance. Nevertheless, for trips to those out of the way places one may avail oneself of local bus (*autóbusz*), trolleybus (*trolibusz*) and tram (*villamos*) systems that tend to start up very early (often before dawn even in summer) and finish similarly early (around 10.30pm). Tickets (*jegy*) are sold in strips at tobacconists, newspaper stands and, sometimes, automatic machines, but not on board. There is a flat fare (ie one ticket) to travel any distance, and usually the same tickets are used on all forms of public transport. However, you must use a new ticket each time you change bus or tram. Once on board, the ticket should be punched in one of the punching machines. Routes are usually marked on town maps. Tickets for one town can not be used in another. Taxis are to be found beside rail and bus stations. Budapest is the only city served by a metro system.

Budapest is quite comprehensively served and most good maps of the city will have bus routes as well as the metro lines marked on. Use of the metro, buses, trolleybuses and trams requires the purchase of a yellow ticket (available at metro entrances and newspaper stands) which must be punched upon entry. You will see few people punching tickets, this is because most citizens buy monthly passes. New tickets must be used when changing tram, metro etc. Ticket inspectors are rare but can fine you on the spot. Day, weekly and monthly passes may be purchased.

Metro line 1 (yellow) is actually the oldest in continental Europe, dating from 1896. Lines 2 and 3 are Soviet wide-gauge and all three meet at Deák tér. Trains run at 5 to 10 minute intervals between 4.30am and 11.10pm. On line 1, punch tickets on the train itself; on the other two lines, punch tickets in the machines by the escalators. You must use another ticket when you change metro trains. Bus stops are indicated by blue-bordered rectangular signs containing a black bus. At most stops there will be a list of the stops on the route together with the time it takes to get to them. The frequency of the bus is also indicated. Some of the busier routes offer an all-night service though generally the system runs from 6am-11pm — as does the 193km (120 mile) network covered by the city's yellow trams. Trolleybuses only constitute a small part of the overall transport network. Budapest also has three suburban commuter lines (HÉV) which are covered by the yellow tickets up to the city limit. Of main interest to tourists is the line to Szentendre (which is outside the city limits) which runs via *Aquincum*. Taxis, both State-owned and private, may be found near the main rail and bus stations and outside the larger hotels. They may be hailed on the street if the sign on the roof is lit or summoned by phone ☎ 122-22-22 or 166-66-66. On arrival at Ferihegy airport one has the choice of a taxi to the city centre or private minibuses that will take you to your stated destination or, much less expensively, city buses that run every half hour to Deák tér (these buses do not use yellow tickets, pay the driver in cash).

Between Cities

Timetable phrases to look out for:

munkanapkon (hetfőtől-péntekig) köz — Monday to Friday only
munkaszüneti napok kivételével naponta köz — daily except Sundays and public holidays
munkaszüneti — Sundays and public holidays
átszállás — change
kivételével — except

There are no internal air services within Hungary.

Train

Hungarian Railways (MÁV) extends to all reaches of the country though the further away from the capital you are the more unreliable the service. Timetables for departures (*indulás*) are in yellow, arrivals (*érkezés*) are in white. Fast trains are marked in red, express trains are marked 'Ex' and cost a little more; pay the supplement at the ticket office as it costs more if you buy it on the train itself. The fastest and most comfortable trains in Hungary are the Intercity trains between Budapest (Keleti) and Miskolc and Debrecen which have compulsory seat reservations and a hefty supplement. At all costs avoid slow trains (*személyvonat*) for long journeys. Seat bookings (*helyjegy*) are obligatory for services marked with a 'boxed' R on the timetable and optional (and advisable) when the R is circled. Reservations cost little and can be made up to 60 days in advance. Timetables are theoretically available at MÁV offices and the major stations in Budapest, if not most hotels and tourist offices will have ones that you can borrow. The *Hivatalos Menetrend* timetable covers all domestic services and also details boat and ferry services on the Danube and on Lake Balaton. Most trains have first and second class compartments and some have a buffet car. International services have sleeping cars and couchettes bookable at MÁV offices but there are no sleepers within Hungarian borders. Tickets may be bought up to 60 days in advance though this will not be necessary except when using an international service. Queuing for international tickets can be a frustrating experience and as well as bringing along heaps of patience you should have your passport and enough hard currency to pay for your journey beyond the Hungarian border. Do not board international trains for internal journeys within Hungary as doing this incurs a large fine. You will not be sold a ticket for such a train at the ticket office.

Season tickets are available but not honestly worthwhile as travel by rail is very cheap and one is likely to lose money on the deal. Concessions of 50 per cent are available for BIJ/Eurotrain ticket holders, 33 per cent for pensioners with rail permits and 25 per cent for groups of ten or more. Inter-Rail allows free travel. Anyone caught travelling ticketless will be fined. Most stations have left-luggage facilities (*ruhatár*), a handful have automated lockers. Bicycles may only be carried in the guard's vans of the slowest trains.

Steam train services are operated on a number of lines in Hungary during the summer, particularly around Lake Balaton. The place to go for information and ticket reservations is MÁVTOURS, Nador utca 19, Budapest V, ☎ 111-0061. The most scenic rail routes in Hungary are those along the northern and southern shores of the Balaton, and the line which runs along the east bank of the Danube between Vác and Szob, north of Budapest.

There is an English-speaking rail information service on ☎ 1228-056. Staff at the information desks of the main Budapest stations also speak English. Budapest has three main railway stations; the Western (Nyugati pu), Eastern (Keleti pu) and Southern (Déli pu). All are served by the metro but be warned that the relative site of the station within the city bears little resemblance to the direction in which the trains actually go and that trains may also leave for the same destination from two of the stations. The other terminus in Budapest is Józsefvárosi pu (no metro) on Fiumei utca, though this is unlikely to be used by many visitors. Another important station is Kőbánya-Kispest, in the south-eastern suburbs of the city (metro line 3), which most trains heading to or from Keleti or Nyugati stations stop at, and at which some trains terminate or begin. This station will be useful to those staying in the south-eastern parts of the city. The main MÁV office in Budapest is at Andrássy út 35 (☎ 122-8049) and is open 9am-5pm Monday to Wednesday, 9am-7pm Thursday and Friday. International railway tickets may be purchased here at the *nemzetközi-jegy* counter.

Times and frequencies of trains from Budapest: Balatonfüred (8-12 daily, 2-2½ hours); Debrecen (11 daily, 2½-3½ hours); Eger (3 daily, 2 hours); Győr

(10 daily, 2½ hours); Kecskemét (8 daily, 1½ hours); Miskolc (11 daily, 2 hours); Pécs (4 daily, 3 hours); Siófok (7 daily, 2½ hours); Sopron (5 daily, 3½ hours); Szeged (9 daily, 2½ hours); Székesfehérvár (10-12 daily, 1 hour); Szombathely (5 daily, 3½ hours).

Bus
Buses (*busz*) are slightly more expensive than trains but in provincial Hungary they are often a more efficient and extensive form of transport. For long distance journeys from Budapest and the major towns tickets and seat bookings may be bought up to half an hour in advance. In rural areas tickets may only be bought on the bus. Children under 4 travel free, children under 10 travel half-price. Bus stations (*autóbusz pályaudvar*) are usually found next to railway stations. The three main long-distance bus stations in Budapest are at Erzsébet tér (Deák tér metro) for western Hungary, Népstadion (metro line 2) for northern, eastern and south-eastern Hungary and Árpád hid (metro line 3) covering the Danube Bend. The best source of timetables and information is always the Erzsébet tér bus station, which is also the main international bus terminal.

Some times and frequencies by bus from Budapest: Balatonfüred (2 daily, 2 hours 15 mins); Eger (8 daily, 3 hours); Esztergom (2-3 hours, depending on route; hourly); Győr (hourly, 1½-2 hours); Kalocsa (8 daily, 2 hours); Keszthely (2 daily, 4 hours); Pécs (5 daily, 4 hours); Sopron (2 daily, 4 hours); Székesfehérvár (hourly or more frequently; 1 hour 15 mins); Szentendre (hourly, 1 hour); Visegrád (hourly, 2 hours). Most towns in southern, northern and western Hungary will have a daily bus service to Budapest — often leaving very early in the morning. However, some places in eastern Hungary (eg Debrecen) have no services linking them with Budapest at all.

Shopping

Most shops open 10am-6pm (some food shops open 6 or 7am) Monday to Friday and until 2pm on Saturdays. Only a limited number of shops open on Sundays — mostly tobacconists and pastry shops. Department stores and some other shops may stay open to 8pm on Thursdays. Budapest and some larger towns have food shops that open 24 hours a day — look for the signs 'Non-Stop' or '0-24'. Hairdressers normally work 7am-9pm Monday to Friday and until 4pm on Saturdays.

bookshop — *könyvesbolt*
butcher's — *hentesáru*
chemist's — *patika*
delicatessen — *csemege*
department store — *áruház*
food shop — *élelmiszer*
supermarket — *közért*
tobacconist's — *trafik*

Tourist Information

Outside Hungary

Tourist information outside Hungary is handled by IBUSZ (the Hungarian tourist organisation) and their appointed agents who can dispense up-to-date information on driving, customs regulations, documents required etc and who have a number of free maps, leaflets and brochures available. They can supply lists of hotels, campsites and other accommodation in the areas you intend to visit and, if necessary, book it for you. They also sell motoring maps and atlases of Hungary and they can supply a very useful booklet detailing the year's festivals and events. In addition to this they also have a number of package holidays available: 3-7 night Budapest City-Breaks, spa holidays, riding holidays, fly/drive deals, car rental deals, coach tours and City-Breaks combining Budapest with Vienna, Bratislava and Prague or Prague and Warsaw.

The main IBUSZ offices abroad are:

GB	USA
Danube Travel	IBUSZ Hungarian Travel
6 Conduit Street	1 Parker Plaza
London W1R 9TG	Suite 1104
☎ 071 493 0263	Fort Lee
	NJ 07024
	☎ 201 592 8585

In Hungary

There is an IBUSZ office in almost every town in Hungary. They are usually very good at supplying maps and information and they often provide money changing and accommodation services. In most offices there will be someone who can speak English, though do not count on it. Tourist offices are plentiful and virtually all will change money and traveller's cheques for you, and will arrange a room in a private house or book hotels, campsites or pensions. In addition to IBUSZ there are also various regional tourist offices (such as Siótour around Lake Balaton, or Mecsek Tourist in southern Hungary), and three other nationwide agencies: Volántourist, specialising in group tours, Cooptourist, specialising in car and apartment hire and Express which concentrates on the cheaper end of the market — campsites, college hostels etc. In Budapest there are information offices at all major points of entry though much the best source of information for the city is to be found at Tourinform at Sütő utca 2 near Déak tér metro (open: daily, 8am-8pm, ☎ 117 9800). There is a 24 hour information, accommodation and money exchange service at the IBUSZ office at Petőfi tér 3 (by the embankment). Addresses of all information offices can be found in the 'Additional Information' sections at the end of each chapter.

Travelling To Hungary

Note these oddities on some Hungarian road signs and timetables: Vienna is known as Becs to Hungarians (often written in its German form, Wien); and Bratislava, the capital of Slovakia, is sometimes referred to by its old Hungarian name, Pozsony.

By Air

From North America there are some nonstop flights from New York to Budapest but chances are you will have to fly to Budapest on a one-stop direct flight via another European city. Connecting services link most other American cities to Budapest. Lufthansa is the only airline to fly from Canada to Budapest (via Frankfurt) though it is obviously possible to fly via the US or to fly to another European city and carry on to Hungary from there either by air or overland. There is at least one flight a day operating between London and Budapest run on alternate days by Malév (the Hungarian national airline) and British Airways. Consult your local travel agent about the availability of concessionary fares (APEX tickets, excursion fares etc). Budapest Ferihegy is Hungary's only airport.

Malév offices:

GB
10 Vigo Street
London W1X 1AJ
☎ 071 439 0577

USA
Room 1900
Rockefeller Centre
630 Fifth Avenue
New York
NY 10111
☎ 757 6480

By Train

The daily connecting service from London Victoria to Budapest takes about 28 hours including the ferry crossing. The Channel Tunnel links London with Brussels, from where one can continue on. The most direct route is via Dover to Ostend then via Brussels (Bruxelles), Cologne (Köln), Frankfurt, Nuremberg (Nürnberg), Passau, Linz, Vienna (Wien), and Győr (Chapter 3) to Budapest. Those who change trains in Cologne could look round the city's fabulous Gothic cathedral while waiting for their connection — it is literally right next to the main railway station. The leg of the journey between Cologne and Mainz, along the valley of the River Rhine, is one of the most scenic railway journeys that can be made anywhere in Europe. The journey from London to Budapest can be done with one change, overnight — either by taking the Cologne-Budapest nightly service, or by using the Ostend-Vienna express and then travelling on from there (NB these services may not run in winter). Couchettes and sleeping berths can be used on these trains. It may be advisable to buy tickets for these in advance (eg at the Deutsche Bundesbahn [German Railways] office in London for the Cologne-Budapest service), though it is possible to buy couchette seats actually on the train itself. Trains from Vienna leave from the Westbahnhof station and take about 4 hours. Alternatively, those who wish to arrive in Budapest in style can use the daily (in summer) Paris-Budapest Orient Express — information and bookings from the British Rail European travel centre at Victoria.

Students and those under 26 can buy discounted Eurotrain tickets which are valid for 2 months and allow unlimited stopovers on the route. Alternatively if you are under 26 you can buy an Inter-rail pass which allows one month's travel on most European railways (including those in Hungary) and offers one third off rail travel in Britain and a discount on cross-Channel ferries. Those people holding a British Rail Senior Citizen Railcard can obtain a Rail Europe Senior Card which allows a 50 per cent discount on rail fares in Europe (again including Hungary). Australians, New Zealanders, Canadians and United States citizens can buy Eurail passes which come in various forms and must be purchased before arrival in Europe. Note that those requiring visas will not be able to purchase them at the border if arriving by train.

International rail fares to Western Europe must always be purchased in hard currency at major stations. Tickets to destinations in Eastern Europe must also be bought using hard currency (for that part of the journey to buy and the Hungarian border. The best place to buy international rail tickets in Budapest is at the MÁV ticket office at Andrássy utca 35, open Monday to Friday 9am-5pm. They accept credit cards and Eurocheques.

International rail services may use any of the three main stations in Budapest. Keleti, however, is the usual station used by long-distance trains to and from Western Europe (though some Vienna services use Deli). Nyugati station is generally used by sevices to and from Berlin and East European countries. Some international destinations and journey times from Budapest (summer only; services are reduced in winter): Athens (29 hours), Basel (14½ hours), Berlin (two daily, 5½ hours), Bratislava (9 daily, 5 hours), Bucharest (4 daily, 17 hours), Istanbul (26 hours), Kiev (2-3 daily, 25 hours), Krakow (12 hours), Moscow (2-3 daily, 38 hours), Munich (3 daily, 9 hours), Paris (2 daily, including the Orient Express - 21 hours), Prague (6-7 daily, 10 hours), Rome, Sofia (2-3 daily, 16 hours), Vienna (8-12 daily, 3½-4 hours), Warsaw (2 daily, 17½ hours), and many other destinations in Germany, France, Austria, Switzerland, Italy and East European countries.

The best book for any rail travellers in Europe is the *Thomas Cook European Rail Timetable*, published every month and available from offices of the Thomas Cook travel agency. This timetable includes details of rail services in and between every country in Europe so it can also be used for travel within Hungary (although only major trains are shown, so it is not comprehensive).

By Coach

There are direct coach services from London Victoria Coach Station to Budapest. Two companies run services; Attila Travel at 36a Kilburn High Road, London NW6 5UA (☎ 071 372 0470) and Eurolines whose head office is in Victoria Coach Station at 164 Buckingham Palace Road, London SW1 (☎ 071 730 0202). The journey time is about 28 hours. For those over 26 this is by far the cheapest way to get to Hungary. There is a small discount offered by Eurolines for those under 26. The international coach terminal in Budapest is at Erzsébet tér, right in the city centre (metro: Deák tér). Cities served by buses from here include Amsterdam (26 hours), Athens (28 hours), Berlin (16 hours), Bologna (20 hours), Bratislava (4½ hours), Brussels (22 hours), Dresden (13 hours), Florence (21 hours), Gdansk (21 hours), Hamburg (20 hours), Helsinki (55 hours), Istanbul (25 hours), Paris (24 hours), Rome (22 hours), Stuttgart (11½ hours), Venice (14 hours), Vienna (3-4 daily, 4 hours), Warsaw (14 hours), and many others (particularly in the Czech and Slovak republics). International coach tickets bought in Hungary must be paid for in hard currency.

By Boat
From April to October there is a hydrofoil service operating on the Danube from Vienna to Budapest. The journey takes 4½ hours Vienna-Budapest, and 5½ hours Budapest-Vienna. Tickets may be bought in advance in Vienna at the IBUSZ office at Kärtnerstrasse 26, ☎ 53 26 86, or at the landing stages on the Danube at Mexiko Platz 8, Praterkai. In Budapest, buy tickets at the international landing stages on the East Bank of the Danube just south of the Széchenyi lánchíd.

By Car
Budapest is some 1,732km (1,074 miles) from London by road. The most direct route is via Ostend, Brussels, Cologne, Frankfurt, Nuremberg, Linz and Vienna. The most popular border crossing from Austria is at Hegyeshalom and queues here are quite long so it may be worth your while instead to head for one of the others (Sopron, Kőszeg, Rábafüzes or Bucsu). There is a car-train from Brussels to Salzburg from where it is a 3 hour drive to Vienna. Alternatively there is a car-train service from Dresden to Budapest. All the border crossings from Austria are open 24 hours a day. Some minor road crossings into Hungary can only be used by Hungarian citizens, or by citizens of the neighbouring country. These borders are marked as being 'restricted' on maps. See also under 'Driving in Hungary'.

INDEX

Page numbers in **bold** type indicate maps

MPC
Visitor's Guides
Itinerary based guides for independent travellers

America:
America South West
California
Orlando & Central
  Florida
USA

Austria:
Austria
Austria: Tyrol &
  Vorarlberg

Britain:
Cornwall & Isles of
  Scilly
Cotswolds
Devon
East Anglia
Hampshire & Isle of
  Wight
Kent
Lake District
Scotland: Lowlands
Somerset, Dorset &
  Wiltshire
North Wales &
  Snowdonia
North York Moors,
  York & Coast
Northern Ireland
Northumbria
Peak District
Treasure Houses of
  England
Yorkshire Dales &
  North Pennines

Canada

Czechoslovakia
Denmark
Egypt

France:
France
Alps & Jura
Brittany
Dordogne
Loire
Massif Central
Normandy
Normandy Landing
  Beaches
North-East France
Provence & Côte
  d'Azur

Germany:
Bavaria
Black Forest
Northern Germany
Rhine & Mosel
Southern Germany

Greece:
Greece (mainland)
Athens &
  Peloponnese

Holland
Hungary
Iceland & Greenland

India:
Delhi, Agra & Jaipur
Goa

Ireland

Islands:
Corsica
Crete
Cyprus
Gran Canaria
Guernsey,
  Alderney & Sark
Jersey
Madeira
Mallorca, Menorca,
  Ibiza &
  Formentera
Malta & Gozo
Mauritius, Rodrigues
  & Reunion
Rhodes
Sardinia
Seychelles
Tenerife

Italy:
Florence & Tuscany
Italian Lakes
Northern Italy
Southern Italy

Norway
Peru
Portugal

Spain:
Costa Brava
  & Costa Blanca
Northern & Central
  Spain
Southern Spain
  & Costa del Sol

Sweden
Switzerland
Turkey

TRAVEL GUIDE LIST

Airline ....
....
....
....
....

Telephone No. ....

Tickets arrived ☐

Travel insurance ordered ☐

Car hire details ....
....
....

Visas arrived ☐

Passport ☐

Currency ☐

Travellers cheques ☐

Eurocheques ☐

Accommodation address ....
....
....
....

Telephone No. ....

Booking confirmed ☐

Maps required ....
....
....